PRAISE FOR *THE FREE WILL DELUSION*

"The Free Will Delusion *is a remarkable book that covers an enormous range of positions, ideas, and writers on free will and moral responsibility, which is already impressive. But to take this often esoteric material and form it into a book that is powerful, provocative, clear, accessible, and a joy to read: that is a singular achievement"*

– Bruce Waller, philosopher, and author of *Freedom Without Responsibility* and *Against Moral Responsibility*

"a terrific book. … bold and provocative, yet rigorously argued. … Miles maintains a hard incompatibilist and anti-utilitarian position against the most prominent defenders of a belief in free will strong enough to support moral responsibility, including Kane, Searle, Dennett, Watson, Fischer, Frankfurt, P. F. Strawson, and the free will illusionist Saul Smilansky. Miles uses the premise of the unfairness of holding persons morally responsible for either determined or non-determined actions to show the intellectual and moral bankruptcy of free will theory. The Free Will Delusion *is passionate, compassionate, and an exciting read. Highly recommended"*

– Richard Double, philosopher, and author of *The Non-reality of Free Will* and *Metaphilosophy and Free Will*

PRAISE FOR THE AUTHOR'S EARLIER WRITING ON FREE WILL

"I greatly enjoyed it and hope it prompts a good response from friends and foes alike. It's a funny one, of course, since it seems so counter-intuitive to disbelieve in free will"
– Richard Holloway, former Primus of the Scottish Episcopal Church, and retired Professor of Divinity, Gresham College

"very fine and provocative. ... [Miles's] account of the downsides of belief in free will in terms of 'deserved inequalities', decreasing concern for unequal wealth distribution and harsher views towards the poor and minorities as responsible for their own condition, is an important challenge to believers in free will like myself and a crucial issue at present for the human future generally. ... Important I believe for raising the issues so strikingly"
– Robert Kane, Distinguished Teaching Professor at the University of Texas at Austin, and Editor, *The Oxford Handbook of Free Will*

"an impressive, powerful, thoroughly informed and eloquent challenge to the entrenched conviction that we have free will"
– Derk Pereboom, Professor, The Sage School of Philosophy, and author of *Living Without Free Will*

"... which I was impressed by and much enjoyed"
- Derek Parfit, Emeritus Senior Research Fellow, All Souls College, Oxford; Global Distinguished Professor of Philosophy, NYU; Visiting Professor of Philosophy, Harvard University

"in general I find [Miles's] reasoning superb"
– Emeritus Professor George C. Williams, author of *Adaptation and Natural Selection* and father of "selfish gene" theory

"has greater chance of changing people's views on free will than anything else available. ... Incredibly important"
– Will Provine, Tisch Distinguished University Professor, Cornell University

"It doesn't get more trenchant than this! ... very well taken indeed ... music to my ears"
– Tom Clark, Director, Center for Naturalism

"a polemical piece (remarkably so, for an academic journal) ... but it's hard to deny that he has a point: there's a dark side to the belief in free will"
– Neuroskeptic

"a violent dissenter from [the orthodox] point of view"
– BioEdge.org

"... [came] at the topic in a way that before now I had not considered"
– Stephen Platten, the Bishop of Wakefield

"I agree with [Miles's] analysis that a world in which human beings lacked free will would require a radically different conception of criminal responsibility"
– Eric Metcalfe, Director of Human Rights Policy, JUSTICE

"I love it"
– David Levitsky, Weiss Presidential Fellow and Professor of Psychology, Cornell University

James B. Miles

The Free Will Delusion

How we settled for the illusion of morality

Matador
9 Priory Business Park
Kibworth Beauchamp
Leicestershire LE8 0RX, UK
Tel: (+44) 116 279 2299
Fax: (+44) 116 279 2277
Email: books@troubador.co.uk
Web: www.troubador.co.uk/matador

ISBN 978-1784621-698

British Library Cataloguing in Publication Data.
A catalogue record for this book is available from the British Library.

Printed and bound in the UK by TJ International, Padstow, Cornwall
Typeset in 11pt Adobe Garamond Pro by Troubador Publishing Ltd, Leicester, UK

Matador is an imprint of Troubador Publishing Ltd

The Free Will Delusion

CONTENTS

ACKNOWLEDGEMENTS

In March 2009 a British publishing house known for specialising in controversial non-fiction offered to publish the earliest draft of this manuscript, but subsequently withdrew that offer on concerns over the difficulty of marketing such a complex message ("highly sophisticated subject matter ... too complicated in the current climate"). A complex message, and for many a deeply unwelcome one. In hindsight, though, this was an important move, as that version was long on outrage and polemic but rather short on fully formed logical analysis. So began the first of many rewrites. Over the period late 2009 to early 2011 an updated version was being used at Cornell University as a text for students on the course LAW 7652, *Human Free Will and Criminal Law*, and I would like to thank the course organiser, my friend Will Provine. I would also like to thank the other Cornell academics – philosophers, natural scientists and social scientists – who have, since 2009, provided me with kind words and feedback on my writing, particularly Derk Pereboom, Yervant Terzian and David Levitsky.

Originally called *The Free Will Delusion*, the working title changed back and forth a few times, particularly after Sam Harris used that title for a 2011 magazine article. The text has changed far more profoundly than the title has, though, and since 2011 my work has acquired a tendency to upset people more thoroughly. In the period 2011–2012 Florida State University funded two separate studies solely to try to undercut my writing on free will. It's worth pointing out that FSU was recipient in 2010 of 4.4 million dollars from the billion-dollar Templeton Foundation; largesse intended to promote a better "accommodation" between religion and academia over the free will issue. The Foundation's interest in free will, and the effect of the myth on the social order, goes back to well before 2010, and one world-renowned academic sitting on the Foundation's board of trustees has called knowledge of the non-existence of free will "one of the world's most dangerous ideas".

I would like to thank the journal editors who have carried my work or who have asked me to peer review others' work on free will, and I would particularly like to thank Philip Laughlin at The MIT Press who in 2013 used me as a consultant on the arguments within the manuscript of one of the world's leading free will philosophers. It was this approach from MIT Press that made me realise that I had moved sufficiently far from pure polemic such that I might once again think of getting a full manuscript published. There are a number of other academics I must single out for their kindness or words of encouragement, including the philosophers Robert Kane, Richard Double and Derek Parfit, but also the celebrated American biologist the late G. C. Williams. George Williams's technical assistance to me on free will was necessarily somewhat less than his incredible assistance during my earlier years writing on selfish gene ("genic selection") theory, the theory he is credited with developing in 1966, ten years before Richard Dawkins popularised his work. However, without the confidence George showed in my early work, and which culminated in his writing the Foreword to my 2004 book, I may not have had the courage, years later, to go straight after the biggest names in free will theory. And including, sadly, being forced to target one of the best-known propagandists of George's work, the philosopher and evolutionary theorist Dan Dennett. It should go without saying that I have benefited both intellectually and in presentation from reading the works of many philosophers, but in particular I have been influenced by the writing of Bruce Waller, Derk Pereboom, Richard Double, Ted Honderich and

Saul Smilansky. Any errors in this work are of course mine alone. I would also like to thank the non-academics who have shown interest in my work, including Tom Clark at Naturalism.Org, and the former Bishop of Edinburgh and *bête noire* of the British tabloids Richard Holloway. And I owe great thanks to Richard Oerton for his invaluable advice on publishing a popular tract on free will. Thanks to all at Matador and particularly my production controller Naomi Green, to my editor Joanne Harrington, and to Cameron Publicity & Marketing for taking up the challenge others thought too complicated in the current climate.

I would like to thank my brother, Dr Chris Miles at Queen Mary University of London, and my sister-in-law Sebnem Zorlu-Miles, for their always excellent advice on the format and for their suggestions for marketing a controversial work. Thanks to Dr Yorick Rahman and Rod Mackenzie for trying to come up with ideas for the cover. There are other friends and family members that I would love to acknowledge here, for their good humour and patience if nothing else, but as the subject matter of this book is likely to upset it is probably kinder to leave them unacknowledged. Richard Oerton recounts the hate mail one distinguished Oxford academic received in 1987 when he pointed out to *The Times* readers and the columnist Bernard Levin that free will was a delusion, and it would be a profound disservice if I dragged family and friends into a vicious intellectual and moral war that they did not ask to be part of.

1

INTRODUCTION

The term free will is widely taken to mean freedom of choice, control such that an individual could have acted otherwise, or true origination of action, although we can and will define it in a number of other ways over the course of this book. Nevertheless, whichever way free will is defined – the libertarian definition, the compatibilist definition, the reactive-attitudinist definition, the illusionist definition, to cite just four instances – the conceit of free will has betrayed truth, intellect, and our capacity for fairness and morality.

"Is it fair, he keeps asking, to hold both of them responsible? Life isn't fair" (Dan Dennett, 'Daniel Dennett reviews *Against Moral Responsibility* by Bruce Waller').

"There is a deep *cultural* connection", writes the philosopher Bruce Waller, between strong belief in self-creation and free choice, and extremes of poverty and wealth and an absence of genuine opportunity for large segments of the culture. The greater the commitment to these conceits, the more the "absence of genuine opportunity, ... the greater the disparity between rich and poor, the weaker the commitment to equal opportunity, and the meaner the support system for the least fortunate". As Waller and the author have independently demonstrated, belief in free will appears to be partially or wholly driving such unappealing characteristics as personal and national vanity, indifference to poverty and inequality, increased cruelty and aggression, greater contempt for ideals of fair play, less concern for protecting the innocent – in other words greater indifference to miscarriages of justice – and heightened toleration of injustice.

The vanity of freedom of the will helped create poverty and destitution, at least in large parts of the West – and in particular the US and the UK – and today it justifies vast inequalities of power, privilege and wealth. It is the affectation of free will which ensures that so many at the bottom are denied any chance of social and economic advancement. In influential work Daniel Dennett, for example, has defended free will with the argument that luck averages out in the long run, and so in consequence everyone in America – rich or poor, black or white – gets just as many chances in life. Dennett suggests that over his long life he has suffered just as much as anyone, and thus no one gets to claim to be any less privileged or less fortunate than anyone else. Free will theorists, secular and religious, advise us to write off between 1 and 20% of our fellows. Some go so far as to argue that justice for the minority should be determined solely by the majority, and even that justice for the majority cancels out injustice for the minority. Other free will scholars seek to split mankind into two types, and deny to the one form the consideration and fairness that we, the apparently more perfect form of human, claim for ourselves. And we shall see arguments from the leading modern free will philosophers that "there is room for the thought" that you and I can take credit for our wonderful health and fine characters, with the deeply distasteful implication that it is to others' discredit when they are born diseased, or into a toxic environment.

> "Is [the system] fair enough not to be worth worrying about? Of course. After all, luck averages out in the long run" (Dan Dennett, *Elbow Room: The Varieties of Free Will Worth Wanting*, p.95).

Free will justification is fundamentally the inability to admit that others have been, or will be, less lucky in life than you. Belief in free will – whether that be belief in free will as free choice, or belief in a free will that eschews free choice – means never having to acknowledge your own great good fortune, or recognise the far greater misfortune of others. It should surely be sad enough that some have forced upon them the losing hands in the lottery of birth and upbringing, while many of us – generally the wealthier, the better-educated, the more attractive, the lighter-skinned – coast though life with barely a hiccup. But to then feel the pressing need to tell untruths about those who suffer misfortune... what does this say about us?

To argue that we don't need *fair*, we just need "fair enough"? To suggest that unfairness is "not to be worth worrying about"? To make up stories about those who didn't get the breaks we did – stories about how "luck averages out" in human life? That they freely chose their own misfortune? That "there is room for the thought" that the child with the progressive motor neurone disease is somehow to blame for being in a wheelchair?

To remain silent when moral philosophers argue that justice for the 99%, or the 80%, wholly extinguishes injustice for the 1%, or the 20%? To say nothing when free will scholars write that the unlucky losers in the lottery of biology and environment are not our fellow humans, that moral and economic apartheid are acceptable and necessary, that truth must be sacrificed to expediency, and that there is no need to extend fair play, or equality, or opportunity, to those not like us?

2

LIBERTARIANISM - FREE WILL AS ERROR

I do not at all believe in human freedom in the philosophical sense. Everyone acts not only under external compulsion but also in accordance with inner necessity.
Albert Einstein, *Ideas and Opinions* (1954, p.8).

In the philosophical literature there are many definitions of free will, all of which we will consider, but when most non-philosophers refer to free will they are referring to freedom of choice, or the possibility that an individual could have done otherwise in any specific situation. Yet whatever definition of free will is being considered - even those which do not presuppose freedom of choice and alternative possibilities - deep ethical and logical problems arise. While we shall introduce more definitions of free will later, we shall start by examining three of the more common, and contrasting, traditions of free will justification. These are libertarianism, compatibilism, and illusionism. This chapter is devoted to the first tradition: libertarianism.

Biology, Environment, and the Third Factor

In free will theory libertarianism is the belief that freedom of choice is actually possible. For libertarians, and in general,

	Can free will and determinism coexist?	Is determinism true (at the human level)?	Do we have free will?
1. Libertarianism	No	No	Yes, but we have no proof
2. Compatibilism	Yes	Yes	Yes (but not free choice)
3. Illusionism	No	Yes	No, but don't tell anyone

behaviour does not just come down to the two factors of biology and environment, because for theorists within this tradition there is a third causal factor that frees us from the dictates of the first two. There is biology, there is environment – but for libertarians there is something else: for libertarians there has to be something else. Because libertarians understand that if man is solely the product of biology and environment (nature and nurture) then moral responsibility becomes deeply problematical, and blame and justified suffering become deeply problematical as well, if for no other reason than that it would be very difficult to argue that a person can be responsible for his or her biology or environment (or argue that being the result of biology and environment gives a person any sort of control over their circumstances).

Not only would it be difficult to argue that a man can be responsible for his biology and environment – or be responsible if he was never given any sort of control or opportunity to do otherwise – but if behaviour comes down to only the two factors of biology and environment then this raises what is called the problem of moral luck. Some of us just happen to have been luckier than others in our biology and upbringing through no credit to ourselves, and through no discredit to them.

The problem of moral luck, and the problem of blame and

5

moral responsibility in a world that reduces to nothing more than biology and environment, is spelled out by the philosopher Bruce Waller. Suppose, says Waller (2015), that we have a best friend John, who is warm, friendly, loving, kind, and virtuous: a credit to our species and a joy to all who know him. Unfortunately a mad scientist – mad scientists are particularly common in philosophical thought experiments – deliberately drips a nasty chemical compound into John's morning coffee one fine sunny Tuesday, which immediately and irreversibly transforms John into a violent and vicious (but still rational and even reflective) person.

In that case, says Waller, most of us would say that John has now become a vicious and awful person, and we would take steps to protect ourselves from his cruel behaviour. But we would not, upon reflection, *blame* our former best friend for his new vile personality, which had been capriciously – and through no fault of John's – forced upon him. We would feel for John's desperate misfortune, for his wife and children, and thank our lucky stars that the mad scientist hadn't just as whimsically chosen us for his bonkers intervention. We would agree that John was now a morally bad person, says Waller, but most of us (though not all) would probably agree that we couldn't blame John for his new personality and the acts that now directly arise from it – and certainly we wouldn't cruelly seek to make him suffer for what was already his great and sad misfortune. We would want him safely incarcerated, sure, but we wouldn't consider taking satisfaction from his incarceration, and might even consider it obscene to take pleasure at the thought of his future suffering. But the point, of course, is that in a universe that reduces to biology and environment, everyone we do blame has no more chosen their vile personality than John had after his transformation by the mad scientist.

Each person we do blame – and take pleasure in the suffering of – has effectively had a mad scientist somewhere in their background, screwing around with their genes or their environment. What... we can't blame our friend John for his personality or wish suffering upon him because he changed halfway through his previously angelic life and against his will, but we think we can blame and wish suffering upon the sixteen-year-old hoodlum from Harlem who has been a problem since infancy? How fair is that, though, that we get to blame and make suffer the one who the mad scientist got to in the cradle but not the one he only finally managed to get to in later life? And largely because John – like you and me – was surrounded by (and then surrounded himself with) the best protection against mad scientists that money can buy? We have no more moral – or intellectual – right to blame the sixteen-year-old hoodlum for his personality or the acts that directly arise from it than we have a right to blame John for what he could not help but become. Or that we only avoided becoming ourselves because the mad scientist dripped potion into his and their coffee (or mother's milk), not ours. We likewise have no moral right to feel superior to the hoodlum from Harlem, nor any ethical excuse to take pleasure in the thought of his future suffering. Some may want to say, *We can't blame John, but we can blame the mad scientist who changed John against his will.* But the mad scientist also has a mad scientist somewhere in his history: someone or something who screwed around with his genes or upbringing. Blame for character fault is profoundly unfair in all circumstances where behaviour reduces to nothing more than biology and environment, and blame and just suffering requires us to be completely indifferent to the overarching problem of moral luck.

If it all comes down to biology and environment our behaviour would be said to be deterministic – would be an inevitable outcome – because biology and environment are themselves recognised as deterministic systems. Determinism is the idea that everything which happens is determined by whatever preceded it, and a deterministic universe is a universe where all current and future events – at least from the point of view of human action – are necessitated by past ones. Determinism is contrasted with indeterminism which recognises events with no cause, as in the quantum world. Metaphysical libertarian free will is the idea – the hope – that humans are not fully determined beings: that although we generally appear to exist within a deterministic universe we somehow manage to break free from this causal chain. For libertarians an individual is truly the ultimate – the originating – cause of his or her actions. The idea is that humans cannot, as above, be the product of only two things – biology and environment – but somehow must be the product of three things: biology, environment, and free choice which exists away from the dictates of biology and environment. For libertarians our actions, at least sometimes, are not solely the product of our cultural and biological inheritance, but are also (and in some significant way) the product of something that can stand outside biology and environment.

The immediate problem for a libertarian view of human action, however, is that it flies directly in the face of both our logical and scientific understandings, and for this reason has tended to be viewed with a profound scepticism by many modern thinkers. Derk Pereboom (2001) has drawn attention to a number of arguments against the libertarian position, including the point that unless the agent was originally responsible for forming his character – in other words that his first ever act was to create his character, and how can anyone create his own character? – then the agent cannot be held morally responsible for any subsequent act, as all subsequent acts will have to flow from that character over which he had no choice or control. Any subsequent act will arise from his character: not a character he freely chose but one that was forced upon him.

However, while these are interesting asides, such arguments remain subsidiary to the wider point that neither determinism nor indeterminism can give us freedom of choice and moral responsibility. Most libertarian authors have traditionally made little or no attempt to offer a coherent explanation for how ultimate origination could even be possible in theory, or for how we might get to stand outside biology and environment at any moment. Origination and free choice are posited but are just supposed to remain a mystery. Origination and free choice are thus proposed as an act of faith by many libertarians. The philosopher Ted Honderich makes the telling point (2002) that in every other area of philosophy concerned with the mind – or philosophy of mind, to be specific – determinism and causality are working assumptions. Honderich says that the theories of consciousness and mental activity nowhere invoke origination or free choice, and instead work quite happily within a deterministic universe of biology and environment. And yet, as soon as we turn to free will, philosophers – very often these same philosophers – invoke origination and an absence of causality with barely a blush.

Given that humans seem to exist within what is termed the quasiclassical or non-quantum universe, where all action exists within a causal chain and all events are the result of preceding causal action, what can be the libertarian explanation? Some libertarians try to found free will on some form of quantum interaction, some form of indeterminism, but that brings its own problems. As Pereboom has written, "aside from the highly dubious idealistic attempts to explain how this might be, the wild coincidences implied by this proposal make it incredible" (2001, p.80). Libertarianism must cling to the hope that indeterminism just happens to appear at exactly the right place and point in time to break the causal chain in a way that would give us control over our moral actions. However, human thought processes involve more than a single neurone, and any attempt to link indeterminism to human mental processing would be not just fanciful but statistically ludicrous. Pereboom notes that interpretations of quantum indeterminacy suggest that it is theoretically possible that all the atoms in a can of soda may suddenly jump one inch to the left, but the probability of such an event at a given moment is so far beyond vastly minuscule as to be laughable, while the mathematics apparently says that you may have to wait far, far longer than the lifespan of the universe for such an event to theoretically occur. Yet similar statistical problems beset any attempt to use quantum indeterminacy to trigger meaningful coordinated determinacy-breaking in human decision-making. Furthermore, the macroscopic universe we inhabit seems to obey deterministic laws because of an effect known as decoherence, which effectively reinstates classical mechanics at the level of systems above the very, very small: this is an effect of universal entanglement that arises from the unavoidable interaction of quantum systems with their environment. Quantum indeterminacy has no implications for human action because we inhabit the macroscopic universe. All such problems are largely irrelevant, though – notwithstanding how interesting they may be – because *even if* quantum theory held implications for human action, quantum effects cannot give us the responsibility that libertarians seek.

The random chance of quantum theory has no connection whatsoever to the concept of ethical freedom: the freedom to choose, the freedom to will. Doing something because (hypothetically) a subatomic particle randomly moves inside your skull offers no more freedom than doing something because genes or culture dictate it. The quantum event may be uncaused, but your hypothetical resulting action would itself be caused by the quantum event. The action is therefore not uncaused, and it is most certainly not chosen or willed. Arguing that human actions are caused by quantum events will not allow free will, but trying to somehow identify a human action with the quantum event is equally meaningless, as self-evidently we have no control over quantum events: they are by definition truly random events that admit no causes, so cannot be identified with the will, or even with the person's desires or character. Acts would sometimes come out of nowhere if quantum indeterminacy was involved in human behaviour: not only would you be unable to predict, trust or rely on others' behaviour, you wouldn't even be able to predict, trust or rely on your own behaviour, because it would be coming out of nowhere and from outside of character. As the mathematician Norbert Wiener once wrote, "the chance of the quantum-theoretician is not the ethical freedom of the Augustinian" (1948, p.49).

The logic of the physical universe - indeed, any possible universe, deterministic or indeterministic - rules out free choice. Why? Because who a person happens to be from a moral point of view cannot possibly be under his or her own control. To be responsible for how they act they would have to be responsible for how they are, and to be responsible for how they are they would have had to have created themselves - and no one can be the *causa sui*, the ultimate cause of himself, because in order to do so he or she would have to be in every sense his or her own parent; his or her own author. Self-creation has been vital to the libertarian project since the time of Aristotle, who argued that it was "at first open to the unjust or licentious person not to become such", and that our dispositions are "voluntary in the sense that it was originally in our power to exercise them in one way or the other" (c.4th BC/1976, pp.124-6).

It was self-creation that the existentialist Jean-Paul Sartre trumpeted when he proclaimed that "man is freedom", and that we have the power to make ourselves, the being-for-itself (*être-pour-soi*) that exists away from causation and determinism. But self-creation is a nonsensical idea. As Nietzsche put it, "the *causa sui* is the best self-contradiction hitherto imagined, a kind of logical rape and unnaturalness. For the desire for 'freedom of the will'... is nothing less than the desire... to pull oneself into existence out of the swamp of nothingness by one's own hair" (1886, pp.50-1). If you try to argue that a person has created himself then you have to posit an earlier self that creates the later self, but then you note that the earlier self could not have created itself but must have been created by an earlier self, and you end up with an infinite regress of selves needed (Strawson, 1994). Yet ultimately for libertarian free will you need an initial creator self, a "prime mover" self, which is impossible to get to because how would it have come into existence? Indeterminism can no more save libertarian free will for mankind than determinism can because – as argued by the British philosopher Galen Strawson – to be responsible for his actions a person would have to be responsible for how he is, and no one can be responsible for how he is for the reasons discussed above. Indeterminism cannot help here, because indeterminism is all about projecting on to the created causal agent an external random factor (if it was internal it would be an internal cause and we would have to ask how the agent authored it, and we are back with the same authorship problems). The prime mover, the self-created self, requires authorship of actions: it requires causal authorship. Just dropping in an acausal indeterministic act gets you nowhere in the free will debates. Responsibility requires causal authorship, and authorship requires one to be the cause of oneself, which is logically impossible. The question is always *Why does the person decide to act as he does?* And, as the answer is *Because of the way he is,* he needs to be responsible for the way that he is: he needs to have created himself. Moral responsibility requires authorship. As Strawson puts it: "in fact, nearly all of those who believe in [libertarian] free will do so without any conscious thought that it requires ultimate self-origination" (1998a, s.3).

Determinism cannot give man freedom, because if we act as we do because we are the causal products of biology and environment we had no possibility of doing otherwise. Determinism cannot give man freedom of choice, but neither can indeterminism, because if the mind is – at least in part – undetermined, then some things "just happen" in it outside the laws of causation for which, by definition, nobody and nothing are responsible. An individual is not responsible if their actions are caused, because those actions were ultimately set in motion before they were even born – set in motion by the determinism of biology and environment. But an individual is also not responsible if some of their actions are uncaused, because those actions just came out of nowhere. To be freely choosing, an individual would have to be free from both deterministic effects *and* indeterministic effects: free from both A and not-A, as a logician would put it. To be freely choosing you cannot have A, but you cannot have not-A either: free choice requires something that cannot logically exist in this or any possible universe.

And to put it another way: if an action is the result of quantum randomness this automatically implies that free will is not present, as a human cannot control quantum events. Even the quantum realm cannot control quantum events: they are, to the best of our current understanding, purely and perfectly random. Hence, when the libertarian theorist Mark Balaguer argues (1999) that we have as much reason to believe that human choices are not determined as we have to believe that they are determined, not only does this argue against all the available scientific evidence – including the principle of decoherence – but it is utterly meaningless for those who need to prove libertarian free will. If our decisions are not determined – are not caused – then we cannot be responsible for them: they just happen by chance, emerging from the fuzzy indeterministic world of quantum rules over which we have no choice, no control. Kant, the doyen of the libertarians, was truthful enough to admit that we have no actual evidence for believing that people make libertarian choices, and no logical argument for how free choice may even be possible or intelligible.

Kant was honest enough to state baldly that libertarian free will was an article of faith with him, but that faith takes us straight into a problematic moral area. The philosopher Richard Double (2002) has pointed out that few libertarians even purport to be able to provide evidence that people actually make free choices. Libertarians, indeed, seem fully aware of the lack of any real evidence for the free will conceit, such as when the libertarian social psychologists Kathleen Vohs and Jonathan Schooler tell us that we should be prepared to "stake our very lives on the introspective certainty" that we are conscious, but "perhaps none of us would be prepared to do the same for free will" (Shariff et al., 2008, p.190). It is interesting to reflect that many libertarians appear unwilling to stake their *own* lives on the possibility of free will: yet surely, then, social psychology "risks appearing far too ready to stake *other* people's lives on the 'introspective certainty' of free will?" (Miles, 2013, p.212). While this is not an argument against the existence of free choice, Double has raised the moral ante by asking how much epistemic justification a reasonable libertarian should need before starting to claim that people make free choices, with all the attendant contempt, loathing, blame, violence, revenge, suffering and retribution this normally entails. "If the practices sanctioned by libertarianism are morally objectionable, the charge of lack of moral conscientiousness seems to apply to libertarian theory" (2002, p.227). Double has suggested that libertarianism should in all decency keep silent unless its suggestions are at least 50% likely to be true, yet notes that few libertarians offer any evidence whatsoever for their arguments, preferring to deal in (wholly refutable) conjecture. He has called this the "moral hardness" of libertarians – which includes almost all Christians and the vast majority of agnostics and atheists – being their unwavering faith in the righteousness of their worldview no matter the lack of any objective evidence and irrespective of the harm caused to others. As Double puts it, "fallibilism about one's views is a desirable quality in general, but it is morally obligatory when dogmatism has potentially harmful repercussions for persons" (p.231).

But returning to the possible arguments for - and thus inevitably against - libertarian free will, other thinkers have tried to use what is called chaos theory, also known as non-linear dynamics, including the interaction of suggested "feedback loops". Yet chaos is just another form of determinism, albeit a highly mathematically complex form of determinism, and not a break from determinism at all. Indeed, one of the scientific working names for chaos theory is deterministic chaos theory. Chaos theory gives us systems that are so complex as to be unpredictable, but unpredictable does not equate to indeterministic. The reason a system can be both deterministic and yet unpredictable can be traced to the system's extreme sensitivity to initial conditions. In the simple predictable systems of elementary mechanics small errors in input description propagate to small errors in output, but in a chaotic system the errors grow exponentially with time, so that the smallest error in input soon leads to complete loss of predictive power. The fact that a system can be highly sensitive to initial conditions simply gives us a rather more complex deterministic system. It thus fails to introduce free choice and a break from the deterministic world, just as any other deterministic - or indeterministic - theory fails to introduce free choice. Chaos theory has thus been almost completely abandoned as a tool by that handful of philosophers still trying to prove free choice, albeit that irrelevant discourses about (deterministic) feedback loops still occur in the literature from time to time.

Kant called free choice an "antinomy", from the Greek *nomos* meaning law - and thus antinomy, meaning in contradiction of the universal law: in contradiction of the rules that run the universe. In other words a paradox, the seemingly impossible: although of course only a paradox for those who try to cling to belief in free choice; for those who try to cling to the impossible. Everything that exists in nature, in the empirical world, is bound by the laws of causal necessity, and yet we think of ourselves as free. To try to resolve this paradox Kant originally had to distinguish between the noumenal and the phenomenal: the former the "thing-in-itself" – involving a timeless realm that lies outside the chain of causation – and the latter the knowable, empirical realm of causality and experience, or things as they appear. There is great controversy regarding Kant's understanding of the two realms, but even most libertarians deny that Kant had any success in connecting the two realms, and thus in making human freedom at all coherent or meaningful. As the Oxford and Harvard philosopher Derek Parfit puts it, "some of Kant's claims about our timeless freedom are not even vaguely intelligible... such claims could not possibly be true" (2011, p.269). Even had Kant managed to connect the causal deterministic realm to an acausal indeterministic realm this would not have proven free will, because we have seen that man cannot possibly be free whether determinism holds, whether indeterminism holds, or whether any combination of the two holds. And, in the more than two hundred years since Kant was writing, libertarian theory has been no more successful at making the idea of free will at all meaningful.

Peter van Inwagen is one of the leading modern libertarian philosophers but in his book *An Essay on Free Will* he bases his belief in libertarian free will on the premiss that we "know" we have moral responsibility for our actions. "To deny the free-will thesis is to deny the existence of moral responsibility, which would be absurd... therefore, we should reject determinism", says van Inwagen (1983, p.223), which is just begging the question, not proving the assertion. If A, moral responsibility (and something that we want, or at least think that we want), requires the existence of B, freedom of choice (as van Inwagen admits it does), A is not then proved by *assuming* the existence of B. There is no proof of B here. B remains unproven, but – more than that – it now throws suspicion upon A as well. Van Inwagen even goes so far as to suggest that his circular reasoning "is as adequate a defence of the free-will thesis as has ever been given for any philosophical position" (p.209). Circular reasoning is now postulated as not only a perfectly adequate argument but seemingly the best argument for free will that philosophy can come up with, at least in van Inwagen's view. And the reason that van Inwagen's argument sounds so much like one of the notorious medieval theological "proofs" of God's existence is that it is indeed based on a religious argument for free will. Van Inwagen's reasoning can be traced directly to the Christian father Origen in the early third century in his *On First Principles*. Even putting to one side van Inwagen's lack of engagement with the modern (or at least post-third century) realisation that free will is ruled out both by determinism and indeterminism, such an assertion is the logical equivalent of suggesting that we "know" God exists so to reject belief in God's existence would be "absurd". Our "knowledge" of God's existence would become the proof of God's existence. It is empty circular reasoning where the conclusion is already built into the premiss.

Another example of the degree of faith necessary to hold to the standard libertarian picture is given by the libertarian philosopher John Searle, probably the best-known academic advancing claims for supposed "gaps" in human consciousness that might leave room for free will. There are different versions of this argument, and often they will invoke some form of distinction between what they call bottom-up, top-down, and even left-right consciousness and causality. Searle is generally held to be the leading exponent of this type of writing. And yet, in a 2000 paper, Searle sought – over almost two dozen pages – to prove free choice before admitting that... er... he couldn't prove it. "I have not tried to solve the problem of free will", Searle wrote, after nineteen pages of trying to solve the problem of free will. The flaw with each of his arguments, Searle admitted, is "to see how the consciousness of the system could give it a causal efficacy that is not deterministic" (2000, p.21). In other words, we are back to the problem of determinism ruling out free choice.

Searle commenced his review by drawing a distinction between his two "most likely possible forms of explanation of human behaviour" (2000, p.20), the first hypothesis being what he called psychological libertarianism with neurobiological determinism, and the second (competing) hypothesis called system causation with consciousness and indeterminacy. Hypothesis One shows bottom-up causation (neurones firing and leading to deliberation; neurones firing and leading to decision) and left-right action (the neuronal firing that leads to deliberation causes the neuronal firing that leads to decision but deliberation does not appear to cause the decision: a "gap" is sensed between deliberation and decision, or more accurately "causes with gaps"). However, this first hypothesis – psychological libertarianism with neurobiological determinism – would not give us free will, says Searle, as the (reputed) gaps are simply failures of experience. Freedom – free choice – must be an illusion so long as there is no freedom in the neurobiology. Under this first hypothesis "free rational life is entirely an illusion" (p.20).

Free will for Searle may only potentially come in under the second hypothesis, which is system causation with consciousness and indeterminacy. Under Searle's second hypothesis the absence of causally sufficient conditions at the psychological level "is matched by a parallel lack of causally sufficient conditions at the neurobiological level" (p.16) and which – remember – had no gaps under Hypothesis One, which was a "completely deterministic system at the neurobiological level" (p.14). In other words down-up causation exists (although Searle cautions us not to consider this up-down causation but rather system causation), yet left-right causation is here truly interrupted. The second hypothesis (he tells us) is not that you get a split between the apparent indeterminacy at the level of the psychology and the determinacy at the level of the neurobiology, but "rather that the whole system moves forward at once" (p.17). Earlier "gaps" theorists were often accused of dualism, of an irresolvable mind-brain split, so Searle hopes that with his Hypothesis Two he has avoided this, and shown that free will is a neurobiological feature; shown that in decision-making "the lack of causally sufficient conditions at the psychological level goes all the way down" to the neurones (p.17).

That's Searle's somewhat tortuous argument: now let's take it apart. Hypothesis One is not an argument for free will, so can it be safely ignored? Unfortunately not, because Searle has already started to smuggle in false ideas, using reasoning that he will later use as evidence to help build Hypothesis Two. So, starting with the first hypothesis, where he has assumed "indeterminacy at the psychological level". This is dangerous language to use, especially in a hypothesis supposedly built on determinism and the rejection of free will, as indeterminacy has a very specific meaning not intended here, or at least not ultimately supported here. Turning to another paper by Searle, from the journal *Philosophy* from 2001, we can see upon what Searle feels the right to assert indeterminacy at the psychological level. It is based on Searle's intuition that he is not determined, that "we typically have the experience of acting 'freely'", that I "sense alternative courses of action open to me" (2001, pp.492-3). But there is no evidence provided here: just faith; just feeling; just intuition. Inability to track one's own thought processes can never be objective evidence of free will. Furthermore, neurobiology has discovered (to almost everyone's surprise) that the mass of neuronal processing occurs below the level of consciousness anyway, so you are hardly likely to have an ability to keep track of it. Hypothesis One is flawed in terms of both foundational logic and neurobiology.

Searle then turns to quantum mechanics. Recall his assertion that "the lack of causally sufficient conditions at the psychological level goes all the way down". He then adds that "if we keep on going down to the quantum mechanical level, then it may seem less surprising that we have an absence of causally sufficient conditions" (2000, p.17). Searle asks: "In some systems the quantum indeterminacies cancel out at the macro level. Is the brain a deterministic system? Right now we do not know" (2007, p.69). The philosopher of science David Papineau has demolished Searle's use of quantum theory and tells us that, actually, we do already know. Searle, says Papineau, misses the point that quantum mechanics tells us that the probabilities of physical effects are always fixed by prior physical circumstances, and that serious physicists are unlikely to start looking for violations of quantum mechanics inside the human skull (Papineau, 2008). Searle then suggests that just because he is invoking a quantum connection "we are not postulating randomness" (2000, p.19) as randomness cannot give us freedom of choice. Searle here argues that the mind actually plays a part in directing brain processes, which are themselves subject to the effects of indeterminacy. He invokes what he calls a "unified conscious field" theory of consciousness, appearing to state that – because humans are known as rational creatures – any random quantum fluctuation on to a rational agent cannot be designated random (or at least as randomness having effects) but can only be designated rational. Rather than trying to argue that quantum fluctuations are not random, Searle is seemingly arguing that quantum fluctuations which purportedly might affect humans have somehow lost their randomness ("we should think of rational agency as a feature of that total consciousness"). Such a claim is extraordinary: it is based on no evidence, suggests no mechanism, makes no sense, and flies directly in the face of an overwhelming scientific consensus. So much for free will "gaps" theories, then.

Libertarian free will – freedom of choice, freedom to have done otherwise – is, in all its guises, an inherently illogical and erroneous concept. To stress again, freedom of choice would require freedom from both deterministic effects and indeterministic effects. Freedom from the noumenal and freedom from the phenomenal. Freedom from the "gaps" and freedom from the bits between the gaps. Freedom from A and freedom from not-A. Free choice requires something that cannot logically exist in this or any possible universe.

Justifications for Belief in Free Choice

Of course, just because belief in free choice is illogical does not mean that we cannot appreciate the current deep emotional attachment to such belief. There may be very good – in the sense of psychologically appealing while being factually erroneous – subjective reasons for belief in free choice, which are nevertheless completely illogical when one pulls them apart. Before considering some of these explanations, though, let us put belief in free will into an historical perspective.

Epicurus (341-c.270 BC) is generally understood to be the first thinker to directly address the issue of free volition, or free will, although his thoughts are mainly known through the writings of his followers and critics, as almost all of Epicurus's own writings are lost. Free will was of little interest to pre-Socratic philosophers, though most would anyhow have been against the idea had they addressed it. Democritus (c.460-370 BC), who gave us the concept of the atom, the indivisible unit – and the Greek atomists, more widely – held to a mechanical, deterministic, causal view of the universe that seemed to leave no room for personal freedom in the metaphysical sense. We shall call this view of the Greek atomists (which seems to give us a universe that rules out the freedom needed for moral responsibility) "hard determinism", although it was the nineteenth-century American philosopher and psychologist William James (brother of the novelist Henry) who first gave us that term. Subsequently – with Socrates, Plato and Aristotle – ethics came centre stage, but there was no true doctrine of free will in Greek philosophy until the appearance of the Epicureans. Over two thousand years ago the philosopher Epicurus tried to convince his Greek listeners that the uncaused and unpredictable swerve – *clinamen* – of atoms may allow room for free will if these swerving movements transmitted their motion to the human body. Epicurus modified the hard determinism of the atomists to try to allow room for free will (by which he meant ultimate origination of action, somehow delinked from prior causation). For Epicurus, and certainly for his followers like Lucretius, the uncaused swerve of atoms represented a random deviation in their otherwise determined movements, and thus would be sufficient to allow free will. For Epicurus free will – self-origination – was necessary for praise and blame, and necessary also to his ideal of the self. "It would be better to follow the myths about the gods than be a slave to the determinism of the natural philosophers. For you can hope to appease the gods with worship, but you cannot appease necessity", he wrote in his *Letter to Menoecus*. Epicureanism is thus the first proper appearance of libertarianism but – as sceptics soon pointed out – how could mankind have freedom to will, how could man possibly be responsible and subject to praise and blame, if a chance physical occurrence simply intervenes in human decision-making? How on earth could the random swerve of atoms affect human decision-making in such a way as to make man responsible? If the only thing that breaks the chain of prior causation – and therefore the only thing that has the possibility for Epicurus of introducing personal responsibility in the sense of origination of action – is a random movement that was not itself chosen or caused by the individual in question, how can this possibly now ground responsibility? This is not the ethical freedom to choose that Pelagius, Augustine and almost all subsequent Jews and Christians would seek.

Epicurus was to be followed by a tradition – Stoicism – that seemingly recognised the impossibility of demonstrating libertarian free will, the impossibility of free choice. Cicero, the great Roman statesman and one of the most famous of the Stoics, would mock Epicurus for the absurdity of introducing uncaused events into the free will discussion. Stoicism by contrast openly debated *heimarmene* (or the concept of determinism) of an ordering and sequence of causes; of necessity under cause and effect. So how did the Stoics manage to fit in free will, given their acceptance of a fully causal universe? Firstly the Stoics showed, quite logically and uncontroversially, that determinism does not imply fatalism – the charge of certain later thinkers such as the Christian father Origen. Fatalism is a resignation to events which suggests that as everything exists in a chain of causation it is pointless to act because of a belief that no matter what one does one's future will not change: people should therefore just stay in bed. The Stoics called this the "lazy" or "idle" argument, and showed that it was nonsense to argue that action will never have any effect. Cicero says that Chrysippus (c.270-207 BC) criticized the fatalist argument by showing that determinism left plenty of room for taking action. Fatalists may argue over the point of calling the doctor if you are ill, as in one very weak sense universal causation has already determined whether you will get better. But Chrysippus showed that you will get better by calling the doctor: it is just that the act of calling the doctor is itself also part of the chain of cause and effect. Determinism is delinked from fatalism. Fatalism for Chrysippus was a stupid argument as it might lead to your death, whereas not having the fatalist view of life would allow you to call the doctor, have a different effect, and save your life.

However, this is not free will, as Chrysippus conceded. It is just having the attitude of being willing to consider – and to listen to argument about – the best course of action in any particular circumstance. To demonstrate free will Chrysippus did something different: he suggested that free will is like a cylinder rolling down a hill that requires a push to start it rolling. The external cause of the action is us pushing on the cylinder, while the internal cause is the character of the cylinder in being a round shape, and therefore capable of rolling once we start it off. Like later compatibilists such as Harry Frankfurt, Chrysippus was to identify "free will" (no longer meaning free choice) with the internal deterministic cause; with our character.

There is still some uncertainty whether all Stoicism was thoroughly deterministic, and the Stoics may have believed that a man was not responsible for his character but was responsible for his actions, although they did not elaborate on how this distinction was possible. Stoicism, though, notwithstanding its inconsistencies, is generally understood as abandoning the possibility of free choice. And the ancient documentary sources, for example Aulus Gellius, provide plenty of evidence that the Stoic conception of free will, later taken up by the compatibilists, caused as much moral outrage over two thousand years ago as it does today. As Harvard's George Foot Moore pointed out in his essay, contemporaries were horrified that Stoic necessitarianism abolished moral responsibility, insisting that to blame men "for doing what they cannot help doing is manifestly unjust" (1929, p.379). Epicureanism and Stoicism are two of the earliest examples of mankind arguing for free will, two of a number of such examples. But why has mankind always believed it is necessary to argue for free will? What, in other words, have been the various motivations, both secular and religious, for arguing for free will and, in particular for this chapter, libertarian free choice?

THE PROBLEM OF EVIL

What is called the Problem of Evil is the question of how a good and powerful God can possibly allow evil to happen. There is no greater obstacle to religious faith, it has traditionally been argued, than the reality of evil. The philosopher David Hume demonstrated the basic problem when he reasoned as follows: is God willing to prevent evil, yet not able? Because then He is impotent. Is He able to prevent evil, yet not willing? Because then He is malevolent. Is He both able and willing to prevent evil? Why, therefore, is there evil?

Theists have traditionally argued that God allows this thing called free will, identified with freedom of choice. This, if it were possible, would (it is argued) possibly let God off the hook for the existence of evil and stop God appearing to be non-existent, impotent or malevolent. There is of course a very large body of writing on the subject of the Problem of Evil, taking a number of stances. Free will is sometimes separated from predestination, and sometimes not. Sometimes it is claimed that God's reasons for allowing evil are unknown or unknowable. Sometimes it is claimed that knowledge of evil allows us to sense the good, or sense God, or prove our faith to God, or prove our love of God, or demonstrate our love of each other, or that pain and suffering are what make us truly human, or that suffering prepares us for the life to come. Anyway, one traditional reason for a belief in free will is the fear that it may take something away from God if we deny the existence of free choice.

PSYCHOLOGY, INCLUDING THE SENSATION OF FREELY ACTING

While some thinkers, such as Darwin and Spinoza, suggested that humans believe we have free will because we are not conscious of the determined nature of our desires, (i.e. we don't know our own minds), David Hume suggested that it was the experience of indecision that made us think we have free will. And just recently Seth Lloyd, a physicist and mathematician at the renowned Santa Fe Institute, suggested that it was perhaps the "intrinsic computational unpredictability" (2012) of the decision-making process that gives us the impression that we are freely choosing. The philosopher John Searle uses this intuition or sensation argument as proof of the existence of free will when he says that "we typically have the experience of acting 'freely'", that I "sense alternative courses of action open to me", and "I do not sense the antecedent causes of my action... as setting causally sufficient conditions" (2001, pp.492-3). Yet suggesting that there are not causally sufficient reasons because we cannot fully sense them has always been a weak argument because, as Darwin and Spinoza noted, it could simply be that we are not sufficiently conscious of the causal nexus that precedes thought and action. One of the most surprising findings of modern neurobiology is just how much processing occurs below the level of consciousness – that indeed the mass of what goes on in the brain occurs below the level of consciousness. In *Subliminal: How Your Unconscious Mind Rules Your Behavior*, the physicist Leonard Mlodinow shows that the brain receives over ten million bits of information each second from various sensory systems, but the conscious mind can handle only about fifty bits per second (Mlodinow, 2012). The unconscious does the vast majority of the work for us, and consciousness itself seems to be a deliberately-simplified model of the world to stop us drowning in data.

Many philosophers apart from Spinoza have believed that it is our lack of awareness of the determined nature of our desires that drives our belief in free will, and other philosophers apart from Hume have believed that it is the feeling of intention that drives our belief in free will. However, neuroscience is now showing the feeling of intention to be an illusion created by the brain. The most famous neuroscientific experiments throwing doubt on classical conceptions of free will were performed by Benjamin Libet in the early 1980s. Libet and colleagues at University of California, San Francisco, got volunteers to watch a clock, move their wrists, and report at what time on the clock they chose to move. At the same time Libet measured electrical activity over their brains, and found that the neural preparation to move preceded the volunteers' conscious awareness of the intention to move by over 300 milliseconds. So there was a spike of brain activity 0.3 seconds before the volunteers chose to move their wrists: or, to put it another way, the volunteers' brains prepared to move before the volunteers consciously decided to move. Libet's work has now been verified, modernised and extended by numerous other neuroscientists such as John-Dylan Haynes, Itzhak Fried and Patrick Haggard, while Haynes co-authored a 2008 study issued by the Max Planck Institute which showed that entire seconds before we are aware of making a decision our brains have already made the decision.

The implications are much debated around questions of subjectivity, predictability and intentionality, as well as the temporal relationships - the last, for example, by Dan Dennett - but many neuroscientists take the results to mean that our sensation of consciously willing is an afterthought that begins after the brain has already begun preparing to move. Free will, for many neuroscientists, is merely a feeling, a sensation put together by the brain. Along with other research, Libet's work seemed to imply that the concept of the self - the unified self, the idea of a real "me" that does the choosing and has free will - is just an illusion. The feeling of intention we get before we decide to act may be nothing more than an effect of neural activity, not a cause. Unconscious brain activity precedes the conscious decision. For the record, Libet himself thought this seemed to rule out standard conceptions of free will, but Libet then argued for something he called "free won't". Libet suggested that we do not consciously cause action, but we can inhibit some actions being made. We cannot originate actions, but we can effectively originate stopping them. Yet Libet's suggestion of course provides no more room for free will than any other libertarian suggestion. We cannot be ultimate originators of our decision to stop our actions any more than we can be ultimate originators of our decision to start actions, because Libet cannot possibly provide an argument that our decision to stop – our decision to veto – lies outside the causal universe. And as the neuroscientist Sam Harris additionally points out, Libet's suggestion "has always seemed absurd… for surely the neural events that inhibit a planned action arise unconsciously as well" (2012, p.73). Free won't, like free will, would still require man to be free from both determinism and indeterminism: free from both A and not-A. Free won't is just as logically impossible as free will.

The last forty years of psychology have been a growing realisation of just how poor our brains are at understanding the real world. Daniel Kahneman won the Nobel Prize in economics by showing that the basis of modern economic theory had been wrong to think of agents as rational and with stable preferences. Kahneman and his long time co-author Amos Tversky showed – in a series of papers over many decades – that experts place far too much faith in their intuitions, that humans are much less aware and rational than we tend to think, and that our thinking can be easily fooled and manipulated by both internal and external factors. Kahneman now believes the brain has two systems of mental operation. One is fast and depends heavily on intuition, but therefore often gets it wrong and can be easily fooled. The second is careful and slow, but lazy – yet it is forever having to make up for the errors of the faster system. Kahneman and Tversky once rigged a wheel of fortune to stop at one of two points. They spun the wheel and then asked people a totally unrelated question. The spin of an unconnected wheel of fortune should not have influenced the answers. But it did, and profoundly. This is known in psychology as anchoring. As Kahneman notes, "we were not the first to observe the effects of anchors, but our experiment was the first demonstration of its absurdity: people's judgments were influenced by an obviously uninformative number. There was no way to describe the anchoring effect of a wheel of fortune as reasonable" (2011, p.120). Another of their experiments was shown (in a mock situation) to significantly influence the sentencing policy of experienced German judges depending on how a loaded pair of dice had been set to roll. The anti-free will philosopher Bruce Waller writes that social psychologists have consistently found that subtle situational factors have a "much greater effect on our choices and behavior" than does underlying character (2011, p.79). And as the neuroscientist Sam Harris points out, "people can be primed in a wide variety of ways, and these unconscious influences reliably alter their goals and subsequent behavior" (2012, p.69). You can manipulate people's mood, charitable inclinations and answers to questions of logic by something as simple as leaving a subconscious auditory or visual cue for them, such as a coin in a phone booth or numbers coming up on a pair of rolled dice. Some readers will know that TV's Derren Brown seems to be the master illusionist for using such primes to fool and manipulate people, although these are often employed to serve Brown's strongly pedagogical intent of making us aware of, and thus mindful against, our intellectual weaknesses.

Psychologists are only too aware now that our minds play tricks on us: we invent reality within our minds, with our brains making up all the missing pieces. Neuroscientists call the explanations our minds invent after the event confabulations, a form of "honest lying", because the individual is unaware that the information is false. Experiments show that eyewitnesses remember far less than they themselves insist upon, because many of their recollections have been filled in or invented by their brains. Furthermore, there is influential work within psychology which recognises that human individual development often involves an acceptance of the constraints on freedom: that maturity goes hand in hand with such an evolving understanding. The psychologist Ellen Skinner, a leader in the field investigating experience of control, has written that "old age brings with it the recognition that many of life's events are the result of happenstance, luck, chance, fate, or coincidence… The development of control during childhood can be thought of as a progressive realization of the limitations of one's own competence… Adulthood can be conceptualized as a time of increasing recognition of the boundaries of 'contingency'" (1995, pp.117-22). There are many fascinating studies in neuroscience that have raised serious question marks over the idea of the fully rational autonomous self, such as alien hand syndrome and schizophrenia, and the fact that neurostimulation can affect which hand people move (volunteers feel they are choosing which hand to move, but a surgeon is using an electric current to the brain to get them to change from the hand they would, statistically, normally choose), but the fact remains that we have a sensation of freely willing. We thus have a sensation of free will that acts as a motive for belief in free will, notwithstanding that that sensation is entirely false and misleading and the belief illogical.

Another interesting piece of human psychology that may help to drive the need to keep alive belief in free will is considered by Bruce Waller (2011) when he examines the retributive emotions. Our desire to strike back – to hurt when we are hurt or frightened – seems to be hundreds of millions of years old. Waller recounts an experiment which shows that when rats are placed in a cage with an electrified floor and then shocked they attack each other. When a rat is hurt its immediate need is to hurt something else, even if that something has not actually hurt it (does not "deserve" it). Similarly, in a monkey colony, a subordinate monkey that is attacked by a senior-ranking monkey will typically seek out a lower-ranked monkey and attack it. Waller's argument is that wanting to strike back – irrespective of the fairness of so doing – is so much a part of our evolutionary heritage that we often deliberately blind ourselves to the fairness of striking back. It isn't fair for the rat to attack its neighbour even though it is not its neighbour which shocked it. It isn't fair for the monkey to attack the lower-ranked monkey after it has been attacked, but that does not stop it. It isn't fair for us to blame and make suffer those who have no choice, and we thus invent the self-justification of free choice as an excuse to strike back, and blind ourselves to the evidence against free choice. Waller suggests that punishment and hurting is psychologically and self-righteously satisfying, notwithstanding that it is morally and intellectually unjustified. So our species – so much more learned than rats and monkeys – can be expected to invent, or at least seek to maintain, profound rationales for such punishment and the barely-concealed desire to inflict significant pain and suffering. We feel the need to take our natural fear and anger and turn it into righteous fear and anger.

THE FEAR OF LOSING A UNIQUE STATUS

"man's free-will and responsibility... [is] utterly irreconcilable with the degrading notion of the brute origin of him who was created in the image of God" (Bishop "Soapy Sam" Wilberforce – 1860, p.258 – writing in response to the publication of Darwin's *Origin of Species*).

One significant motivation for belief in free will has always been species conceit, and the desire for a unique status for the human animal. This craving is seen in the work of the American philosopher Robert Nozick, for example. "Without free will, we seem diminished, merely the playthings of external forces. How, then, can we maintain an exalted view of ourselves? Determinism seems to undercut human dignity, it seems to undermine our value" (1981, p.291). Or as the former chief writer for *Scientific American*, John Horgan, put it in *The New York Times*, "free will is something I cherish. I can live with the idea of science killing off God. But free will? That's going too far" (2002, p.3). If we have no free will, goes the argument, aren't we merely *ordinary*? Aren't we rather unexceptional? Aren't we suddenly less "exalted"? Yet, as the psychologist Ellen Skinner noted above, adulthood can be – or should be – conceptualized as a time of increasing recognition of the boundaries of contingency, so clinging to a fantasy exalted image of ourselves is not necessarily evidence of maturity or a healthy psychological development. And yet such motivation also tends to come from a deep misunderstanding of what is left behind once one accepts the non-existence of free choice. The human animal may be just an animal but we are a truly wondrous and deeply unique animal at that, as we shall see in a later chapter: and notwithstanding that we have no free will.

One of the mistakes made by theorists is this fear that accepting there is no free will would somehow make the universe and ourselves less complex and less fascinating. We have already touched on the fact that deterministic systems can be so sensitive to initial conditions that the results end up completely unpredictable. Human systems are generally far too complex to predict in detail, and this complexity has nothing to do with free will. In his rejoinder to the influential humanist Corliss Lamont, Tom Clark (1999) has also made the important point that it is a false supposition that determinism and novelty are incompatible. As Clark puts it, given the massively complex interaction of natural forces, fresh, never-before-seen configurations of phenomena are both commonplace and inevitable at all scales. We are still part of an unfolding process of unimaginable complexity, novelty and wonder even without free will. We are in no way diminished by accepting the absence of something that does not exist and could never have existed.

MISTAKING DETERMINISM FOR FATALISM

There is another mistaken fear as great as that of being unexceptional, of being ordinary – and that is the fear of fatalism, which we have already touched upon. A lack of understanding that determinism does not imply fatalism has existed in both philosophy and theology for many hundreds of years. Determinism means that every action in the quasiclassical universe has a cause. In contrast, fatalism is a resignation to events which suggests that as everything is determined it is pointless to act because of a belief that no matter what one does one's future will not change. Almost 2,500 years ago the Stoics first demonstrated that determinism should never imply fatalism, because determinism left plenty of room for taking action. Actions and efforts still have effects and change the outcome from what it would have been if the effort had not been made where there is no free will: it is just that the outcome can still be defined in terms of prior causes.

The philosopher Derek Parfit argues that even a thinker of the status of Kant mixed up determinism and fatalism. Kant made this mistake, Parfit asserts, when he implied that if determinism is true there would be no point in our trying to decide what we ought to do – that we would have to be *passive*, waiting to see what sort of decisions we shall be caused to make. "That is not so. Even if determinism is true, we can be *active*, by trying to make and to act upon good decisions", writes Parfit (2011, p.262). Christian writers have been guilty of mistaking determinism and fatalism since the time of Origen, but leading libertarian philosophers still indulge in this palpable error.

In a 2001 paper John Searle stated that even a determinist must act on the supposition of freedom: his argument was that a determinist in a restaurant would not be able to refuse to exercise his or her free will. "So if you say to the waiter, 'Look, I'm a determinist... I'll just wait and see what I order', that refusal to exercise free will is only intelligible" if you take it as an exercise of free will (2001, p.494). But this is to be deliberately blind to the distinction between determinism and fatalism. A determinist will make as many decisions as a hopeful libertarian: it is just that he or she will recognise their decisions as fully determined. The determinist will still select the fish over the woodpigeon; he or she just won't cast the runes seeking instruction, offer up a quick prayer for guidance, or invoke this as proof of either God or free will. No determinist has ever refused to make a decision: that is fatalism, not determinism. Indeed, as a determinist understands that all effects need causes, and that all change only comes about through effort, a determinist is perhaps more likely to strive harder than most. I make the considerable effort to write this book in order to have an effect, in order to try to trigger significant change both intellectually and morally. Abraham Lincoln is probably America's most famous determinist who, although he daily rejected the idea of free will, made multiple decisions that define contemporary America. The Lincoln scholar Allen Guelzo has even suggested (2009) that it was Lincoln's understanding of the true constraints on human freedom that impelled him to action. Guelzo has argued, in line with similar suggestions from Lincoln's friends and colleagues, that Lincoln's fine character – made up of charity, of tolerance, of forgiveness and of a lack of malice – stemmed at least in part from what Lincoln termed his "doctrine of necessity", which was his understanding of determinism and the absence of free choice.

Mistaking determinism for fatalism exists across the academic writing on free will, although particularly within the libertarian literature. The legendary biologist E. O. Wilson wrote the following in *Consilience*: "because the individual mind cannot be fully known and predicted, the self can go on passionately believing in its own free will... Without it the mind, imprisoned by fatalism, would slow and deteriorate" (1998, p.120). Wilson himself has historically moved between libertarianism and compatibilism, and his mistakes on free will go back a further two decades to his first attempt to apply his sociobiology to the human animal, in *On Human Nature*.

Roy Baumeister and Kathleen Vohs are influential North American social psychologists who claim that believers in free will (and disbelievers in determinism) are more pro-social, less aggressive and less selfish, and more likely to work hard but their analysis is undermined through the confusion of determinism and fatalism, and through having apparently led test subjects into the same confusion, as the author has previously shown (2013, 2013a). For example, Baumeister and Vohs make the error themselves: "a deterministic view... suggests that efforts do not matter" (Stillman, Baumeister, Vohs et al., 2010, p.44), and Baumeister has inadvertently led his participants into the error: "apparently disbelief in free will subtly reduces people's willingness to expend that energy" (Baumeister et al., 2009, p.267). The philosopher Bruce Waller has likewise noted of this North American social psychology research, which has "drawn significant attention... from the popular press" – and indeed has been lauded in influential and respected publications from *Nature* and *New Scientist* to *The Economist* – that "the researchers primed their experimental group not toward belief in determinism, but rather in the direction of a diminished sense of self-efficacy, to acceptance of helplessness" (2011, pp.279-82).

OTHER INTELLECTUAL MISTAKES

There is a very common argument which is often made in the popular press that free choice must exist, as otherwise why do only some children who are abused become abusers? Similar to this is the assertion of the leading American legal scholar Stephen J.

Morse that free will simply must exist as the "vast majority" raised in poverty do not turn to crime (1976, p.1254). Putting aside the fact that both these arguments are blind to the understanding that biology, and not just environment, may also have a role to play in behavioural differences, the fact that two children will have quite different experiences apart from the abuse, or apart from the poverty, never seems to occur to the people who raise this argument. To quote the psychological profiler Paul Britton, who helped the police track down the two children who in 1993 killed the British toddler James Bulger, and as interviewed on the 1998 BBC series *Children of Crime*, "People will say: 'Well there are thousands upon thousands of children who have these negative experiences, and they don't all go on to do this... '. ... Well of course not everyone goes on to do this, because for many people there are other mediating factors in their experience. They come across particular teachers at school... other friends... other families that provide alternatives. The key thing about the children who killed James Bulger is that they didn't find those external sources of correction, they found each other". Even behavioural geneticists have stopped arguing that any two humans, any two brothers, even any two identical twins, can ever have had "the same upbringing". The evolutionary psychologist Robert Wright put it quite nicely in *The Moral Animal*, when he noted that the larger point here "is about 'nonshared environment', whose importance geneticists have grasped only over the last decade" (1994, p.387). Wright explained that though two brothers do share some aspects of their environment – same parents, same school – a large part of their environment is "non-shared": relationships with parents, siblings, teachers and friends. No two humans, not even the most closely-raised identical twins, have ever shared the same upbringing, as to do so they would have had to have looked out from the same pair of eyes. Not all abused children go on to commit abuse, and not all raised in poverty turn to crime, not because free choice exists, but because – even ignoring any possible contribution from biology – they all come from very different environments and have very different formative experiences.

While we are on the subject of the complexity of genetic action, the complexity of environmental action, and the additional confusion of gene-environment interaction, let us mention epigenetics. The author has generally been using the term biology over genetics (and in contrast to environment) because biology is more encompassing. However, the distinction is somewhat unimportant, as the larger point is that however one draws one's boundary there is no hiding place for free will. Hence the term biology over genetics allows for the inclusion within the former of hormonal influences on a developing foetus, with biology being genetics plus maternal hormonal influences in the womb, and environment as everything else. Epigenetics (literally "above" genetics) is the study of heritable changes in gene expression which are not caused by changes in the DNA, so is therefore a bridge between genotype and phenotype.

It was noted after the Second World War that a devastating famine in the occupied Netherlands in winter 1944 had not only, and as expected, produced children who were smaller than normal, but that – wholly unexpectedly – the well-fed children of that first generation were also smaller than average. Still sometimes mistakenly confused with long-discredited anti-Darwinian Lamarckism (the inheritance of acquired characteristics: giraffes' necks lengthening as they stretched to reach the highest leaves), epigenetics is a rigorously scientific understanding that, as the author comprehends it, includes processes such as methylation, acetylation, ubiquitination and phosphorylation. Some have tried to suggest that epigenetic effects add something new to the free will biology-environment discussion (e.g. Bókkon et al., 2014), but epigenetics is simply a further complication on the boundary question. Whether you talk about genes/culture and define everything outside the gene, including perhaps womb effects, as culture – or whether you talk about biology/environment and add womb effects, methylation of DNA and the subsequent switching on and off of gene expression to the non-environmental side of the boundary – this is immaterial to the wider free will debate.

Finally for this chapter, there is another reason for the persistence of arguments for free will that we need to mention, and that is the willingness to turn a blind eye both to the lack of evidence for free will and to the evidence against the possibility of free will, even among leading scholars. Because when it comes to free will, and apparently only when it comes to free will, "an absence of evidence is not necessarily evidence of an absence", writes the North American social psychologist Jonathan Schooler (Shariff et al., 2008, p.195). While it is gratifying to see here a clear recognition that there is absolutely no objective evidence for the existence of free will, this only serves to highlight the incongruity of such a statement within modern academia. The author can think of no other area of current intellectual debate where something could be posited with zero external evidence. Furthermore, the neuroscientist Sam Harris notes that "more than in any other area of academic philosophy" the vast literature of free will justification "resembles theology", with parts of it, he says, "deliberately obtuse" from both a scientific and a moral perspective (2012, p.18).

We appear to be moving well away from the type of scholarship where evidence and logic are paramount, and towards the realm of disinformation, faith or ideology. As we shall see in the next chapter, the standards of evidence required – and the quality of debate involved – in modern free will study often appear to be far below what is expected in perhaps any other branch of contemporary academia. When even the world's highest-paid philosophical thinker, the consciousness theorist and evolutionist Dan Dennett, defends belief in free will with the comment that we should be "highly motivated to look on the bright side and find the case for free will compelling if we possibly can", and that although "the circumstances are ripe for self-deception... still, what one hopes very much to be true may be true" (1984, pp.168-9), we seem to have left academic best practice far behind. Dennett's argument that we should just assume free will and moral responsibility "within limits we take care not to examine too closely" (p.164), and notwithstanding that "any defense of free will against the skeptics invites the suspicion of wishful thinking at best, hypocrisy at worst" (pp.168-9) at least suggests that defences of free will may have more to do with species vanity and maintenance of the *status quo* than they have to do with the search for truth or with concepts like justice, equality of opportunity, and fairness.

3

COMPATIBILISM –
FREE WILL AS MISDIRECTION

> The general delusion about free will obvious… One must view a
> wrecked man, like a sickly one… more proper to pity than to
> hate & be disgusted with them… nor ought one to blame others.
> Charles Darwin, *Notebooks* (edited Barrett *et al.*, 1987, p.608).

Given the fundamental illogic of freedom of choice – the ability to
have done otherwise – the great majority of contemporary
philosophers have given up attempts to prove or hold to libertarian
free will. So far we have considered the single tradition that openly
declares its belief in something beyond biology and environment;
openly declares belief in the third factor of contra-causal free
choice. We shall from this point forward be considering the
traditions that have – at least in their official statements – given
up belief in free choice, and generally either hold that they can
advance a belief in free will in the absence of free choice, or that,
notwithstanding their own awareness of the absence of free choice,
they can find reasons to continue to dissemble to the public over
the possibility of free choice.

The most influential of the traditions putatively rejecting the
ability to freely choose is today called compatibilism, although the
libertarian philosopher William James originally called it soft
determinism to contrast it with hard determinism. Compatibilism,
or soft determinism, was initially supposed to be the position that

	Can free will and determinism coexist?	Is determinism true (at the human level)?	Do we have free will?
1. Libertarianism	No	No	Yes, but we have no proof
2. Compatibilism	Yes	Yes	Yes (but not free choice)
3. Illusionism	No	Yes	No, but don't tell anyone

even if determinism is true we may have the free will (no longer defined as free choice) required for moral responsibility. This is in contrast with hard determinism, a form of incompatibilism, which avows that moral responsibility is incompatible with determinism at the human level. For the record, libertarians are also incompatibilists in that they too reject the idea that determinism could be compatible with moral responsibility – although, as we know, libertarians try to keep both moral responsibility and free choice by rejecting the understanding of determinism at the human decision-making level. Interestingly, though, and as Bruce Waller has shown better than anyone, when you scratch beneath the surface of compatibilism you rarely find a wholehearted rejection of belief in that third factor, free choice. It appears that compatibilists, at least to judge from the writing of the leading exponents, often lack the desire to consistently and continuously recognise the absence of free choice. And the main reason for lacking such desire seems to be the acknowledged moral difficulty of blame and justified suffering in a universe without free choice.

Philosophical compatibilism dates back to the early Stoics. It is supposed to be the idea that free will is compatible with a fully deterministic, choiceless, universe, and that free will can coexist with the understanding of humans as fully determined persons lacking choice or the ability to have done otherwise. As we already know, for humans you can fit quantum indeterminism into a deterministic picture of actions because the quantum event may be uncaused but our resulting actions would be caused by the quantum event, just as they might otherwise be caused by biology or upbringing. The *OED* defines determinism as the doctrine that action is determined by motives external to the will. So if the quantum decay is triggering – and thus determining – the act it would still technically be external to the will, and a deterministic system at the human level. But how can free will be compatible with, at the human level, a fully determined universe? Because, for free will compatibilists, free will is redefined as being something other than freedom of choice; something other than freedom to have done otherwise; something other than freedom to have willed otherwise. Within compatibilism the general rule is supposed to be that free will can be defined as anything so long as it is never defined as freedom of choice; freedom for any actual individual to have done otherwise. But as the neuroscientist Sam Harris has already noted for us, the vast literature of the compatibilists "resembles theology" more than any other area of academic philosophy and is, he says, "deliberately obtuse" from both a scientific and a moral perspective (2012, p.18). So, for example, Susan Wolf (1989) has redefined free will to mean sanity, whereas others have redefined it as freedom from constraint, as unpredictability, or as acting in accordance with Reason. Possibly the most influential – and certainly the most widely-read – compatibilist, the philosopher and evolutionist Dan Dennett, has defined free will as mechanical self-control (1984). Dennett has written that the Viking spacecraft had free will as soon as it got so far from Earth that NASA left it to float freely into the beyond (1995, pp.366-7).

Free will, according to Dennett, is possessed by yeast, chrysanthemums and some plastic toys. Under Dennett's formulation were you to take your son's toy car, put in new batteries and then set it to race away, it would not have free will. However, as soon as you turn your back and walk away from it never to return, you have blessed it with free will. In other words, free will has deliberately been defined so generously that it becomes almost a meaningless term, a morally empty concept; a capacity we can share with both the Energizer Bunny and fungal infections. At one point Dennett even tells us that he is not concerned with the underlying fairness of blame, only with the need to justify blame even if such blame is not fair. He writes that "free will is whatever gives us moral responsibility" and thus, for Dennett, the perceived ability to blame and justify suffering (2008, p.254). Or to rephrase (and as we shall see) Dennett will always claim, by fair means or foul, that we have just enough free will to allow us to blame and justify suffering, because he has prejudged that blame and suffering are *socially necessary* even if they cannot be *morally justified*.

This, then, is not a defence of the concept of free will. It is a defence of the desire to blame and make suffer. Dennett's is a utilitarian conception of free will. The idea of free will, however it is to be defined, is simply a tool that philosophers must use to govern, and to control, their ideal – but not necessarily just – society. But the immediate problem is content, particularly given that most people still want and need free will to incorporate some element of free choice, the ability to have done otherwise, in order to justify blame, suffering and retribution. Saying you believe in free will after taking away free choice is a little like saying you believe in God after taking away the omnipotence and the omniscience. You would not be left with much of a God in that case, and possibly with little more than a really good stage magician. You have bought divine existence, but at the cost of meaning and content. You have proved your point that "God" can exist, but at the expense of giving the human race a God with no meaning. Similarly with free will. If you want free will in order to be able to ground blame and suffering, but take away free choice and the ability to have done otherwise, you are not really giving people much freedom against which to be measured and blamed. Free will without the freedom; God without the godhead. Empty word games like this are what compatibilism very often boils down to. This is why Kant in 1788 called compatibilism a "wretched subterfuge... petty word-jugglery"; why William James in 1884 called compatibilism "a quagmire of evasion".

There are of course a range of compatibilist theories within such a vast literature. It was the influential Harry Frankfurt, for example, who introduced hierarchy into free will theory – the idea that free will should be seen as compatible not with choice, but with identification of desires: desires to have desires. In Frankfurt's (1971) estimation all one needs for free will is that one is making authentic decisions, decisions that on reflection one identifies with. You are not necessarily free if you have a desire, but you are if you have a desire to have a desire. Frankfurt has been criticized over the years, including over such technicalities as where the hierarchy ends (is a desire to have a desire to have a desire even more free?), and the philosopher Bruce Waller is one of many who point out that Frankfurt's hierarchy concept leads to some disturbing implications. Waller (2011) tells us to consider Jamal, a fiercely independent warrior who is captured and transported to a plantation. At first Jamal is an unhappy slave, and therefore according to Frankfurt's hierarchy model is without responsibility for his situation. Jamal tries to escape at every opportunity. However, at every attempt he is caught, mutilated and humiliated. Eventually, after many attempts, he gives up. His spirit is broken: every attempt has just led to worse conditions, writes Waller. Jamal gives up hope of freedom and lives, dead-eyed, as a slave. He now *identifies* with his slavery, with no further spark of anger or wilfulness. Yet because he is now a "satisfied" slave under the

Frankfurt model – because he identifies with his slavery and has given up identifying with the desire for freedom – he is free and responsible for his condition according to the model. He is now responsible for being a slave. As Waller puts it, "blaming the satisfied slave for his acquiescence in slavery seems to me morally repugnant" (2011, p.66). The unwilling slave is not free, Waller notes, but the willing slave is even less, not more, free and cannot be blamed by privileged and lucky academics for having been unlucky enough to have been broken down by years of torture and hopelessness.

> "In a deterministic picture there was no real opportunity for us to be people who do otherwise. If in the end it is only our bad luck, then it is not morally our fault – *anyone* in 'our' place would (tautologically) have done the same... and the fact of *our* being such people as do it, is ultimately just a matter of luck. Matters of luck, by their very character, are the opposite of the moral – how can we ultimately hold someone accountable for what is, after all, a matter of luck? How can it be fair that she 'pay' for this?... It makes perfectly good sense to say that a person is being punished unjustly for what is ultimately (basic, identity determining) luck, in one sense just as if she were being punished merely for her skin colour" (Smilansky, 2000, pp.45-7).

Bruce Waller cites Martin Seligman's research into learned helplessness, where dogs were placed into harnesses, held helpless, and given electric shocks. Although they initially struggled desperately, they soon learned that escape was impossible, and struggled less and less. These dogs and a group of unshocked dogs were then placed in a cage with a low barrier to freedom. When new shocks were introduced through the floor of the box, the previously unshocked dogs jumped to freedom, while the dogs that had been subject to repeated inescapable shocks just cowered, enduring the pain, making no attempt to escape. Like the willing slave, the hopeless broken-down slave, these dogs had developed learned helplessness. The Frankfurt model's description of the beaten-down slave, or the cowering dog, as "free" because they had identified with their captivity has been widely criticized in the literature, and writers have come up with a multitude of examples. The battered wife who is so beaten down by life that she can't imagine living without her abusive husband is not "free" and responsible for her continuing toleration of the abuse. The abused child who clings to the abusive parent is not "free", and the abused child who has given up hope of escape to a better life is not now "responsible" for his continuing toleration of the abuse. And although there have been attempts, by philosophers such as Gerald Dworkin, to save Frankfurt's model by introducing additional requirements – such as the absence of coercion – this is simply to ignore the fact that we can be coerced as much by internal constraints as we can by external constraints. An addict's body is no more free from internal biological coercion than a slave's body is free from whips, chains and external coercion. Both are completely coerced by their internal and external constraints to live lives that few of us on the outside looking in would want, and neither is free nor responsible for his unfortunate condition. And all hierarchical models cannot help but fail morally because they refuse to acknowledge the *unfairness* of the fortunate trying to hold someone responsible for pure biological and environmental misfortune.

Pereboom (e.g. 2001) develops a four-step series of arguments to furthermore show that compatibilism is neither morally nor intellectually coherent. Starting with a thought experiment somewhat similar to our best friend John from the last chapter, Pereboom shows that almost all compatibilists would agree that if we start with an agent who is being directly and immediately controlled by a team of mad scientists then that agent is not free or morally responsible. Imagine the situation where the scientists have inserted a computer chip in the agent's brain, which runs him like a puppet on a string from second to second, or like a remote control robot. But Pereboom then shows that the difference between such an agent (who it is agreed is not responsible for his actions) and real life cases is in effect nothing more than a morally irrelevant time lag. What if, instead of being controlled second by second in real time, the chip is designed to intervene and trigger his actions a few hours – or even years – later, perhaps similar to the delay under a post-hypnotic suggestion? Having agreed that he was not morally responsible when a chip runs him in real time, how on earth can he then be judged responsible when the only difference is the chip designs in a time lag? And then what if instead of a team of scientists using a real-time microchip or a microchip with a delay we have intense behavioural training, deterministic brain-washing for want of a better term. These are all scenarios that start *wholly outside* the agent, and over which the agent can *do nothing* to change the common outcome, so what really is the (morally) relevant difference? How can he not be responsible when programmed by a team of mad scientists, but responsible when the only change is that his programming comes through the brutal mechanistic learning process he was subjected to? And, in the final instance, what of everyday, more "normal" development? Compatibilists, suggests Pereboom, have great difficulty pointing out the morally relevant differences. The influential compatibilist John Fischer, for example, tells us that it "would be uncontroversial" that the agent would not be morally responsible in Pereboom's first case of the real-time microchip control, or even if there were to be just a mad scientist using a "laser beam", because it is "clandestine" and "unconsented-to" manipulation (2007, p.54). But in even the final two of Pereboom's four cases the manipulation is similarly clandestine and unconsented-to, at least initially and *until* the personality that might agree with the original manipulation has been successfully formed. The character formation still starts wholly *outside* the agent and is necessary to *create* the agent that later identifies with both the manipulation and the resulting character.

Pereboom notes that Fischer and Mark Ravizza have tried to respond to the damage that such a series does to the integrity of compatibilist distinctions by suggesting that the "externally" manipulated person would not be "a coherent self… or genuine individual" (2001, p.121). But there is no difference in coherency or genuineness between the agent who is intensively and relentlessly brainwashed and the putatively normal developmental human. It would be insulting and intellectually wrong for Fischer and Ravizza to suggest that Patty Hearst was not a coherent self because through weeks of intense deprivation and one-to-one Maoist propaganda she gradually began identifying with her captors rather than her upbringing. Why was her previous identification with a translucently white background and indifference to poverty any less of a manipulated existence, any more genuine, than her later identification with colour-blindness and violent social revolution? All our developmental processes, biological and environmental, are ultimately, relentlessly, one might even say brutally, mechanistic – even the chaotic chemical ones – and deterministic. Compatibilism does itself few favours when it needs to argue that mad scientist intervention would be theoretically less genuine than the messy non-free developmental soup we all grow up in. Medical cases of non-coherent selves do exist in split personalities and the like, but such cases teach us nothing of importance for the free will debates. Indeed, Fischer and Ravizza's argument would probably have to deny coherent and genuine selfhood to at least half of all Americans – those deluded souls who have been manipulated and brainwashed (any other terms cannot really do justice here) into believing the bonkers absurdity that evolution is a scientific conspiracy, and even that mankind and dinosaurs coexisted six thousand years ago. Did any of these people really consent to being raised with such ludicrous and, frankly, embarrassing beliefs? And if not, how is Pereboom's first case clandestine and unconsented-to but his third and fourth cases non-clandestine and consented-to?

Such thought experiments from Waller and Pereboom arguably do deep damage to the free will and moral responsibility-asserting traditions, but such thought experiments (no matter how persuasive in themselves) are secondary to what is called the *problem of moral luck*. And such that compatibilism appears to be completely indifferent to the fact that all that separates the willing slave – or Patty Hearst, or the creationist or the cold-blooded killer – from the professor of philosophy is simple dumb luck, and the wholly unfair lottery of biology and environment. We originally highlighted the problem of moral luck in the last chapter, when we considered our former best friend John and the mad scientist who dripped potion into his morning coffee. The problem of moral luck seems to strip away all our moral pomposity, all our holier-than-thou posturing, and furthermore we seem to lose our ability to blame, our ability to feel righteously superior to life's screw-ups. As Notre Dame's Alvin Plantinga – rare in being both an academic philosopher and a Christian – puts it indignantly: "if determinism is true, then on any occasion when I do what is wrong, it isn't possible for me to refrain from doing wrong. And if it isn't possible for me to refrain from doing wrong, then I can't really be responsible for that wrong-doing – not in the relevant sense anyway… The relevant sense involves being properly subject to disapprobation, moral criticism, and even punishment… I am not properly blamed for doing what it was not within my power not to do" (2013). This is what Fischer terms the common-sense view: "our commonsense theorizing about our moral and legal responsibility presupposes that sometimes at least we could have done otherwise" (2007, p.72).

And as we shall see (and having started by highlighting how compatibilism is meant to be defined) it appears to be the insurmountable problem of moral luck within the deterministic lottery of biology and environment that forces most – though not all – compatibilists to need to look beyond biology and environment and for some form of divine intervention, for a quasi-mystical universal guiding hand, or for the self-origination that they hope might still bring free choice – or at least an absence of pure chance – back into the equation.

	Can free will and determinism coexist?	Is determinism true (at the human level)?	Do we have free will?
1. Libertarianism	No	No	Yes, but we have no proof
2. Compatibilism	Yes	Yes	~~Yes (but not free choice)~~ Yes, and free choice
3. Illusionism	No	Yes	No, but don't tell anyone

Dennett's Law, or the Unluckiest 20% Do Not Matter

"Is [the system] fair enough not to be worth worrying about? Of course. After all, luck averages out in the long run" (Dennett, 1984, p.95).

Libertarianism accepts that if everything were to reduce to the lottery of the two factors – biology and environment – then blame becomes unfair, blame reduces to a matter of circumstantial luck… and that you can no more blame a man for his biology and the acts that arise from his biology than you can blame a man for his upbringing and the acts that arise from his upbringing. Libertarians bring back blame by positing a third factor, free choice (*self-origination*) which might then offer an escape from the lottery of biology and environment. This third factor is supposed to undercut the problem of moral luck in the way that the first two factors on their own could not. But what if, as recognised by compatibilism, you only have those first two factors? How do you then justify blame and suffering? Mainstream compatibilism at first seems to have no answer to the problem of moral luck, or rather to have the single answer of - like Frankfurt and Dworkin - simply ignoring the problem: of turning a blind eye to it. But it is turning a blind eye that causes compatibilism its greatest ethical problems because by ignoring the problem of moral luck all we end up with is the justice of the lucky: all we have is winners' justice. Harry Frankfurt's theory of hierarchy, as one example, could not get around the fundamental problem that in a deterministic causal system everything reduces to luck and the lottery of two factors that were not chosen. The sort of justice that the Frankfurt model was offering could be nothing more than the justice of the winners over the losers, of those with opportunities over those with no opportunities - and the justice of, if not of the abuser over the abused, then at least the justice of those somewhat indifferent to abuse over the abused. However, there are compatibilists who think that compatibilism *can* find an answer to the problem of moral luck where Frankfurt, or Frankfurt and Dworkin, could not. We will now spend some time examining the work of the influential compatibilist theorists Dan Dennett and Gary Watson.

It is important to spend time on Dennett's work, and not only because he is a household name or because he is often viewed in the popular realm as one of the leading thinkers of our time. We will spend time on both Dennett and Watson because their compatibilism seems to offer a crucial component that other compatibilist theories do not and cannot. In a radical departure from earlier compatibilist theories both Dennett and Watson promise to give us – in a universe that reduces to nothing more than biology and environment – the right to blame *without* triggering the problem of moral luck, without the system reducing to winners' justice, the justice of those with opportunities over those with no opportunities. It is difficult to overstate how important the work of Dennett and Watson potentially is, because they seem to offer the possibility of a just and moral compatibilism that theorists like Frankfurt and Dworkin cannot even attempt to provide. Turning to Dennett's work first, then, let us introduce what we shall hereafter call Dennett's Law.

Dennett's Law, the first of the two major compatibilist attempts to overcome the problem of moral luck, is fundamentally the argument that we need have little sympathy for others who are not doing so well in life because moral luck does not actually exist as we all get approximately the same breaks.

> "Dennett does not argue that our moral responsibility system is fair; rather, it is *fair enough*… Dennett seems comfortable with 'fair enough', and he can champion such a system and not blink" (Bruce Waller, 2012).

A system that is not actually fair, but that apparently is still *fair enough*. Ethically, how can this be justified? Because *luck averages out in the long run*, says Dennett. Dennett has written that although people are born with different opportunities and then get different breaks ("luck") throughout life, this means nothing over the longer term. Over the long term the differences we are born with, and are raised with, confer "such a relatively small initial advantage" as to "count for nothing" (1984, p.95). Dennett seems to be arguing something very close to the idea that human life is nothing more than an endless series of random coin tosses. We all know that if you toss a coin enough times then over the longer term it will come up heads as often as it comes up tails: that you are as likely to win as often as you lose. So you can see the intuitive appeal here. If, and obviously it is a big if, Dennett is right that in human life luck averages out over the long run, then the supposed lottery of biology and environment would seem to disappear. Not because biology and environment would not still be two lotteries – each time you toss a coin it is still a lottery whether it will come up heads or tails even if over the longer term we know there should be as many heads as tails – but because each lottery and also the interaction of the two lotteries would be driving towards a result where you get to win as often as you get to lose. Dennett is potentially offering something immense, and something that the Frankfurt model, and the Frankfurt-Dworkin model, could not: the absence of moral luck in a system comprised of just two deterministic causal factors. So, to summarise Dennett's Law: over a sufficiently large number of coin tosses the heads and tails will, statistically, even out. And exactly the same happens, suggests Dennett, in human life. Over our long lives we are all exposed to good and bad luck, and this evens out because we are just as likely to suffer good luck as bad luck: thus we all get (or will get) approximately the same breaks. Over the longer term none of us can claim to be any less (or more) fortunate than the rest. We all have temporary periods when our luck is reduced but, according to Dennett's Law, we have to recognise that these will only be temporary, and we should just wait for luck to run back our way again as it undoubtedly will over the longer term. Dennett's Law is an argument for the fundamental *fairness* of blame in a deterministic universe because, it is suggested, the so-called problem of moral luck is really nothing more than an illusion and not a problem.

And yet this idea that, in human life, "luck averages out in the long run" seems, at least on the face of it, to be an extraordinary claim and surely at odds with our experience of the world. There seems to be a huge difference between the luck of repeated coin tosses and human luck. After all, a coin is chosen to stand in for – to play the part of – randomness precisely because inherent design symmetry means that it is equally likely to come up with either face under the impersonal and indifferent rules of physics and the natural world. Human luck not only has no such inherent design but has to factor in that we are not dealing with the impersonal world of physics but the very personal world of human interaction, including intent, prejudice, stupidity, psychology, and vindictiveness. Furthermore, each coin toss carries exactly the same weight of outcome as any other, whereas one single event of human good (or bad) luck can easily swamp all the other bad (or good) luck that you might have in your life. But perhaps we are missing something important that only a professional thinker like Dan Dennett can understand. Obviously some do start life with very unfortunate biological and/or environmental hands, and Dennett does not deny this, so what is Dennett's Law really trying to tell us? We need to examine such a radical and comprehensive solution to the free will problem, or at least the moral luck problem, more closely than we have done so far.

Dennett freely admits that some can certainly start with a markedly more unfortunate biological and/or environmental inheritance than the typical. We shall identify these positions as B_U, E_U, and BE_U (to signify unfortunate biology, unfortunate environment, and unfortunate biology plus unfortunate environment). If Dennett's Law is valid the only way that luck can average out for those who start off in such unfortunate circumstances is if B_U, E_U, and BE_U are subsequently offset. And the only way they can be offset is by the initially unfortunate individual benefiting at some point, either contemporaneously or later in life, from a more fortunate biological and/or environmental inheritance. We shall identify these options as B_F, E_F, and BE_F.

Starting position: B_U, and/or E_U, and/or BE_U

Offsetting position: B_F, and/or E_F, and/or BE_F

B_U can potentially be offset by any of B_F, E_F and BE_F (and indeed must be offset by at least one of these options if Dennett's Law is to hold for someone starting from position B_U). E_U can likewise potentially be offset by any of B_F, E_F and BE_F. And BE_U can also potentially be offset by any of B_F, E_F and BE_F. We need to examine each of the options.

DENNETT'S LAW 1 – IT'S THE BIOLOGY, STUPID

"Is [the system] fair enough not to be worth worrying about? Of course. After all, luck averages out in the long run" (Dennett, 1984, p.95).

Let us consider, in particular, the case where someone starts with severe biological handicaps. We are all aware that there are many people in poverty, and many in prison, who have unfortunate biological pedigrees, such as schizophrenia, autism, and Asperger's. Remember that Dennett is proposing that luck averages out – and thus that we need feel no guilt for those we naively describe as less fortunate – as *a general, and universal,* rule. Dennett may be allowed to claim that there are very occasional breaches to his rule – the sick child who doesn't live long enough to get the corresponding breaks he or she would have got as an adult – but Dennett is still trying to claim that in a standard lifespan luck averages out, and that responses to crime (and presumably poverty and social inequality if Dennett is being consistent) must reflect this. Hence we could consider an initial biological hand leading to low impulse control, or low IQ, but equally we have the right to — and, morally, should, if we are to truly test Dennett's Law — consider the case of someone born with severe physical and mental handicaps.

Firstly, is Dennett, a respected Darwinian theorist, suggesting that there is some sort of even-handedness attached to genetic mutation akin to the physical world's indifference to a coin toss, where the coin has an inherent design that makes it equally likely to come up heads or tails? Is he indeed giving us some deep philosophical insight about the world similar to "every cloud has a silver lining", or some atheistic variant upon "when God closes a door He opens a window"? Luck averages out, so is he perhaps arguing that Stephen Hawking's huge success as a mathematical thinker only came about because of his life spent motionless in a wheelchair, a life spent doing nothing other than think? That the bad is not only offset by the good, but that the bad may bring about the good? Is he suggesting that Hawking would have been nothing more than an academic hack had he not been lucky enough to have been struck down with a debilitating and progressive motor neurone disease that gave him the opportunity to do nothing other than sit and think? Or is he perhaps arguing that physical handicaps are offset by better life chances as thereafter sufferers get an easier ride in life, and that in fact Professor Hawking may be an indifferent mathematician whose great intellectual success owes far more to journal editors giving him an easier ride? And if such questions are starting to make you feel uncomfortable do remember that we must strive to understand what Dennett's Law is telling us because, whether you realise it or not, it is one of the more ambitious and promising justifications underlying our own questionable championing of human suffering and indifference to the problem of moral luck. Furthermore, and as we shall see later, Hawking has himself used his enormous scientific credibility to help justify the conceit of free will, so I think it only appropriate that we ask what Dennett's "luck averages out" explanation might mean in his particular situation.

If you start life suffering from biological misfortune this is often the result of genetic mutation. It is true that we undergo genetic mutation throughout our lives, leading perhaps to cancer. Our bodies will actively protect against many of these mutations through error-checking and repair, particularly when we are young, and we also possess genetic redundancy that allows us to live happily with a degree of harmful mutation. But there is a fundamental flaw in Dennett's Law if it is trying to suggest that biological change, or mutation, evens out in the long run. That fundamental flaw is because the vast majority of genetic mutations are, or would be if not cleaned up by our protective mechanisms, deleterious to the body. A random walk in genetic design space almost always takes you over a cliff, because our bodies (and hence our genetic codes) start out rather well adapted, thanks to millions of years of evolution.

There are vastly more ways for a random genetic mutation to hurt the body than to help it. A mutation that causes the loss of just three nucleotides on a single gene on chromosome 7 is the most common cause of cystic fibrosis. This mutation in just three nucleotides out of three billion base pairs causes an illness where thick mucus builds up in the lungs leading to life-threatening infections. So further biological mutation is vastly unlikely to bring a happy ending, will not "average out" the initial biological bad luck. This is not a coin toss with one head and one tail. This is a coin toss with one head and about a million tails. Some genetic disorders can simultaneously engender benefits, such as sickle-cell anaemia which has survived in the human population because it protects against the worst effects of malaria, but this is a very rare parallel to Dennett's would-be coin-toss effect. People with cystic fibrosis, and that mutation in chromosome 7, do not at the same time inherit the ability to leap tall buildings in a single bound. Their bodies are basically wrecked. And the same is true for the bodies, and minds, of people with – for example – schizophrenia, autism and Asperger's. Drugs will help to ameliorate the effects, but only to a certain extent. Luck will not average out for them – at least, not biological luck.

Well, can biological luck at least average out a poor environmental hand? We all know of the sports stars who rose to greatness, as their natural skill allowed them to rise to the top in soccer, baseball, basketball (or whatever) thus allowing them to escape the slums and the barrios. The problem, of course, is that there are so few of these examples, which is why we remember them. Yes: occasionally, someone will have such natural talent that it will let them beat the odds. But therein lies the problem for Dennett: this is against the odds, while Dennett's Law, to be valid, needs it to be much closer to 50:50 if we are to get some sort of reliable averaging-out. It is hugely rare, however. For every child who escaped the barrio through football we all know there are a multitude who did not escape – who did not have the talent, did not have the luck. Biological luck may (or may not) be more likely to offset an initial bad environmental hand than it will offset an initial bad biological hand, but it is only a little more likely. Instead of odds of millions to one we are now perhaps dealing in odds of hundreds to one. It is still very unlikely. And a problem that we shall return to below is that not only is such against-the-odds-leading-to-success natural talent rare, such skill still depends on the unfairness of random luck. The problem of moral luck cannot be solved by further appeals to rare and random genetic chance. Dennett's Law finds no succour in biological luck. So what about environmental luck, then?

DENNETT'S LAW 2 – IT'S THE ENVIRONMENT, STUPID

Obviously Dennett's Law cannot be suggesting that biology is providing the averaging-out, the evening out. Hence Dennett's Law can only be supposing that environmental good fortune will offset initial biological misfortune and/or initial environmental misfortune. But now we have another problem. There is no evidence proving, or even suggesting, that environmental good fortune will reliably offset either early biological misfortune or initial environmental misfortune. Turning first to early biological misfortune, on what basis could we say that environmental misfortune averages out initial biological misfortune? If nothing else, surely this is for the person suffering the affliction to judge whether environmental benefits offset the affliction? Ancient law, and modern insurance, may have set tariffs on what recompense was due for the loss of a body part, but it's hardly a convincing guide. According to the internet, Aviva bronze cover in the UK is currently paying £25,000 if you are unlucky enough to lose both your eyes in an accident, but the author would suggest that almost all of us would far rather have our eyes than £25,000. So how much would you be willing to settle for in order to suffer from schizophrenia? Or autism? Or Asperger's? It is nonsensical to claim that environmental fortune could ever even out for significant biological disadvantage, even if there were a kind of Cosmic Aviva ready to make the trade. But there is no Cosmic Aviva, and no guarantee in this life that someone who has suffered biological disadvantage will receive any form of parallel offsetting environmental advantage. In fact, experience tells us that usually the opposite is true.

It is profoundly upsetting that in the twenty-first century disabled people often encounter hostility and even ridicule and violence due to their disability, particularly in non-Western countries, but also sometimes here in the West. The lives of those with mental, physical and learning difficulties are often horrendously difficult and unjust, notwithstanding the efforts of the many very fine people who dedicate themselves to trying to stop this being the case. We all know that we have a natural tendency to be drawn towards attractive people (much of this is probably an evolutionary inheritance as body symmetry tends to signal reproductive health), but the flipside is that so many people make no attempt to hide their fear and loathing of those with physical and mental defects. When a few years back BBC children's television employed a presenter with a malformed arm, middle-class parents – quite unbelievably – wrote in to complain. So in reality, rather than environmental luck reliably averaging out for biological misfortune, environmental misfortune often follows and enhances biological misfortune.

As a follow-on from the point above that it is perhaps for the person suffering the affliction – and not the person standing in life's winners' enclosure – to judge whether their life chances have seen an averaging-out of luck, there is a wider point here. Compatibilists like Dennett tend to need to suggest that we all get similar chances in life, or that the current system is sufficiently just and fair (not fair but "fair enough"), but it is a mainstay of contemporary liberal political philosophy that you should be highly sceptical of winners' comments on how level the playing field actually is. John Rawls famously suggested that an impartial view of social justice would require participants to choose from *behind the veil of ignorance* of where one stands or will eventually stand. It should be unsurprising that the winners tend to overestimate the fairness in life. Winners tend to be too quick to claim that the game is fair, that we all get the same chances in life, that luck averages out in life, and that any American can become President of the United States. Furthermore, it has long been recognised that such claims are a staple of political ideologies that make a fetish out of actively blocking a more equal distribution of resources. One needs to at least make the effort to consider the question of fairness from the point of view of the losers, but unsurprisingly the losers don't tend to have the publishing contracts, the political influence, or the leading positions in the philosophy departments of American universities. Rawls's insight, this touchstone of contemporary liberal political philosophy, was of course a development from earlier ethical thinking, including that oldest of moral maxims: *Do unto others as you would be done by*. Rawls's insight was also a development upon the Christian philosopher Immanuel Kant's first categorical imperative: that one should act only according to that maxim whereby one can at the same time will that it should become a universal law. It is open to question how far most compatibilist theory, with all its not-actually-fair-but-fair-enough, with all its within-limits-we-take-care-not-to-examine-too-closely, can honestly be argued to be operating from behind the impartial veil of ignorance, or to be operating as an example of *Do unto others as you would be done by.*

Of course, as Dennett's Law is unable to show that environmental good fortune can reliably average out biological misfortune, we actually need go no further. To be a valid answer to the deep problem of moral luck Dennett's Law had to be a *general and universal* rule. So even if it were true that environmental good fortune can be relied upon to even out initial environmental misfortune, Dennett's Law is neither general nor universal as it is certainly not true that environmental good fortune can be relied upon to even out biological misfortune. However, despite the fact that there is a proven fallacy within Dennett's Law already, let us for completeness examine the final option: the idea that subsequent environmental good fortune can be relied upon to at least even out initial environmental misfortune. And again, there is absolutely no evidence for this hypothesis, and plenty of evidence for the exact opposite. While there are of course heart-warming instances of someone from the wrong side of the tracks making it big, these tend to be very rare exceptions. Rags to riches tales are the exception, not the norm, and it usually takes money to make money – or if not money, at least unusually good luck. For every child who climbs out of the trailer parks there are dozens who do not. For every child who climbs out of the slums and the barrios, there are scores who do not. And even the one who does climb out requires either significant good fortune or unusual ability – good fortune or ability not shared by those who remain behind in the trailer park or the barrio. This is not the averaging of luck over a lifetime: for most this demonstrates only a lifetime of non-averaged-out poor luck and hopelessness.

There are occasional inspiring instances of complete change of direction in life. The true story of the black American football star Michael Oher that lies behind the hugely successful Sandra Bullock movie (and Michael Lewis book) *The Blind Side* is a tale of a lad with everything against him whose life was turned around when he was accepted into a Christian school to pursue sports, and later adopted by a white Christian evangelical family. But even that change in life story required a significant degree of vastly improbable environmental luck, as well as Oher's own considerable physical and psychological talents, his biological luck or good fortune – not just in his size, but also in his speed, coordination and single-mindedness. And the point is that luck does not average out. Fewer than ten children in a hundred from the slums will get the education and the breaks to be a relative success in life, but in contrast perhaps around 70% of middle-class children will get the education and the breaks to be a relative success in life. There is no averaging: this is not 50:50, and we all recognise this. None of us who have the resources leave things up to luck, and we deliberately skew life chances in our families' direction. The wealthiest in the land ensure that their offspring get the best education money can buy, largely because they recognise that initial environmental good fortune is vastly important for good fortune in later life. It will not guarantee it, of course, but it makes it very much more likely.

Initial environmental good fortune feeds back on itself, as does initial environmental misfortune. As Neil Levy writes in *Hard Luck: How Luck Undermines Free Will and Moral Responsibility*, Dennett is just plain "wrong" to argue that environmental luck averages out, because luck "tends to ramify" (2011, p.199), both the bad and the good. If you start off with a poor environmental hand, it will largely follow you and limit your future opportunity, particularly in countries like America and Britain. Levy tells us that 63% of black Americans born into the bottom income quartile will die in that quartile. Bruce Waller (1999, 2011) also reminds us that luck does not average out in human life – including discussion of the halo effect, leading to a spiral of biased behaviour, upward and downward. A child can start at school simply giving off the wrong aura – such as the unwillingness to make eye contact within certain ethnic groups being mistaken for hostility or disinterest by his or her teachers – and from such a simple misunderstanding a downward spiral in relationships may easily result. Does even Dennett – "everyone comes out more or less in the same league" (1984, p.96) – truly believe that in America anyone can be president? Those who get to be president tend to come from vastly privileged social and educational backgrounds, to be of excellent health – it is thought that Franklin D. Roosevelt would not have become president in a global media age where his crippled body would have been common knowledge – and to be generally of the "right" skin colour, gender, religion and sexual orientation. Dennett is forced to admit the truth of the halo effect, such as when he accepts that "physical beauty gives a huge undeserved advantage to those who have it, and it is just one of a variety of unequal endowments that challenge any account of moral responsibility" (2012). But Dennett's simultaneous suggestion that the differences we are born with, such as physical beauty, skin colour or wealth, and are initially raised with, confer "such a relatively small initial advantage" as to "count for nothing" (1984, p.95), and that "many of the differences that survive are, in any event, of negligible importance" (2003, p.274), is both intellectually false and morally obnoxious. The differences, advantages and disadvantages turn out not to be small and not to count for nothing: in a world that reduces to biology and environment they count for everything. The effect is not of negligible importance but of overriding importance.

DENNETT'S LAW 3 – RENDER UNTO DENNETT...

There is an axiomatic flipside to Dennett's Law, and indeed to the work of other compatibilists. The converse to blaming the unlucky for their misfortune is praising the lucky for their good fortune. As per the title of one of Jonathan Jacobs's works, *Choosing Character: Responsibility for Virtue & Vice*, compatibilism is not just about the fortunate blaming the unfortunate. It is also about the fortunate slapping themselves on the back. Vice *and virtue*. The effect of free will propagandising is very much to maintain the *status quo*. While the intention might only be to keep things unchanged at the bottom of the heap, the simultaneous effect is to likewise keep things unchanged at the top of the heap. Not only does free will justification mean that offenders continue to be subject to blame and retribution and that the poor are in danger of meeting blame and indifference, but those at the top of society also get to stay where they are too, untroubled by deeper questions of merit. When you "take care not to examine too closely" (Dennett 1984, p.164) what is going on at the bottom, you ensure also that we are unable to examine closely what is going on at the top.

The neuroscientist and campaigner against the free will myth Sam Harris has written: "Consider the biography of any 'self-made' man, and you will find that his success was entirely dependent on background conditions that he did not make and of which he was merely the beneficiary ... And yet, living in America, one gets the distinct sense that if certain conservatives were asked why they weren't born with club feet or orphaned before the age of five, they would not hesitate to take credit for these accomplishments" (2012, pp.61-2). We will examine later whether liberals are not actually just as guilty of this prejudice as Harris's conservatives, but his larger point stands. There is something unseemly and apparently self-interested – even where this may not be the underlying motivation – about academics who have benefited from the most extraordinary biological and environmental good fortune refusing to acknowledge that luck is the single ultimate dividing factor in social position. For recipients of such good fortune to lend their names and reputations to the beliefs and theories which act to deny the self-evident driving role of luck in human life… well, it at best leaves a nasty smell.

DENNETT'S LAW 4 – THE UNLUCKIEST 20% DO NOT MATTER

The final point to cover in relation to Dennett's Law is of it being completely meaningless from any rational standpoint. Dennett, by his own admission, is a naturalist and a determinist. For Dennett, the only things that exist, and which can produce subsequent behaviour, are biology and environment. The point, therefore, is that it is completely without meaning (and perhaps even insincere) for Dennett to say that our different lives come down to more than luck, or that luck averages out. Why so? We started to consider this point when we noted that human life is not a series of (deterministically) random coin tosses, where each of us is as likely to meet success or failure with each new door we open. Coin tosses are completely unpredictable – as likely to be heads or tails, wins or losses – because the utter indifference of physics is driving the result. Human futures are anything but random because they are driven by the power, partiality and vested interest of human systems. George W. Bush did not become president because of a random coin toss that any one of a hundred million Americans could have won. He became president because his father had been president, and because he came from a very powerful and politically-connected family, a family with considerable wealth to fund his campaign, and even – arguably – due to the ideological partiality of the US Supreme Court. And almost the same can of course be said of so many politicians across the world – of left, right and centre persuasions.

Elsewhere Dennett tries to claim that luck averages out because skill will tell in the end, and that "there is elbow room for skill in between lucky success and unlucky failure" (1984, p.97). To claim that there is elbow room for skill between good luck and poor luck is exactly equivalent to arguing that $(+1) + (-1) = +1$. According to Dennett there seems to be something left over when one takes away the lottery of biology and environment. You can have good or bad fortune in internal causes (biology), and you can have good or bad fortune in external causes (environment) but, for Dennett, there is something beyond normal causation – some form of uncaused skill. Not just a third elbow, but seemingly an uncaused, spirit-guide elbow. We have already gone through all the possible (non-mystical) permutations: all we have available to us is B_U, E_U, BE_U, B_F, E_F and BE_F. It is meaningless gibberish for either a determinist or an indeterminist to try to claim that skill somehow lies outside fortune or misfortune. In a universe without free choice – and be that a deterministic universe or an indeterministic universe – "luck swallows everything", as Galen Strawson puts it (1998). Not luck swallows everything... oh, apart from skill, of course. And good looks. And male-pattern baldness. And lotteries, perhaps. It does philosophy no favours to be caught out making such outrageous claims, even where – perhaps especially where – Bruce Waller (2015) argues that even Dennett can't really believe what he is writing when he suggests that luck averages out in human life, or that skill lies outside the causal universe of biology and environment.

So, returning to the wider point about Dennett and the meaninglessness of claiming that luck averages out within human systems. If it all comes down to biology and culture then a bad life can be only the product of bad biology and/or bad environment. But Dennett is self-evidently trying to deny that any biological and/or environmental loading can be bad, because luck averages out in the long run, and therefore no biological and/or environmental loading will be any worse than any other in the long run. In one sense *no upbringing – no life* – can be truly bad, as all upbringings, for Dennett, will be fully compensated for (positively or negatively) later in life. Indeed, the worse your upbringing, the more of an offset you can expect in later life as your luck still has to average out. If you fall off your bike in childhood you can expect to one day win ten dollars in the state lottery, but if you are repeatedly raped in childhood… hey, you must surely be able to look forward to winning millions in life's lottery. Every cloud has a silver lining and, at least under Dennett's Law, the darker the cloud the more silver in the lining. Falling off your bike is starting life with two tails, and will be compensated for in this coin-toss universe by two heads later in life. Being repeatedly raped as a child is starting with ten tails, and will be compensated for one day by ten heads – the jackpot in the lottery – in this farce of a toss-of-a-coin philosophy. Dennett is here so close to suggesting that there really is no such thing as an abusive upbringing, and certainly no such thing as an abusive (long) life. Harry Frankfurt's model made the willing slave and the clinging abused child free and responsible for their abuse. Dennett, in contrast, offers the willing slave and the beaten-down child the largely false promise that their lives will get better, while denying that their lives can be judged to be any worse or less fortunate than his in the long run. Whichever way he turns, Dennett is on the horns of a dilemma, caused by his pathological need to deny the problem of moral luck. What he has written is either completely meaningless or runs the risk of being wholly offensive, as it downplays human pain and suffering. Luck "averages out in the long run"? But just how do you average out in later life for a childhood of repeated rape? And should Dennett even be the one to judge when such averaging-out is complete? Just to suggest it –

and Dennett is very much at risk of suggesting it by positing his universal law – is deeply troubling.

So let us assume that Dennett means something different. Let's assume instead that he doesn't believe that in the long run a biological and/or environmental loading can be no worse than any other. Where would this leave him? Well… nowhere, really. First off, we can now make no sense of his statement that luck averages out. If a lifetime ("long run") loading is now accepted by Dennett to be bad, how has luck ever averaged out for this person? Secondly, if the lifetime loading is bad, but the system "fair enough", where is the fairness? Is Dennett trying to suggest that the individual is somehow to *blame* for his lifetime loading, that he somehow chose his bad lifetime loading? But for Dennett this is also meaningless, as that choice – for Dennett – was determined by bad biology and/or environment. So, again, how can this be fair enough? When the anti-free will philosopher Bruce Waller took Dan Dennett to task for his extraordinary claim that, in human life, luck averages out in the long run, Dennett hit back – but his new defence is so wholly surprising that it should be quoted at length:

> "Waller often resorts to sports examples, provoked perhaps by my example of the marathon with the uneven (but fair) start, which he raises but dismisses by just saying that it is absurd to suppose the luck averages out. It is not absurd; more on that below… Waller… dismisses as absurd my claim that it is fair because luck averages out in the long run, and offers realistic examples that exhibit good head starts amplifying fortunate outcomes in the long run and bad beginnings spiralling down into worse and worse conclusions. There are of course an abundance of such examples to point to, but they don't in fact make the point he thinks they do. To make the logical point, suppose that in a population of 300 million, there were 3 million examples of manifestly amplified good fortune and bad fortune

of the sort he details—but *only* 3 million! The luck averaged out in ninety-nine percent of the population: there were as many deprived childhoods that led to happy outcomes as not, and equally many privileged childhoods that led to deplorable ends. If anything like that were true, my claim would not be absurd at all. But *could* anything like that be true? Of course it could, because society is actively engaged in all manner of compensatory feedback mechanisms designed (imperfectly) to *make* it true... If a child is growing up alarmingly wild and irresponsible, parents and teachers offer compensatory programs of one sort or another. It doesn't always work, of course, but we keep monitoring our successes and failures, devising new, hopefully better, schemes" (Dan Dennett, 2012).

Dennett's evidence here that we are still treating the unlucky 1% fairly – the system is fair enough remember – *is that the system is to the benefit of the other 99%*. Because intervention ("compensatory feedback mechanisms") might have worked for some of the previously unlucky, those it didn't work for are obliged to regard it as a universal averaging-out. This is an absurdly unjust argument that we shall return to below, but even for the lucky 99% his argument is extraordinary and wholly unrealistic. Suppose 25% start in wealth, 25% in poverty, and 50% in the middle. He is then suggesting, for his thought experiment, that the 50% in the middle do not move, but that all 25% of the deprived childhoods end in happy outcomes and all 25% of the privileged childhoods lead to, to quote, "deplorable ends". This is at first only a slightly strange thought experiment, until he actually tries to connect it to contemporary America by asking "*could* anything like that be true?" and responding "of course", and because of political action. So previously Dennett appeared to be arguing that luck averaged out because life was a long series of random coin tosses where any individual is as likely to experience good luck as bad at each new decision we make. Since 2012 Dennett has revised his work to tell us there is no luck involved at all in his luck averages out maxim: life opportunities average out, not because of the interplay of chance outcomes, but because of active and concerted state intervention.

Even if Dennett were describing opportunities in the culturally strongly egalitarian Nordic countries this would be patently false, but to suggest that state intervention causes life chances to average out in a country like America, with its market fundamentalism and almost pathological aversion to state assistance (particularly assistance to the poor) comes close to being downright insulting. And having started with a rose-tinted view of the American Dream, telling us that everyone in America has exactly the same life chances overall, Dennett then gives us faith in the American Dream with a novel twist. For Dennett, luck – actually state intervention – can and does average out life chances because of two opposite but converging tendencies. The first driving tendency is that, for Dennett, *all* those who start at the bottom will end up at the top (not so much anyone can be president even if born into poverty, as everyone will be president so long as they are born into poverty) – but minus, of course, 1%: the perhaps one and a half million of unfortunates experiencing "manifestly amplified … bad fortune", whom Dennett has simply refused to take into account. And the second driving tendency is that, for Dennett, *all* of those who start at the top ("privileged childhoods") will end up in poverty and coming to "deplorable ends". This is thus the American Dream seen through rose-tinted spectacles yet with a particularly vindictive class-hatred inversion. Not only will black offensive tackle Michael Oher one day be President, suggests Dennett, but Bill Gates must some day freeze to death next to his shopping cart on the winter streets of Boston.

Even if it were true that there was an active attempt in a particular country to intervene to try to even out unfair starting positions in life, Dennett's assertion that luck averages out in the long run still reduces to nothing more than the suggestion that B_U, E_U, and BE_U are subsequently offset by any of B_F, E_F, and BE_F. Why so? Because to the extent that state intervention had been somewhat successful, all it would have done is to have reduced the gap between starting point A (let us call this the unlucky start in life, be that for reasons of B_U, E_U, or BE_U) and starting point B (let us call this the lucky start in life, be that for reasons of B_F, E_F, or BE_F). There is still a gap, and that gap is explained completely in terms of the luck of biology and upbringing. It is whatever is *left over* – the residual difference between states B_U and/or E_U and/or BE_U and states B_F and/or E_F and/or BE_F – that matters to the free will debate. No one is denying that even in America there isn't some attempt to assist at least some of the poor some of the time, in part through the fine American tradition of philanthropy which grew up to fill the vacuum that may otherwise be filled by a working welfare safety net. Even in a strongly egalitarian culture like Iceland it is profoundly wrong to try to pretend that what separates the most ethical and successful from the least ethical and successful is not simply a matter of luck that can be traced directly to biology or upbringing or to some complex interaction of the two. Why is it necessary to stress this point? Because Dennett's assertion that luck averages out in human life is just as meaningless even if we allow for state intervention as it is when he is suggesting a form of coin-toss existence. Indeed, his state-interventionist existence still presupposes the coin-toss existence in order to try to get the necessary averaging-out he needs. Unless state intervention is set to level *all* differences for *all* people *all* of the time – theoretically impossible, for reasons we covered in the first two sections, not to say practically bonkers – then there will be differences remaining: and those differences will be the result of a less favourable biology, environment or biology-environment. Even with theoretical massive state intervention, Dennett's luck averages out hypothesis collapses in upon itself because (as we showed in the first and second sections) unfortunate biology, environment or biology-environment cannot be and will not be reliably offset.

Having said all this, please put to one side Dennett's extraordinary suggestions for Bill Gates, America and the 99%, and just concentrate on what he is saying about the 1%. The question is: *Are we treating X fairly?* Dennett's response is that evidence that we are treating X fairly isn't provided by investigating our treatment of X, but instead by investigating treatment of a completely unconnected and extraneous Y. If someone asked the question: *Is access easy for the disabled?* and yet got back the singular response: *Access is easy for the able-bodied*, the questioner would legitimately feel that the respondent had (just possibly) not understood the question or was not an English speaker or – far more likely – was deliberately refusing to answer the question asked. It would be a rather foolish tour guide who turned up expecting easy access for the disabled after receiving this particular response. Likewise, it would be a rather foolish person who expected fairness for the unlucky 1% after receiving Dennett's assurances above. Fairness to the 1%, for Dennett, is not to be judged by reference to that 1%: according to Dennett, the fact that it doesn't work to the benefit of that 1% is utterly unimportant and meaningless. That 99% have a good deal is enough to completely excuse the fact that 1% get a raw deal. Dennett's argument for why this is still fair enough? Because it doesn't need to be fair. Apparently life isn't fair. "Is it fair, he keeps asking, to hold both of them responsible? Life isn't fair" (2012). So the effects on 1% of the American population, no matter how unjust, can effectively be wholly ignored when assessing whether the system is fair enough.

Yet it is not only 1% of Americans that Dennett's Law is completely dismissive of. At the time of writing one in five American children receives food aid in the richest nation in the history of the world. More than fifteen million US kids regularly go to bed hungry, which is almost more children than there are people in Chile. Over forty-five million Americans are now thought to depend on food banks: the poor or near-poor living in deep neglect. It is not just offenders who are unjustly targeted by the free will fraud: the free will fraud is central to keeping alive the conceit held by a large proportion of voting Americans that poverty, as much as crime, is the product of free will. As the Republican presidential candidate Herman Cain put it: "If you don't have a job and you're not rich, blame yourself" (see Pearlstein, 2011). So it is emphatically not 1% of Americans who are being hurt by the free will myth: it is at least a fifth of Americans, including perhaps 20% of American children. Dennett says as much above, when he painstakingly links the debate around free will to bad fortune, compensatory feedback mechanisms, and both deprived and privileged childhoods. The free will myth, Dennett here admits, doesn't just speak to us regarding offenders, but to the far larger grouping known as the undeserving poor. Dennett can only defend free will by writing off not just 1% of Americans, but at least 20% of Americans. Of course, Dennett's attempt to delink the free will debates from the problem of moral luck would be just as odious if he were only telling us that 1% of children (or 1% of the population) do not matter as it is when he is telling us that 20% of children (or 20% of the population) do not matter.

Dennett needs to deny the existence of moral luck in the free will debates. However, Dennett recognises that if life comes down to just biology and environment then the existence of moral luck becomes impossible to deny, as no one can be argued to be responsible for the biology they were born with or the environment they were born into. Therefore Dennett is driven to posit something that *compensates* for moral luck – something that would allow us to shrug the problem away. This compensatory mechanism – either the even-handedness of random coin tosses in life or state intervention – can only solve the problem of moral luck if it *reliably* offsets moral luck, and for Dennett for all but 1% of the time it *does* reliably offset moral luck. But this leaves Dennett with a new problem that we have not fully fleshed out yet. As, in Dennett's argument, this compensatory mechanism does reliably intervene – or for 99%, and excepting three million Americans – then, as almost fifty million Americans do depend on food banks (and, as experience tells us, that most of this fifty million will die in poverty) they must now be somehow *responsible* for their lifetime of poverty. And they must somehow be responsible for their lifetime in poverty as there is no more luck left in the system, because the compensatory mechanism has, for Dennett, taken away the random luck of biology and environment. For Dennett, their poverty is somehow now up to *them* as it is delinked from any unfair lottery of biology and environment, because luck has averaged out. Hence we not only have the most extraordinary attempt to get around the problem of moral luck, but we also have the situation where this attempt makes life's unfortunates wholly responsible for their ill fortune as all luck and misfortune has disappeared from the system over the longer term.

Gary Watson, Moral Apartheid, and the Two Types of Human

"There is room for the thought that there is something 'in me' by virtue of which I would not have become a vicious person in Harris's circumstances. And if that factor were among my essential properties, so to speak, then that difference between Harris and me would not be a matter of moral luck on my part, but a matter of who we essentially were… [and] this difference still might explain what is to my credit" (Watson, 2004, p.248).

Recall now that Dennett's work had the potential to be deeply important because it promised to square the circle and do what Frankfurt's work, or Frankfurt and Dworkin's work, could not do:

legitimise blame in a deterministic universe by getting around the problem of moral luck. Dennett failed in his argument because he could neither show that biology and environment are not a lottery nor that there is anything to offset the lottery. Gary Watson thinks that he has an alternative, and valid, argument which does not rely on denying the obvious fact that biology and upbringing are a lottery, something you are just born into. Gary Watson and his fellow "essentialists", as they have been described, believe that they can bypass the problem of moral luck by instead giving us an argument based on essential human differences.

First, the intellectual background. Compatibilists are naturalists, materialists, and philosophical determinists, and are therefore supposed to be capable of accepting that behaviour is nothing more than the interaction of biology plus environment. But as it is the case that human behaviour is nothing more than the product of biology plus environment this can lead to some rather uncomfortable conclusions – including the recognition that had you been exposed to the horrific experiences some of your fellow human beings have had to suffer, you might have turned out to be a very different person (and possibly even a malign and deeply vicious person). Admitting this to oneself might start to induce some sympathy for those who have been less fortunate in their upbringing or biology. Both history and social psychology appear to confirm that those we came from, and those we most closely resemble, were and are capable of acting in deeply nasty ways. As such, surely we must all have had the potential to have grown up behaving in malign – even evil – ways, at least at some earlier point in our lives? Yale's Stanley Milgram showed in the early 1960s that volunteers were prepared to subject other volunteers (actually actors) to what they believed were lethal electric shocks when encouraged to do so (and assured that they would not be held responsible for their actions) by an authority figure in a white coat. Apparently most of us are prepared to behave quite abysmally when the peer pressure is turned up or our social status turned down. Philip Zimbardo – whose recent book is tellingly titled *The Lucifer Effect: How Good People Turn Evil* – conducted the famous Stanford Prison Experiment in 1971 which showed how almost all ordinary college students, randomly divided into guards and inmates, quickly became either bestial sadists or cowering victims according to the situation they were put into.

Such experiments, and any review of human history, have always raised challenging questions about the nature of good and evil, and of the human predisposition to both good and evil. These are deeply troubling questions, such as: *Are you absolutely sure you wouldn't ever have been a slave owner?* Abraham Lincoln, the liberator of millions and that great critic of the conceit of free will, once said that Northerners couldn't feel too morally superior to Southern slaveholders because "if we were situated as they are, we should act and feel as they do; and if they were situated as we are, they should act and feel as we do; and we never ought to lose sight of this fact in discussing the subject" (Guelzo 2009, p.39). Deeply troubling questions, such as: *Are you absolutely sure you wouldn't have been a concentration camp guard if you had been raised in the paranoia of early 1920s Germany?* Yet many are deeply uncomfortable with such considerations, almost taking as a personal slight the thought that they might have been raised to be different people, perhaps even not very nice people. The philosopher Gary Watson, for example, has admitted to an "ontological shudder" and even a (to him) "troubling... sense of equality with the other", the troubling thought that "I too am a potential sinner" (2004, p.245), when he ruminates upon, but quickly rejects, the possibility that he might have been raised to be a quite different, and quite nasty, person. He quickly rejects the thought that he, too, might ever have been raised to be a "sinner".

Essentialists are theorists who argue that there is something essential in them that means that even with the most terrible of upbringings they would still have turned out effectively virtuous, or at the very least lacking in vices and "sin". Essentialists, in other words, like to suggest that they somehow stand *outside* any real lottery of biology and environment and that, at least to an extent, they were always destined to win in life. Discussing the case of the American serial killer Robert Harris – who was tortured by his sadistic and wholly unpredictable father (who believed that Harris was not his natural son), hated by his mother because she blamed her son for the beatings she received at her husband's hands, and bullied by merciless classmates, before being incarcerated in an American prison for children where he was repeatedly raped from the age of fourteen – Gary Watson tells us that had he ever been subjected to such experiences he might very well *not* have become a scarred or violent person. "There is room for the thought that there is something 'in me' by virtue of which I would not have become a vicious person in Harris's circumstances. And if that factor were among my essential properties, so to speak, then that difference between Harris and me would not be a matter of moral luck on my part" (2004, p.248). In this passage Watson is explicitly recognising that *if* all human difference reduces to moral luck then our economic, social and judicial attitudes towards life's losers would have to fundamentally change. "The thought about moral luck turns one's gaze inward. It makes one feel less in a position to cast blame" (2004, p.245). And yet, like Dennett, Watson is keen to find an argument that life does not just reduce to moral luck. As with Dennett, blame requires the denial of moral luck, at least for Watson and the essentialists. So what does Watson's essentialism really reduce to, when we take a closer look? It reduces of course to the following equation:

Harris (bad) behaviour = $B_B + E_B$

Watson (good, or at least not bad) behaviour = $B_G + E_B$

Watson is implying here that all really bad behaviour – subscript B for bad, and contrasted with subscript G for good – reduces to biology. Watson argues, or at least is making "room for the thought", that even if he had been subject to the same horrific abuse as Harris, he'd still have turned out fine. Watson is suggesting that as a young child he could have been brutalised and buggered on a daily basis, and at least to an extent he'd just have shrugged it off; viewed it as a salutary lesson about life's rich tapestry. Watson, or at least the essentialist Watson, is suggesting here that no matter the environment he started with it would not have thrown off *his* moral compass – that he would not have turned to the bad: he would never have been a killer or a sinner. And that he could probably never have been a Southern slaveholder either, or a concentration camp guard.

No matter how extreme the environment E in Watson's case, the argument is that his behaviour would have remained good, or at the very least not bad. So whether or not Harris's behaviour was triggered by purely bad biology, or bad biology in a bad environment, the point here is that bad biology – fundamentally different biology from Watson's – was the overriding factor. They could have had an identical environment, but Watson would never have behaved badly in either a good or bad environment (he was in effect *fated* to be a good, or at least non-sinful, person), while Harris was effectively *doomed* to be a bad person, at least in a bad environment. Watson does not tell us how Harris might have behaved in a good environment, be that well or just as badly, but this is largely irrelevant to the above argument. In the naturalist biology + environment world (supposedly) inhabited by Watson, the only way we can *always* get acceptable behaviour from Watson in a bad environment while simultaneously always getting bad behaviour from Harris in that same environment is if Watson is suggesting that Harris (and violent offenders in general) possess a fundamentally different biological code from the fated-to-be-good people like him and you and me.

In Watson's view, or at least Watson's essentialist view, the world is *clearly and permanently* divided into the non-sinning (who owe no gratitude for their fine upbringings but simply possess better, non-toxic, biologies) and the sinful and violent who – no matter what environment we give them – will always be marked out for suspicion because they are carrying those worse, toxic, biologies. But although he has divided mankind into two forms, will Watson actually go so far as to deny to one form the consideration and rights he claims for the other form? Yes, he will. Remember Watson telling us that he has a sudden "sense of equality" with "the other", a sense of equality that disappears once we split mankind into two forms; a sense of equality that disappears as soon as he can convince himself that he could never have been like that? Watson adds to this, and tells us that although sympathy, along with outrage, is the appropriate emotional and moral response to "the other" – which justice demands that we *simultaneously* view with sympathy and outrage – he has found a reason to deny Harris the sympathy that would otherwise be his moral due. "The sympathy toward the boy he was is at odds with outrage toward the man he is… each of these responses is appropriate… Harris both satisfies and violates the criteria of victimhood" (p.244). The important word here is "violates".

We view victimhood, according to Watson, as digital, not analogue. Violates does not mean that we balance out or temper our sympathy. Violates means that we disregard the formerly appropriate moral response: that Harris has now lost the right to our sympathy. Sympathy and a sense of equality, remember, that he would still be entitled to if we could believe that we could ever have been like this; sympathy that he is entitled to where there is that residual "sense of equality with the other". Sympathy can, for Watson, ethically be abandoned where there is no sense of equality with the other. Sympathy, for Watson, is either on or off, yes or no, 1s or 0s: digital, not analogue. There is a clear admission from

Watson that at some level justice *demands* that we recognise the victimhood of the offender, because such offenders meet the criteria necessary to be regarded as victims (p.244), yet at the same time the instruction from Watson that the right that we (the biologically fortunate) would have to claim victimhood *no longer* applies to the offender who is, biologically, not like us. Irrespective of what justice originally demanded, only the B_G has the right to claim victimhood now: only the B_G has the right to sympathy and that "sense of equality with the other". The other form of human, the B_B, has lost the basic rights to equality that we still claim, notwithstanding that justice would otherwise have demanded he share those rights. There is no longer "equality" between the two types of human. One has more rights than the other; gets more justice than the other. This is beyond Frankfurt and Dworkin's winners' justice: this is – at least in the author's opinion – philosophical eugenics bordering on moral apartheid. As with Dennett's Law, we are denying to "the other" – to the 1 to 20% – fundamental rights that we claim for ourselves. One form of human has more basic rights and claims to respect and consideration than the other. Skin colour and nose shape do not drive this ghettoisation, but biology still does.

So what is the supposed effect? For Watson life does not come down to moral luck – not because there is no lottery of biology and environment, but because mankind is divided into two forms, and the luckier form need sense no fellow-feeling (what Watson terms "equality") with the unlucky form. They are *not* equal to us. They are not our fellows. In other words, we have no more duty to address questions of sympathy, fairness and justice when considering the unlucky form of human than we – the higher apes – have an obligation to consider questions of sympathy, fairness and justice for the chimpanzee, or any other of the lower apes. We don't unnecessarily torture chimpanzees, sure, but we don't have to extend them considerations of sympathy, fair play and justice.

Essentialists do not go so far as to describe "the other" as non-human or sub-human, but they are nonetheless looking to deny the other any common fellow-feeling or sense of equality. *In the literature the other remains a human, just not a fellow human.* Moral luck is extinguished, according to Watson, by the simple expedient of denying some humans the right to expect the considerations of fellowship, equality, and fair play that those like him and you demand. According to Watson, we can avoid talking about a lottery – avoid all problems of moral luck – by defining the losers out of existence: by denying the unlucky are even allowed to take part in our lottery in the first place.

Watson's essentialism and denial of moral luck moves beyond suggesting two essentially different types of human, and the need to feel no fellow-feeling with the losers or even gratitude for environmental good fortune, when he further argues that he may be able to take credit for his fine essence: a fine essence which (we have seen) reduces to a fine biological hand. Watson tells us that the hypothesised difference between himself and a violent offender would then not be a matter of moral luck "but a matter of who we essentially were … [and] this difference still might explain what is to my credit" (2004, p.248). We have previously encountered the anti-free will polemicist and neuroscientist Sam Harris asserting that "living in America, one gets the distinct sense that if certain conservatives were asked why they weren't born with club feet or orphaned before the age of five, they would not hesitate to take credit for these accomplishments" (2012, pp.61-2). Harris's epigram is supposed to be amusingly satirical, and yet Watson, this well-educated mainstream American philosopher, is trying to claim exactly such credit. It might still be "to my credit" that I possess the better biology than most of America's incarcerated population, asserts Watson. It may still be to Watson's credit that he does not possess the genetic weaknesses of so many who make up America's imprisoned, from schizophrenia to dyslexia. And it might still be to Watson's credit, presumably, that he does not have club feet and was not orphaned before the age of five.

Essentialism comes down to pure biology for Watson. But if you can find credit in the biology you are born with, the corollary can only be that others should take the blame for the biology they were born with. To the extent we allow any "room for the thought" that Watson's biology is to his credit – an argument proposed solely to provide a necessary platform to reject the problem of moral luck – then we are self-evidently allowing room for the thought that others' biologies are to their discredit. The whole point is to deny moral luck, and as Watson is trying to find an argument that good biology is not just down to luck and must be somehow deserved, the corollary must be that bad biology is not just luck either but is also somehow deserved. When Herman Cain claims credit for being rich it is so that he can blame those who are not rich. When Watson tries to claim credit for his biology he is simultaneously suggesting that others, including Robert Harris, are to blame for their biology. But Watson will not be able to limit it to Harris, because what applies to Harris must surely apply equally to the child born with half his face and brain missing, because there is no agency to DNA that logically allows him to draw a line here. "There is room for the thought that… if that factor were among my essential properties… then that difference… [would be] a matter of who we essentially were… [and] this difference still might explain what is to my credit." But the genetic abnormality that caused the child to have half his face and brain missing is as much a part of who the child essentially is – it is as much among his "essential properties" – as is the genetic blessing that caused Gary Watson to have such a very fine character, and which he is then looking to claim credit for. So there is exactly as much room for the thought that all unfortunate biology is to one's discredit as there is that fine biology is to one's credit. Malign biology for Watson is somehow also deserved, but in trying to get around the problem of moral luck malign biology has had to be identified as biology that is unlucky – be that a tendency towards crime or a tendency to have half your face and brain missing. To extend Sam Harris's epigram, Watson is looking not just to claim credit for not having been born with club feet, he is looking to make others to blame when they were born with club feet.

In his strange attempt to sidestep the problem of moral luck Dan Dennett forced us to ask what *luck averages out* might mean in the case of the free will propagandist Stephen Hawking and his progressive motor neurone disease, including whether Dennett was suggesting that Hawking might need to display some gratitude for being in a wheelchair. In his bizarre attempt to sidestep the problem of moral luck the essentialist Gary Watson seems to go one step further and suggest (make "room for the thought") that it might be to Stephen Hawking's discredit that he ended up in a wheelchair in the first place (one of the essential properties of a leading academic so immediately recognisable through his disability that he even appeared on *The Simpsons*). To stress again the reason that such smart, liberal, and senior philosophers paint themselves into such absurd corners is that they are trying to find a solution to the most difficult problem in the free will and moral responsibility debates – the problem of moral luck. It is easy to ridicule their attempts, but with a request for understanding do remember that Dennett and Watson are desperate to provide a moral justification for the current (mis)behaviour of the vast majority of us.

Essentialism is relatively widespread among philosophical naturalists. Michael McKenna has written against Watson's expressions of disquiet over the robust defence of retributivism and the more violent reactive attitudes in a world where, essentialist screens lowered for a moment, "the thought about moral luck turns one's gaze inward… makes one feel less in a position to cast blame". Watson described for us his "ontological shudder" and sense of equality and fellow-feeling with the offender when considering, albeit very briefly, the possibility that he might have turned out to be as violent and as vile. McKenna, in contrast, has no time for such liberal uncertainties, and no time for any expressions of fellow-feeling with the other. Also citing the case of Robert Harris, McKenna concludes that "the thought that we ought not blame does not seem compelling in these cases since it is hard to take seriously that we might have been like that" (2008, p.216). As Bruce Waller (2011) has pointed out, McKenna's work is a little unusual in that it bases the right to blame specifically upon the fact that others are not like us, which has some further extraordinary implications. Mankind, McKenna's writing is suggesting, is comprehensively and permanently divided into *them* and *us* – into at least two distinct biological types of human. And we have the right to blame them *because* they are not like us, and because we could never have been like them. There is of course something deeply suspicious about any argument that bases the entire rationale for blame upon the division of the world into two biological types of human that are distinctly different and can never meet. There is now a significant body of psychological research (summarised in Kraus & Keltner, 2013) suggesting that biological essentialism is attractive to many within the privileged classes as it serves as an excuse to ignore the plight of the less fortunate.

Yet not only do we have the traditional suspicion of any permanent notion of them and us – of irreconcilable forms of human – we also get some even more unusual outcomes with McKenna's work. Had it been possible that we might have been like them, then McKenna seems to be suggesting that we would not have the right to blame. "The intuition that we ourselves ought not cast blame seems only to gain purchase upon our sentiments when the condition of our present selves shares the same kind of moral fault or (minimally) shares the *potential* for the same kind of fault" (2008, p.216). McKenna suggests, as an example, that he might not be able to blame drunks to the extent that he has similarly drunk too much. So the implication seems to be that if we – the light-skinned middle classes – fiddle our taxes then hey, no one can blame us as we have all considered fiddling our taxes (and thus all have the "*potential* for the same kind of fault"). Our form can never be blamed for those normal middle-class peccadilloes, including insurance fraud, casual racism and tax evasion. But crimes associated very largely with the slums, poverty and toxic environments? Well, then, we – the comfortable middle classes – can go to town on those, as they are not our weaknesses. No one can blame us, but we get to blame everybody who is not like us. This is winners' justice on a scale undreamed of under the Frankfurt and Dworkin models: they can't judge each other because they are alike, but we get to judge them because they are not like us – and furthermore, if it could be shown that we have weaknesses like them… well, hey, then no one gets to judge us.

McKenna here bases his right to blame on two very different approaches. His first is that we can blame, as who we are now could not be like "the other" (the intuition that we "ought not cast blame seems only to gain purchase… when the condition of our present selves shares the same kind of moral fault or… the *potential* for the same kind of fault"). His second approach, which he still needs to try to sneak in for reasons we will discuss, is that we could never have been like the other ("the thought that we ought not blame does not seem compelling in these cases since it is hard to take seriously that we might have been like that"). As regards the first approach, it may be true that most working American philosophers could not now be induced to torture or butcher another human being, though personally the author would not try to hold up Western philosophers as exemplars of non-violence, kindness, morality, fair play, or justice. The first approach, though, is useless to us, as it entirely avoids addressing the question of moral luck: it just takes us back to where we were earlier with the winners' justice of the Frankfurt model, and that model's indifference to the problem of moral luck. The second approach does, like Watson and Dennett, offer a vital attempted solution to the problem of moral luck, though not one that has not already been attempted more comprehensively by Gary Watson. The first approach fails as it is a non-moral approach: it is deaf to unfairness and the problem of moral luck. The second approach has greater potential, but will be shown to be almost certainly factually false.

Even if there was something to be said in favour of essentialism's general claim that there are two types of biological human – and history and social psychology provide little evidence for such a conceit, while we shall see later that biology provides much to suggest that a young Gary Watson could probably have been raised to rape and butcher with abandon – there is nothing in the work of Watson, or McKenna, which answers the problem that Robert Harris, like all in his situation, was simply the product of great misfortune that he did not choose or author: being the product of unlucky biology and/or unlucky experiences. To fail to see the injustice of lording it over Harris because you were just more lucky and had real opportunity – including, as with Watson, taking away his rights to equality with our form because he was less lucky in his putative biological inheritance, which really does smack of positive eugenics – seems to speak volumes against our form's, or the philosopher's, supposed noble essence and innate goodness. The argument of the philosopher Peter French, best known for championing the virtue of "hostile" vengeance, is that the gap between them and us is unbridgeable – "vengeance theorists are realists… there is an unbridgeable moral chasm between people who regularly do wicked deeds and those who typically do good deeds" (2001, p.89). An unbridgeable moral divide or chasm: one might as easily say an essential moral difference – two essentially different forms of human, perhaps. This suggestion seems to the author not only historically and ontologically suspect but deeply conceited and self-serving.

Essentialism is morally troubling even where we credit the general idea that it might be true: that it might be the case that some of us – most of us – would never have behaved as badly as some have done. Essentialism is morally problematic even where we give credit to the assertion that we are a breed apart from the biologically unlucky, and would never have become drug users or begged from a position of the direst poverty; never have brutalised after the worst upbringing. As morally troubling as essentialism would be even if it were true – because it divides humanity into two biological types and denies to the not-so-perfect type of human the inalienable rights still claimed for our more perfect form – it becomes more troubling still given that it is almost certainly factually incorrect. We all appear to be descended from ancestors who have committed the most depraved behaviour, behaviour that matches that of any serial killer. While there is cultural variation, and we may one day discover some Amazonian tribe of which such behaviour was never the case, you usually only need to go back a hundred years or so within Western, African and Eastern cultures to come across our suitably depraved ancestors: from the German, Austrian, and Italian mid twentieth-century behaviour that needs no reminder, and the Eastern European cultures that eagerly embraced a similarly thuggish fascist worldview, to other European cultures' embrace of the mass murdering insanity of Marxist-Leninism. Indeed, the true extent of some horror is only now coming to light, as historical archives are opened and codes of silence are lifted. In *The Spanish Holocaust*, Paul Preston, a leading expert on twentieth-century Spanish history, has catalogued in excruciating detail the utter barbarity of that country's civil war. Both left and right committed vast atrocities but, according to Preston (2012), only the right used genocide and terror as an actual instrument of policy. The planned gang rape to death of teenage girls, the deliberate murder of children in front of their parents, the wholesale slaughter of pregnant women, systematic extermination, concentration camps, slave labour: the dehumanisation and cruelty of twentieth-century Spain was almost beyond belief. Likewise, in just the last couple of hundred years Africa has seen many, many home-grown genocides, plus imported European inhumanities, from the apartheid of Dutch settlers to various French and Spanish barbarities, and not forgetting the Belgian horrors in the Congo, that real life "Heart of Darkness". Eastern cultures have seen their own examples, from the unspeakable killing fields of Cambodia and Year Zero to the similar ideological barbarities of twentieth-century Maoist China. Even today, Japan does not teach most schoolchildren of its own early to mid twentieth-century guilty horrors, with the Rape of Nanking at such a level of bestiality and dehumanisation that it perhaps deserves to be especially singled out.

In the New World, eighteenth-, nineteenth-, and twentieth-century militaristic horror was often imported via European settlers, albeit that such horrors were taking place in a region that had, sometimes only a few years before, seen the unparalleled human sacrifice by indigenous people and their blood-crazed gods. Meanwhile, North America, home to so many intellectual essentialists, has little to crow about, with segregation following hard on the heels of slavery. In *The Barbarous Years*, Bernard Bailyn, the nonagenarian double Pulitzer Prize-winning Harvard historian, argues that the horrors of American slavery were a by-product of the physical and intellectual "savagery" (Bailyn's term) of the early settlers, the white European-descended Americans and their intolerant apocalyptic worldview. And it is difficult to credit essentialism with much intellectual respectability when even our most holy of books actively celebrates bestial dehumanisation, including genocide, infanticide, the rape of children, and slavery:

> "And the children of Israel took all the women of Midian captives, and their little ones... And Moses was wroth with the

officers of the host... And Moses said unto them, Have ye saved all the women alive?... Now therefore kill every male among the little ones, and kill every woman that hath known man by lying with him. But all the women children, that have not known a man by lying with him, keep alive for yourselves" (the *Bible*, Numbers 31, verses 9-18).

According to Deuteronomy 20 verses 16 to 18, and Deuteronomy 7 verse 1, to the extermination of the Midianites was added the genocide of the Hittites, the Amorites, the Canaanites, the Perizzites, the Hivites, the Jebusites, and the Girgashites ("you shall save alive nothing that breathes, but you shall utterly destroy them"). When we have even the most sympathetic of human religions celebrating infanticide and the raping to death of children – in verse in the Pentateuch, and in deed as with the Spanish Catholic Church – the essentialist conceit that some of us could never have been raised to act thus – even under such systems of extreme paranoia, hatred and an inculcated contempt for human life as existed in early twentieth-century Spain, Germany and Japan – appears laughable. It is difficult to avoid the recognition that we all come from those who have committed every kind of barbaric atrocity, every deed that we despise when such acts are committed by headline-grabbing individuals and serial killers. Remember that Watson and McKenna (or at least McKenna when he is trying to address the problem of moral luck) are refusing to accept that they could ever have committed bestial act A (say, brutal infanticide). But in a world without free choice act A can only be the product of biological inheritance B_B and/or environmental inheritance E_B. Now for it to be the case that Watson and McKenna would never have committed act A ("hard to take seriously that we might have been like that"), it must be the case not just that they could never have existed in environment E_B but that they never had the biological propensity B_B. Yet their forefathers almost certainly committed act A, and must therefore have either carried biological inclination B_B or been raised in a conducive environment E_B.

Even if it was not a biological inclination but only a biological propensity, their forefathers suffered from it, and it was all that was needed to permit them to undertake act A when in conjunction with environment E_B. If the act is wholly environmental in origin we need look no further, as it is preposterous that we could not manufacture a similar enough environment such that they would not have acted as their forefathers did. Remember, we are not saying they would so act: to destroy essentialism's attempt to answer the problem of moral luck we need only show that an earlier version of them could have been so programmed ("might have been like that"). Biology would seem to offer Watson and McKenna greater security than trying the environmental argument route, but since – if act A is not wholly environmental in origin – their forefathers almost certainly had such biological propensity, or at least susceptibility, there is nothing to suggest that they too do not – or at least cannot, which is all we need to show – carry similar biological programming, propensity, or susceptibility. Essentialism, which says they could not have behaved so, seems wholly false and self-serving when one accepts only that our ancestors behaved appallingly. The only way Watson and McKenna could realistically claim that they could never have acted so, given that their forefathers almost certainly have acted so, would be for Watson and McKenna to be theoretically able to stand outside both B_B and E_B – for Watson and McKenna to have been able to override B_B and E_B. Since Watson and McKenna are trying to argue that they could never have behaved so, and despite full knowledge of our ancestors' behaviour, it is arguably fair to say that Watson and McKenna may, in essence, be trying to argue that they do stand outside B_B and E_B – which might suggest that Watson and McKenna may be as guilty of contra-causal libertarian flights of fancy as are John Searle, Peter van Inwagen and Dan Dennett.

We have now seen two attempts to square the circle: two attempts at finding an answer to the compatibilists' overarching problem of moral luck. The first, from Dennett, was to deny that biology and environment are in the longer term a lottery as they are, for Dennett, no more than a temporary uncertainty to the fair unfolding of events (although first we may need to write off between 1 and 20% of the public). There is no lottery because the losers are eliminated from any assessment of the luck of the system. The second, from Watson and the essentialists, was not to deny that biology and environment are a lottery but instead to argue that there are two types of human and that questions of moral luck are no more relevant when considering the other form of human than they would be when considering our cousins the chimpanzees. Two solutions. Both seemingly deeply flawed, intellectually and morally.

Compatibilism as Self-Creation

The idea of self-creation is central to the libertarian project. Recall Aristotle, who argued that it was "at first open to the unjust or licentious person not to become such", and that our dispositions "are voluntary in the sense that it was originally in our power to exercise them in one way or the other". But just compare Aristotle's famous libertarian assertion with this from the reputedly compatibilist Dan Dennett: "common wisdom has it that... I have created and unleashed an agent who is myself... I think this common wisdom is indeed wisdom" (1984, p.85). But the common wisdom referred to here is the third factor: freedom from biology and environment; man as *causa sui*; man as the contra-causal originator of himself. And Dennett certainly appears to be giving us libertarian self-creation when he writes that "one can be as responsible for one's character" because it is the person who "managed to turn himself into a monster" (1984, p.167).

One crossover point between mainstream compatibilists and libertarians, then, is self-creation. Like Dennett, Gary Watson is another such compatibilist-libertarian. "A plea of this kind is, on the other hand, grist for the incompatibilists' mill… [as Robert] Harris's history reveals him to be an inevitable product of his formative circumstances… In this instance, however, an incompatibilist diagnosis seems doubtful… [T]he force of the example does not depend on a belief in the *inevitability* of the upshot. Nothing in the story supports such a belief. The thought is not 'It had to be!'" (2004, p.243). Watson is simply wrong where he is here trying to suggest that Harris was not the inevitable product of biology and environment; that Harris somehow created himself away from the imperatives of biology and environment. In a world without free choice it was inevitable that Harris would turn out the way he did, given the particular set of biological and environmental factors in play, the here-admitted "formative circumstances". And yet compatibilism is supposed to be able to accept this understanding. It was most definitely the case that *It had to be!* given the acknowledged formative circumstances. We exist in the quasiclassical universe, which is deterministic at the human level, but even if this were not the case indeterminism would not have given Harris a freely chosen could-have-done-otherwise moment. To suggest otherwise, as Watson is here doing, is simply untrue. Dan Dennett likewise writes erroneously that when we are making important decisions we undertake an internal monologue or debate but at some point we stop the deliberation "in the full knowledge that I could have considered further" (1978, p.297). Yet as Bruce Waller notes, the "glib suggestion" that everyone, no matter what their capacities and resources, could have carried out the same level of self-deliberation, additional monologue and self-criticism "is both shallow and false" (2011, p.163).

The philosopher Jonathan Jacobs is another ostensible naturalist who tries to sneak in self-creation, as when he writes that it is sometimes easier to insist that one was not wrong "in having done something quite awful than to admit that one knew better or could have acted differently", and that "the inability of the ethically disabled agent to overcome that condition is not exclusively a matter of bad constitutive luck. It is something the agent has brought about" (2001, pp.79-81). In this work Jacobs quite shamelessly conflates free choice with our well-understood mental plasticity when he uses as evidence of free choice the fact that an agent might one day be a better person.

$$B_1 + E_1 \rightarrow O_1 \; (\checkmark)$$
$$B_1 + E_1 + E_2 \rightarrow O_2 \; (\checkmark)$$

There is no possibility of free choice when we first consider the deterministic outcome such that biological state B_1 plus environmental state E_1 gives rise to outcome O_1, yet then acknowledge the possibility of mental plasticity such that biological state B_1 plus environmental state E_1 *as added to by future environmental state* E_2 would give rise to the wholly different outcome O_2. And yet Jacobs (2001) has misused the above two deterministic statements to suggest that in his view there is a third option, where biological state B_1 plus environmental state E_1 just might have given rise to alternative outcome O_2 even in a deterministic universe:

$$B_1 + E_1 \rightarrow O_2 \; (\text{Jacobs}; \; \times)$$

Both $B_1 + E_1 \rightarrow O_1$ and $B_1 + E_1 + E_2 \rightarrow O_2$ are fully naturalistic and determined outcomes with no element of free choice, yet Jacobs (supposedly a naturalist and determinist) is misusing logic to suggest (like any libertarian) that there might have been a contra-causal third option – a free choice, a could-have-done-otherwise possibility of self-creation – hidden in here somewhere. $B_1 + E_1$ could never have given us any outcome other than O_1; could never have given us outcome O_2. Suggesting that it could have makes no more sense than the idea that although the sum of $20 + 30 = 50$ (outcome O_1), and the sum of $20 + 30 + 40 = 90$ (outcome O_2), Jacobs can offer us the hope of the sum of $20 + 30$ alternatively turning out to be 90 (outcome O_1 magically flips to outcome O_2).

Pace Dennett and Jacobs, no one could ever have "considered further" than they actually did at any particular moment and specific situation, and no one should admit that they "could have acted differently" in any particular situation (such as $B_1 + E_1$, or $B_1 + E_1 + E_2$). In a different setting at a different time – environment ($E_1 + E_2$) rather than environment E_1, say – then yes, the consideration and outcome would axiomatically have been different. But determinism requires that for a person at biological state B_1 combined with environmental state E_1 (producing unique interaction I_1) will be determined outcome O_1. If we are at unique interaction I_1 then determinism says that biology and environment will only allow single unique outcome O_1. Compatibilism is supposed to be based on a deterministic understanding, so for Dennett to argue that this person "could have considered further" is for him to pretend (against every scientific belief he holds) that there is a way that biological state B_1 combined with environmental state E_1 will result in alternate unique interaction I_2 – which would have produced a second, alternative, outcome O_2. That is of course not possible if man is the product of just two deterministic factors (biology and environment) but may be hoped for by some if man is a product of three factors – as libertarians might suggest – which are biology, environment, and something that stands outside biology and environment. Then biological state B_1 could combine with environmental state E_1 and a factor outside determinism (or indeterminism) and causality F_X to reach outcome O_2. However, it is vital to stress again that even if we could throw in supra-causal factor F_X (which may get us to alternate outcome O_2) this is not free will. This does not give us freedom of choice. We already know from the previous chapter that we have not achieved freedom of choice by throwing in a hypothetical acausal event on top of determinism.

Bruce Waller (2011, pp.115-31) provides a whistle-blower list of other examples of supposed naturalists and philosophical compatibilists ultimately espousing, like Dennett, Watson and Jacobs, a form of voodoo libertarianism and self-creation. This list includes Charles Taylor: "self-resolution in a strong sense… is within limits always up to us", and George Sher: we can only not talk about desert "if the difference between them has made it impossible for N to achieve as much as M. However, differences… are rarely so pronounced as to have this effect", as well as Nancy Murphy and Warren Brown: "there is no limit, other than lack of imagination, to the ability of the agent to transcend earlier conceptions".

Many of the most influential legal compatibilists also appear to be seeking human-level indeterminism, alternate possibilities and self-creation. For example, Stephen J. Morse, for three decades the doyen of the legal compatibilist tradition, writes that "all of us choose our behavior… behavior *is* a matter of choice" (1976, pp.1251-2), and that "hard determinism can neither explain our practices nor ground a theory of desert" (2004, p.431). Morse tells us approvingly that "most theorists believe that a moral decision for conviction requires… an actor who 'could have done other'" (1976, p.1257). Or there is University of Illinois law professor Michael S. Moore, possibly the most influential retributivist scholar in Western legal theory and second only to Morse in the ranks of the legal compatibilists, who nevertheless suggests that an actor could have done otherwise "*if* he had chosen (or willed) to do otherwise" (1985, p.1142). This latter argument, staged between compatibilists and incompatibilists, has a long pedigree within the literature, though is today largely discredited – as to say that an individual could have done otherwise *if* he had willed to have done otherwise is the logical equivalent of saying that a dog would have a curly tail *if* it were a pig: it is completely meaningless within this debate. Conditionality ("if") is not applicable here as no individual ever could have willed to have done otherwise in either a deterministic universe or an indeterministic universe. Two factors, and two factors only, determine human behaviour: these are biology and experience; nature and nurture. Behaviour is the product of character, and character is the product of biology and experiences. At any particular moment an individual could only have willed to have done otherwise if his character, his biology or experiences to that date (including hypothetical indeterministic triggers), had been different. Hence an individual could only have done otherwise if, in effect, he had happened to have been a different person formed under different circumstances. It is therefore factually wrong to say that an individual "could have done otherwise", as it is not this individual who could ever have done otherwise, but only a completely different person.

Outcome $O_1 = B_1 + E_1$
Outcome $O_2 = B_1 + E_2$ *or* $B_2 + E_1$ *or* $B_2 + E_2$

If you are saying that an individual could have done differently at a particular instance, you are saying that there could have been two different outcomes at that particular instant: two different outcomes notwithstanding an identical biological and environmental starting point. But in our universe of cause and effect (at least at the quasiclassical non-quantum level), $B_1 + E_1$ could never give anything other than outcome O_1. To have instead have got to outcome O_2 you would have needed to start with either the same biology and a different environment, or a different biology and the same environment (or, for completeness, a different biology and a different environment). But we are our biology and our formative experiences. The individual gave us outcome O_1 because of his biology and formative experiences $B_1 + E_1$, so to say that "he" could ever have given us outcome O_2 is clearly false, as "he" would never – in the situation under discussion, the situation we want changed – have been anything other than the product of $B_1 + E_1$, and therefore never anything other than the person who gave us outcome O_1.

The author was asked by the editors of a leading experimental psychology journal to assess for publication a paper by five North American academics linking counterfactuals and belief in free will. Counterfactuals are the thought that one situation could have resulted in a different outcome, but there is a significant difference between using counterfactuals to provoke creative thought and actually believing that some outcome might have been different. Hence the idea that Germany might have won the Second World War if the country had had access to a larger U-boat fleet is an example of a counterfactual, as is the thought that the Holocaust may never have taken place had Hitler died in childhood or been slightly more happily successful as a painter. Both are counterfactuals, but while the first may be of value at West Point in triggering creative discussion of military strategy and resourcing, the latter's use is largely restricted to being the script for the next Quentin Tarantino revenge fantasy. Indeed, conditional counterfactuals – of the sort above, which ultimately reduces to the suggestion that someone would have acted differently *if* they had happened to have been a different person – may be one of the least wholesome defences of the myth of free will because we are no longer even seeing arguments for individual freedom but for freedom for a completely different person. These are arguments invoking an alternative universe's version of "you", if you like. A different upbringing version of "you"; an alternative methylation of DNA version of "you"; a there-but-for-the-grace-of-God version of you; a taller and better-looking but unfortunately also more explosively flatulent version of you, perhaps. And none of which, self-evidently, is "you". The argument that alternative possibilities for short individual A would be demonstrated by considering the alternative behaviour of different and taller individual B seems to be on a moral and intellectual par with Dan Dennett's argument that justice for the unluckiest 1% is evaluated by completely discounting consideration of that 1% and asking only after the other 99%.

Compatibilism as a Moral and Intellectual Failure

"It is those two charges – of shallowness and of complacent compliance with the injustice of not acknowledging lack of fairness and desert, and in particular ultimate-level victimization – which form the backbone of my case against compatibilism… There is a sense in which 'compatibilist justice' is very often, at best, 'justified injustice', and in which the proper compatibilist order can be seen as, in one way, morally outrageous" (Smilansky, 2000, pp.54, 99).

There is a significant intellectual and moral problem with blame in the recognised absence of free choice. If a person's environment is A and their biology is B, and the person's character is nothing more than the sum of A+B, then blaming the person for being the product of A+B is really the same as blaming the person for A and/or blaming the person for B, both of which are problematic propositions. Blaming the person for their biology smacks of the worst excesses of 1920s American eugenics, while blaming the person for their environment suggests blaming an abused child for their abuse. Because what is it that we are doing when we are blaming a person? We are either blaming the person's underlying character which produced the act, or we can try to avoid reference to character and just blame the person for the act. But, in a world without free will, character is the direct result of biology and upbringing (environment). If you blame the person for their character, C – but C is nothing more than the product of environment A and biology B – you are by extension blaming the person for being the product of A and B. You are blaming the person for their biology and environment (or at least for their biology and/or environment). OK, then: forget blaming character and just blame the person for the act. But if you are blaming the person for the act, you are still blaming the person for their biology and/or upbringing. If you blame the person for the act D, and D is likewise the result of character C – which was the result of nothing more than the product of environment A and biology B – then you are again by extension blaming the person for being the product of A and B – blaming the person for their biology and environment (or at least for their biology and/or environment).

Whichever way you turn when you blame you are, in a world without free choice, either blaming the person for their environment – which is going to mean at least on occasion blaming an abused child for its abuse to the extent you ever blame children – or you are blaming the person for their biology, which is likewise hardly just or fair. Whichever way, it reduces to environment and/or biology, and when you blame you blame for one or for both. It reduces to moral luck, and you are effectively blaming the person for being less lucky than you. Dennett once told a hard determinist colleague (personal communication, 5 May 1998, and seen by the author) that even though he (Dennett) accepted that no one gets any choice whatsoever over their position in life that his (Dennett's) attitude to maintaining blame within the context of the American social, economic and penal systems is "not, I think, heartless; it is bracing (in a 'tough love' type way)". But, with respect, and even allowing for a noble didactic intent, there is a real problem with trying to suggest that Dennett's advocacy of the free will conceit is motivated by love, no matter how tough. Tough love is always supposed to be in the interest of those it is directed against. Yet in whose interest is the free will and moral responsibility myth? Surely not those it is generally being used against.

We will come on to the evidence that the myth of free will maintains and enhances the widening disparities of wealth and power in the United States, and prevents so many at the bottom getting any real chance to climb out of poverty. While we are still to come on to such evidence we have already seen that Dennett's apologia for free will is built upon both turning a blind eye ("within limits we take care not to examine too closely") and writing off that portion of the American population that does not fit within his "Is it fair...? Life isn't fair" worldview. I find Dennett's tough love excuse disturbing, because I can find little evidence of love or even minimal reflective consideration as his main motivation. "Waller... dismisses as absurd my claim that it is fair because luck averages out in the long run... The luck averaged out in ninety-nine percent of the population... If anything like that were true, my claim would not be absurd at all", writes Dennett (2012). Life is fair, suggests Dennett – what he elsewhere describes as sufficiently fair or "fair enough" – because it is fair for 99% of the population. That it is wholly unfair for 1% is seen as completely irrelevant by Dennett. But you cannot be acting in the interests of a minority when you are both turning a blind eye to the effects on them and have written them off – formally excluded them from the very calculus of justice and fair play. This is not a form of love, and hardly qualifies as "bracing" except in a pathological sense. It is not even that there is a suspicion that such tough love is more to the benefit of the winners than the losers: there often appears to be zero benefit to the losers here, and not just a lesser benefit, given that you find the need to formally exclude them from your equation of consideration.

Compatibilists often resort to claims that leave a sour taste in the mouth. We have already seen Dennett's suggestion that (almost) everyone in America gets the same breaks over the course of a long life, and that the seventy-two-year-old man surviving on food stamps has been just as lucky in life – has had all the same breaks in life – as Dennett himself. Although, to be fair, we must point out that what Dennett actually says is that perhaps ninety-eight out of the one hundred seventy-two-year-old men surviving on food stamps (pretty "deplorable ends" under anyone's estimation) have been, over their lifetimes, just as blessed as him, while he is happy to admit to the perhaps two out of the one hundred who suffered "manifestly amplified... bad fortune" and so sit outside his 99% "fair enough" guide. We have seen Dennett's claim that over the course of his long life he will (99% probability) suffer on average just as much as the child who was tortured by its father, hated by its mother, mercilessly bullied by its classmates and then repeatedly raped in that US prison for children. Another Dennett argument, influential in the compatibilist literature, is his "plateau of development" argument. Moral development is not a race, Dennett writes, where we need to recognise differences in ability, but a process that brings people "sooner or later" to a plateau of development. Some come slower as they "overcome initial disadvantages", but we all have the capacity to make it, he says: "everyone comes out more or less in the same league" (1984, p.96). Dennett has reformulated his plateau as a "threshold" in a more recent work, where he writes that it is "not in any way your own doing that you were born into a specific milieu, rich or poor, pampered or abused, given a head start or held back at the starting line. And these differences are striking… [but] many of the differences that survive are, in any event, of negligible importance to… the threshold of moral responsibility" (Dennett 2003, p.274). So just compare these words of Dan Dennett, supposed liberal and humanist, with the words of Charles Murray, arch paleoconservative and co-author of that notorious book *The Bell Curve*: "People – all people, black or white, rich or poor – may be unequally responsible for what has happened to them in the past, but all are equally responsible for what they do next" (1984, p.234).

These statements are effectively identical, yet the great moral difference between Dennett and Murray is that Dennett does know that there is no freedom of choice and probably knows that luck does not average out in human life, while Murray remains in ignorance about the absence of freedom of choice and the deep problem of moral luck. Murray continues a few sentences later with the comment that his view of the level playing field between rich and poor and black and white is valid because "the options are always open. Opportunity is endless" (p.234). But the point is that options are *not* always – or indeed *ever* – open for so many. Opportunity is *not* endless, unless one believes in free will – believes in something that allows the embedded individual to rise above the pure luck of biology and environment. And Murray truly seems to believe in such free will, and that anyone can be president. Dennett, however, is fully aware that not everyone can be president: that a president is overwhelmingly more likely to be male, white, heterosexual, Christian, wealthy and connected, and that to be president you have to be vastly lucky. Dennett's suggestion that many of the differences that survive "are, in any event, of negligible importance" is as profoundly untrue as is the suggestion that "anyone" can be president. Dennett himself understands – the evolutionist Dennett, that is, if not the libertarian Dennett we are seeing here – that the differences that remain are of the *greatest importance*, as they are the necessary and sufficient cause of the different behaviour. Dennett, unlike Murray, is fully aware that we have no third factor – free choice – that allows us to transcend biology plus environment, that would allow the unlucky to transcend their "initial disadvantages". For Dennett, one of America's deeply fortunate souls, to simply pooh-pooh the "initial disadvantages" of America's more unfortunate souls seems rather odious and self-serving.

Compatibilism also leaves a sour taste in the mouth when it advocates an appeal to mass beliefs. For example, Dennett writes that "in fact, I will argue, it is seldom that we even *seem* to care whether or not a person could have done otherwise" (1984, p.133). But who is this "we" that Dennett refers to? As we shall see, mainstream religion has almost always cared about whether or not a person could have done otherwise. As the Christian philosopher Alvin Plantinga writes: "If determinism is true, then on any occasion when I do what is wrong, it isn't possible for me to refrain from doing wrong. And if it isn't possible for me to refrain from doing wrong, then I can't really be responsible for that wrong-doing – not in the relevant sense anyway... The relevant sense involves being properly subject to disapprobation, moral criticism, and even punishment... I am not properly blamed for doing what it was not within my power not to do" (2013). Moral philosophers have almost always cared whether or not a person could have done otherwise: for Kant it was the cornerstone of his moral philosophy. Indeed, Dennett himself admits that this is the common intuition when he says that "as van Inwagen notes: 'Almost all philosophers agree that a necessary condition for holding an agent responsible for an act is believing that the agent *could have* refrained from performing that act'" (1984, p.131). This is Fischer's "common-sense" view: "our commonsense theorizing about our moral and legal responsibility presupposes that sometimes at least we could have done otherwise" (2007, p.72). The great majority of theologians have cared whether or not a person could have done otherwise, if for no other reason than if God set up the world, but set it up without the ability for humans to have done otherwise, this seems to cause significant difficulties for theology. Erasmus was aware of the problem almost five hundred years ago: "Why, you ask, is anything attributed to the freedom of the will, then? It is… to prevent calumnies attributing cruelty and injustice to God" (1524, p.93). And those Christian traditions which have not cared about an ability to have done otherwise – such as extreme Calvinism – have usually had to build their theology on a disastrous contempt for the value of individual human life, as we shall see in a later chapter.

As it matters very much to moral thinkers – Catholic or Protestant, religious or secular – whether or not a person could have done otherwise, who exactly is this "we" Dennett is trying to appeal to as an authority? It turns out to be the jingoistic and poorly-educated American masses who Dennett, a self-styled "bright", often seems to have so little time for. (I will not explain what a bright is supposed to be, as it is not overly relevant here. You can easily find out, but even Dennett's friend the late Christopher Hitchens described this particular Dennett and Richard Dawkins's conceit as "cringe-making".) Yet even here Dennett is misleading us, as the public also seems to care about – and to see the world in terms of – could-have-done-otherwise. There is a branch of philosophy termed experimental philosophy – a hybrid of philosophy and the methods of psychology – that investigates folk psychology, or lay beliefs. Shaun Nichols is the most high-profile of those who wish to show that the masses have libertarian sensibilities, while Eddy Nahmias is probably the most visible of those who wish to try to prove the masses have compatibilist tendencies. But even Nahmias has to admit that his own studies have appeared to show that between two thirds and three quarters of the public appear to believe that at any given moment people can choose to do otherwise. In one scenario 67% thought so, and in another "76% of participants responding that both Fred and Barney could have done otherwise" (Nahmias et al., 2005, p.570). Experimental psychologists have recently been castigated for taking their samples from both an educationally and culturally unrepresentative source (Henrich, Heine and Norenzayan, 2010), with Western college graduates tending to make up an atypically large proportion of respondents. The level of belief in could-have-done-otherwise in a fully representative population is likely to be even higher than Nahmias is here admitting to. Meanwhile, within the literature – and including Nahmias – there are acknowledged to be significant problems with interviewing lay folk that revolve around their seeming lack of understanding of the concepts involved – concepts including determinism, freedom, fatalism, and could-have-done-otherwise – not to mention their complete lack of awareness of the underlying moral paradoxes. And it is not just open to question how capable respondents are of understanding the concepts under discussion, because even the researchers themselves sometimes cannot be relied upon to keep the definitions exact and problem-free.

"When you ask people if they 'believe' in free will you are self-evidently asking them if they believe in free choice, the ability to have done otherwise. If free will is just fulfilling one's desires there is nothing to 'believe' in; it definitionally exists as we all pursue our desires, as all animals do. Similarly, if you redefine God to be a small mouse living in Knightsbridge there is nothing left to 'believe' in; it can be proven that He exists, and that He is partial to cheese. But God as an immaterial being who takes physical form at the Eucharist? That needs belief. Jonathan Schooler and Kathleen Vohs are not afraid to stake their lives on the possibility that humans pursue their desires; they are afraid to stake their lives on the possibility humans make free choices. I cannot help feeling that Baumeister appears to have a slightly too flexible approach to defining free will... [And] if the interviewer appears to have a slightly too flexible approach to defining free will, what hope for the interviewee in this complex and highly technical area?" (Miles, 2013a, pp.232-3).

Finally, and *pace* Dennett, it doesn't actually matter what lay folk believe when it comes to free will – the research subject of experimental philosophers like Eddy Nahmias and Shaun Nichols and of social psychologists like Roy Baumeister and Kathleen Vohs. Things are not true or false (or right and wrong) because the majority of Americans believe them. A survey from 2003 reported that around 70% of Americans still believed that Saddam Hussein was involved in the attacks of 9/11. The important question has never been *What do lay folk believe?* The important question – the moral question, the intellectual question – will always be *What should lay folk believe?* And here compatibilism has nothing to teach us.

Justifications for a Necessary Belief in Free Will

But just because compatibilism is an intellectual and moral failure does not mean that there are not strong subjective perceptions underlying the attachment of intellectuals to such free will self-justification. Compatibilists – and the illusionists, attitudinists, and semi-compatibilists of the next chapter – often share concerns about a world stripped of the illusion of free will.

UTILITARIANISM

So far we have tended to consider the intellectual mistakes which convince people that free will and even free choice exist. We will now start to consider something different. This is not a belief in free will, nor even free choice, but a belief in the need to convince others of the existence of free will and the non-existence of the problem of moral luck, and irrespective of any underlying doubts about the existence of free will or the problem of moral luck. The most obvious example of this tendency comes under the umbrella of what is called utilitarianism.

Utilitarianism founds all practical reasoning in the concept of utility, or of maximising the happiness of the community: the greatest happiness of the greatest number. Originally synonymous with intellectual liberalism, utilitarianism has been attractive to many traditions of humanist political philosophy since the Enlightenment because it seems to offer the hope of a truly coherent and systematic moral system – a system that does not owe allegiance to any particular preconceived belief (including religious belief) or depend on some contingent point of view. But the weakness of utilitarianism has always been that, in their understandable craving for an objective table of values, secular philosophers have been attracted to a system that is capable of excusing startling injustices. The greatest happiness of the greatest number is seen as somehow not just trumping the unhappiness of the minority, but as justifying such unhappiness, of making such unhappiness "just". All injustice is defined away once justice becomes only justice for the greatest number. When philosophers and scientists were first attracted to utilitarianism it was seen as progressive and reform-minded but – notes the ethical philosopher, the late Bernard Williams – modern utilitarians have been keen to suggest that their work will not challenge the existing social order and are "surprisingly conformist" (1972, p.102). There has always been the risk that utilitarian intuitions can justify scapegoating the innocent, weak, or unlucky, because when your only yardstick is the "greater good" there are no wider moral concerns to keep you centred. Under utilitarianism – and in contrast to, for example,

Kant's system of justice – people are considered as a means to a more important end, and not as ends in themselves. To quote the political philosopher Will Kymlicka, "Utilitarianism could justify sacrificing the weak and unpopular members of the community for the benefit of the majority" (1990, p.45).

> "Waller… dismisses as absurd my claim that it is fair because luck averages out in the long run… The luck averaged out in ninety-nine percent of the population… If anything like that were true, my claim would not be absurd at all" (Dan Dennett, 2012).

When the compatibilist Dan Dennett is asked to defend the free will conceit – "Is [the system] fair enough not to be worth worrying about? Of course" – he does so by brazenly writing off any duty to consider the effects on the unluckiest sections of the population. The happiness of (fairness towards) the majority doesn't just trump the unhappiness of (unfairness towards) the minority. For Dennett it makes considerations of the minority henceforth morally irrelevant. And when Dennett says that we should blame people for their social position – "within limits we take care not to examine too closely" (1984, p.164) – or Harvard's Dan Wegner tells us that "sometimes how things seem is more important than what they are" (2002, p.341), they both mean that turning a blind eye will allow the interests of one group, the unlucky, to be sacrificed to the interests of the rest of the community. In *Elbow Room*, Dennett's argument for holding people responsible within limits we take care not to examine too closely is that "we are rewarded for adopting this strategy" by the greater number going on to display responsible behaviour (1984, p.164). The benefit of doing injustice to the minority is inculcating responsibility in the majority, according to Dennett. Even putting to one side Dennett's extraordinary assertion that the majority learn responsibility through the practice of injustice towards the minority, this is classic utilitarianism. Life is judged to be sufficiently just and fair ("fair enough") because it is just, fair and beneficial for the great majority of the population. Those who fall outside the utilitarian algorithm – be that 1% or 20% – don't even get a say; they are the ones deemed "not to be worth worrying about" in this calculus.

In some of his more recent writing Dennett (2012, 2012a) states clearly that he is espousing a consequentialist defence of the free will conceit. Consequentialism says that the value of an action should be judged purely by its consequences and not, for example, by its original motive or intent: all consequentialism is ultimately the argument that the ends justify the means. While consequentialism is not synonymous with utilitarianism, utilitarianism is itself a consequentialist system of ethics, so Dennett is here flagging up his weakness for utilitarian arguments. Similarly, Gary Watson and the essentialists effectively give us a utilitarian defence of free will, albeit not so much a greatest happiness argument as a perfect happiness argument. Watson and the essentialists seek to achieve this by writing off anyone who is not happy. Remember that the "sense of equality with the other" was removed from one form of human, and thereafter consideration of (and rights to) justice, fair play, sympathy, and happiness only apply to the other form of human – the more perfect form of human. Under the Watson utilitarian calculation there is perfect fairness, and perfect happiness – as those treated unfairly, and those who are unhappy with the system, are excluded from the calculation. Likewise, when the free will illusionist Saul Smilansky writes about the "justness of deeply unjust practices" (2000, p.279), he is placing the interest of those against whom the deeply unjust practices are targeted well below the interest of those doing the targeting.

In contrast to secular utilitarianism, orthodox Judaeo-Christianity has always argued that morality is not a zero-sum game, that ends do not justify means, and that happiness and a social good for 80% (or even fully 99%) does not average away unhappiness and a moral bad for 20%, or even just 1%. Within philosophy this is perhaps most famously represented in the work of the Christian-inspired philosopher Immanuel Kant who wrote that people, all people, should be treated as ends in themselves, and not as means to an end. Utilitarianism takes the opposite view, and people become means to achieve a desired social end. The utilitarian calculus says that human life comes down to numbers, and that in consequence it is not only efficient but morally right to sacrifice one child to save two. Utilitarianism is very often not only an argument that the practical effect of sacrificing one child to save two is that you will be up one child. It is an argument that sacrificing one child is the morally right thing to do. Utilitarianism here does not view the sacrificing of the child simply as the least worst option, but as a moral good in and of itself. Utilitarians tend to argue that society is worth saving whatever the cost, and even if it means having to build society on gross unfairness and gross injustice for some. In contrast, and at its best, Judaeo-Christianity has recognised that whatever the practical effects may be – whatever the practical least worst option may be – it is always still morally wrong to treat individuals as means and not ends, or to sacrifice one unwilling victim to save others, and that sometimes a society which does not get this is perhaps not one that should be saved.

Utilitarianism as a self-justifying belief system has always had a dangerous appeal to liberal intellectuals because (on the face of it) it seems to offer – in contrast to religious belief systems – one of the few chances of a non-contingent moral system; a system that does not depend on some conditional point of view for its fairness. But there is no impartial, non-conditional point of view here. This is not *a priori* justification (justification before the fact). Dennett, Watson, and Wegner are making their utilitarian calculation *a posteriori*: they are making their decision after the fact. Utilitarianism is all about the sacrifice of others, and has nothing to do with self-sacrifice. Self-sacrifice is a virtue within Judaeo-Christianity, and one of the most admirable attributes of the human animal, but when Dennett and Smilansky recommend sacrifice for the benefit of the community it is never themselves or people like them who are being sacrificed to the "greater good". Dennett and Watson are like the gambler trying to throw down his chips after the ball has stopped rolling round the roulette wheel: they rationalise as they do after they know the outcome will privilege them. Smilansky and Wegner are recommending that we accept the utilitarian calculus because in effect they have no stake in the game, and their chips were never at risk. They are not effectively even playing the game – as they wager nothing – but are dictating the rules of the game to those who are playing, and who are forced to wager much (if not everything). It was never going to be the Dennetts, the Watsons and the Smilanskys of this world who ended up sacrificed to the greater good, so their utilitarian justification for the free will conceit becomes highly suspicious at best.

THE PERCEIVED NEED TO SUPPORT MORAL VALUES

Many philosophers argue as they do from a secular weakness for utilitarianism, with its siren call about the moral acceptability of sacrificing others for the greater good. However, this can only ever be part of the story, as many philosophers also maintain deeply-held views that ending the free will myth would undermine moral values. Thomas Hobbes wrote in *Behemoth* that the Catholic Church was using the myth of free will to control the common people, although this was justified as being in their own interests. In our own day the philosopher the late Leo Strauss is generally credited with reintroducing the idea of Plato's "noble lie" into political philosophy: the idea that the lay folk can best be governed, and possibly only be governed, through being deceived. Dan Dennett has frequently drawn attention to what he sees as the danger of admitting to the public the non-existence of free will, a danger he finds "almost too grim to contemplate" (1984, p.168). The entire philosophical tradition of reactive-attitudinism likewise holds to the belief that Western civil society would collapse into anarchy if we were to admit to the non-existence of free will, while the illusionist Saul Smilansky says that disabusing people of the free will myth will lead to apathy and cynicism (2000, p.227).

Propagandising free will from the perceived need to maintain existing social and moral values tends to come both from those who do not themselves believe in the existence of free choice but think others should believe (illusionists, attitudinists, and sometimes compatibilists), and from those who believe in free choice and think others should too (libertarians, and at times compatibilists). Over the last few years a number of works have been published in North American social psychology asserting both the putative prosocial benefits of belief in free choice and the possible dangers of disclosing doubts about the existence of free choice. Roy Baumeister has suggested that belief in free will reduces aggression and promotes selflessness (Baumeister, Masicampo, & DeWall, 2009). Kathleen Vohs, Jonathan Schooler, and Azim Shariff have argued that disbelief in free will encourages cheating and undermines moral behaviour (Shariff, Schooler, & Vohs, 2008; Vohs & Schooler, 2008). Tyler Stillman, Baumeister and Vohs have asserted that believers in free will make better employees (Stillman et al., 2010). And Stillman and Baumeister (2010) argue that belief in free will facilitates learning from emotional experiences, while disbelief in free will reduces learning. Yet the above corpus of work appears to be built on some major misunderstandings. Every single North American social psychologist named above, and a multitude of unnamed co-authors, appears to be a libertarian. As the intellectual world is moving to distance itself more and more from free will libertarianism, with (for example) a steep drop by 2009 to only 13% of philosophers clinging to the possibility of free choice (Dennett, 2014), the overwhelming direction within North American social psychology is for a faith-based embrace of free choice. Furthermore, there appear to be significant methodological problems with the research, not the least of which is the overarching confusion of fatalism for determinism. Bruce Waller writes that "the experimenters started from the assumption that determinism equals helplessness... The researchers primed their experimental group not toward belief in determinism, but rather in the direction of a diminished sense of self-efficacy, to acceptance of helplessness" (2011, pp.281-2). In other words, they weren't investigating the effects of disbelief in free will, but the effects of belief in fatalism (two wholly different things). Confusing fatalism and determinism is a hallmark of libertarian thinking, and a mistake that Christian scholars have been making for close on 1700 years.

The methodological errors in this North American social psychology tradition – work that Dan Dennett has nevertheless (and perhaps, again, taking care "not to examine too closely") described as "pioneering" (2012a) – seem to go beyond the simple confusion of fatalism and determinism, though. We have already mentioned that the leading experimental philosophers from across the traditions agree that it is remarkably easy to unintentionally mislead participants when it comes to free will responses, and remarkably difficult to interpret what participants' responses imply for their understanding of the questions being asked. North American social psychology nevertheless seems largely unmindful of the need for such slow and cautious interpretation, notwithstanding that social psychology would appear even more prone to leading participants astray. The author

(2013a) had to upbraid Roy Baumeister for changing his definition of free will without acknowledgement or recognition, with the thought that if the experimenter cannot keep track of his experimental method what hope is there for his participants? Furthermore, researchers sometimes appear to be inattentive to their own results, such as when Andrew Vonasch and Roy Baumeister (2013) failed to recognise that their latest surveys actually demonstrated the injustice of the free will myth (see Miles, 2013a, pp.233-4). There is also a significant unacknowledged ontological problem with the North American social psychology research. The tradition appears almost wholly oblivious to the problem of moral luck, a key confounding factor in any attempt to claim moral benefits arising from the free will conceit. It becomes impossible to assess the morality of the free will belief outside of the larger problem of moral luck, as otherwise researchers are simply unmindful of moral paradoxes and the problem that morality is no longer being defined objectively or independently. For all the varied and trenchant criticisms of writers like Dennett, Watson, Smilansky, and Fischer that you will find in this book, each of these theorists is nevertheless acutely aware of the problem of moral luck and is trying to somehow reconcile or answer that problem (even if their answer is to direct attention elsewhere). Their work may be wrong both intellectually and morally, but because it at least tries to reconcile the problem of moral luck it is not automatically self-negating in the way the work of (for example) Baumeister, Schooler, and Vohs can be argued to be.

Against the charge of a threat to moral values, it should also be noted that even leading free will justifiers have suggested that the hard determinism of Waller, Pereboom and Abe Lincoln may be a purer ethical system than any of the alternatives. As the illusionist Saul Smilansky has observed, "the hard determinist agent we are considering enquires after the right thing to do and goes on to do it *despite* realizing that he is not praiseworthy for doing so and would not be blameworthy were he to act differently" (2000, p.237). Smilansky is here suggesting that only the hard determinist can be considered ethically pure. The hard determinist acts as he does not from thought of his moral salvation or moral worth but rather from his concern for what Smilansky terms "morality alone". If you like, it is somewhat similar to the concern that has been raised about theism since the Enlightenment: do theists try to behave well because they know this is the right thing to do, or simply because they are being told by their god and their neighbours how to behave (and possibly even because they are being coerced or bribed by the hope of some recognition or reward)? The hard determinist, under Smilansky's view, has internalised the right moral behaviour whereas, for example, the libertarian may still be acting off external compulsion (be that fear, praise, control or perceived sanction). The hard determinist, according to Smilansky, is a pure moral agent, while everyone else is still acting from, at least in part, impure motives.

Other erroneous suggestions from those who want free will because of a perceived threat to moral values include the fear that we cannot legitimately judge or sanction others without the conceit of free will. As the philosopher Thomas Nagel puts it, when recognising the limitations on free choice "the area of genuine agency, and therefore of legitimate moral judgment, seems to shrink under this scrutiny" to an extensionless point (1979, p.35). But this suggestion is simply false.

> "When the assumption that wrongdoers are blameworthy is withdrawn for hard incompatibilist reasons, the conviction that they have in fact done wrong could legitimately survive" (Pereboom 2001, p.212).

We can still analyse, draw moral distinctions between people, and judge and criticize character and effect. It is just that we just cannot blame, or invoke anything beyond moral luck to differentiate. Hard determinists like Bruce Waller (1990, 2006) and Derk Pereboom (2001, 2007) have written extensively on why this is the case, and why we can and should make such a differentiation. (As above, Pereboom prefers his term hard incompatibilist over hard determinist, but we shall retain the more common taxonomy used by Smilansky above, even though Pereboom is entirely correct when he says that modern hard determinists are actually hard incompatibilists in that they deny the possibility of free choice under both determinism and indeterminism.) We still punish children even when we do not believe them morally responsible, because they have to learn that they cannot behave in certain ways, and we are trying to make them better people. We can, and will, still incarcerate dangerous people even for perhaps their whole lives in a world that recognises no free choice, no free will. But incarcerating adults for public protection, even once we take steps to minimise their likely suffering, is not the same thing as punishing children for their own good, and we may ultimately have to face up to Isaiah Berlin's controversial recognition half a century ago (e.g. Berlin, 1971) that not all moral values can be reconciled. Such incarceration may indeed never be wholly morally justifiable, but our current practices are not even vaguely morally justifiable (or, rather, are not justifiable outside utilitarian scapegoating). And at least we will then have stopped the further injustice of "within limits we take care not to examine too closely" misrepresenting such injustice as justice. We will also in other ways be reducing the injustice by, for example, minimising the suffering relative to the current situation of often seeking to maximise the suffering. Hence, although we may never have full moral justification we will have done the best we can to maximise justice and minimise injustice in a universe where not all moral values can be reconciled. In fact, we will see that, with great irony, it is only under the ethic and practices of free will apologists like Dan Dennett, Gary Watson, and Saul Smilansky that we lose the moral high ground to be able to fairly judge and justly incarcerate those who would do us harm.

4

ILLUSIONISM, SEMI-COMPATIBILISM, ATTITUDINISM – FREE WILL AS INDIFFERENCE

> And thus we come to understand that the history of moral feelings is the history of an error, an error called "responsibility", which in turn rests on an error called "freedom of the will"... No one is responsible for his deeds, no one for his nature; to judge is to be unjust. ... The tenet is as bright as sunlight, and yet everyone prefers to walk back into the shadow and untruth – for fear of the consequences.
>
> Friedrich Nietzsche, *Human, All Too Human* (1878, s.39).

We have now considered the two most influential traditions of free will justification. Libertarianism is the belief that free choice, the ability to have done otherwise, is actually possible. Compatibilism is a tradition which generally maintains that whether freedom of choice is even possible is nonetheless irrelevant, in part because it is suggested that there is no overarching problem of moral luck. In this chapter we start to address a very different class of thinker: those who (like the compatibilists) generally recognise the impossibility of free choice and could-have-done-otherwise, but who (unlike the compatibilists) acknowledge the persistent problem of moral luck. However, this class of thinker nevertheless believes that we can find wider considerations to offset the problem of moral luck – but in doing so we will be turning from free will as a largely intellectual mistake to free will as a largely moral mistake. The linking theme between illusionism, reactive-attitudinism, semi-compatibilism, and what we shall call hard compatibilism is the conviction that we can afford to be indifferent to questions of individual injustice and an absence of fair play.

Interlude – Lesser Libertarianism and Lesser Compatibilism

Before we turn to the traditions just mentioned, for completeness we need to briefly consider two attempts to reintroduce intellectual rigour into both libertarianism and mainstream compatibilism. We shall refer to these – for reasons which will become obvious – as lesser libertarianism and lesser compatibilism.

LESSER LIBERTARIANISM

One of the most influential libertarian philosophers of recent years has been Robert Kane. Kane's significant contribution has been to provide a libertarian justification that appears somewhat intellectually rigorous in the way that the libertarianism of Kant, van Inwagen or John Searle does not. A degree of self-formation is possible for Kane, but it only exists on the edge of quantum indeterminism, when we are torn between two courses of action we struggle to resolve. Kane (2002, 2007) hypothesises a situation where we are in two minds as to whether we undertake a course of action. Either course is one that we could identify with (is within our personality profile) but instead of a deterministic resolution – of biology and/or environment forcing our hand – it is an indeterministic event that ultimately forces our hand. In other words: we are wavering between two courses of action, either of which we could identify with, but due to the indeterministic nudge (for Kane, separated off from determinism through chaos in the brain) we end up with an outcome that was not determined and thus freely chosen. We have broken free from determinism yet made a decision we identify with (one that we can endorse). For Kane, under this specific set of circumstances, it becomes both a non-determined and a free decision. Kane is not trying to argue for could-have-done-otherwise, but is still trying to offer us a self-formed character for our subsequent decisions.

Unfortunately, though, Kane's influential model is not giving us any form of decision that people are responsible for in the sense of having made a free choice. All Kane is giving us here is a deterministic system with a little bit of arbitrary randomness thrown in on top. We have already seen that we do not have free choice under a deterministic system, we do not have free choice under an indeterministic system, and we do not have free choice if we mix in both. The problems with Kane's model include both that there is absolutely no evidence that indeterminism can act this way in the brain, and a modern understanding (including decoherence) that it cannot. Further, even if the brain could work this way we could never have any evidence in a particular situation that it had worked this way, giving us the impossibility of firmly asserting even weak self-formation (and thus zero additional practical utility). And, as many have noted, if what finishes the act is separated off from our existing determined character then what makes the final choice – what completes the act – isn't really "us" anyway. It isn't "you" then forming the subsequent self in these supposedly self-forming acts. It is random indeterminism. This still doesn't give us the free will, the conscious free choice, or the true self-formation, that libertarians – and even compatibilists like Dan Dennett, Gary Watson and Jonathan Jacobs – crave. Furthermore, the mind is undecided between two options, both of which it identifies with. But the reason the mind identifies with each of those actions is that it has already been deterministically set up to value such action: that is, it had no free choice over the original identification. Assuming that at least one (and probably both) of those possible courses of action are good/bad (as we are almost certainly trying to attribute praise or blame here), whichever one our actor is ultimately forced into he will not be ultimately responsible for, as what he identifies with he had no initial choice over. This actually takes us back to the argument by Pereboom (2001) that we considered briefly in an earlier chapter: that unless the agent was originally responsible for forming his character – unless his first ever act was to create his character – then the agent cannot be held responsible for any subsequent act even if he identifies with it, as all subsequent acts would have to flow from that character (over which he had no initial choice or control).

As has also been noted by others, if the first option is a morally bad option and the second is not, then if indeterminism tips him over into choosing the first he has just been unlucky – whereas if it tips him over into choosing the second he has been lucky. If both are morally bad options then he is going to be unlucky whatever indeterminism does to him. It doesn't matter that he identifies in advance with both options: that identification is purely down to the lottery of biology and environment, and thus we are back with the overarching problem of moral luck. If indeterminism does or does not tip him into a poor choice he identifies with because (under at least one of the options) he has again been on the losing end of the moral luck equation, then we still haven't escaped the moral luck problem. Kane's criticism of compatibilism is that we can't hold someone accountable for what is a matter of luck. Yet his model gives us no stronger basis to attribute blame, as Kane often seems to recognise. Whatever the actor gets to do here, the cards were either stacked against him (as with the serial killer Robert Harris) or stacked for him (as with an elite and privileged philosopher like

Gary Watson), and the deck doesn't stop being stacked if occasionally indeterminism gives the actor a slightly luckier (or slightly less lucky) hand than he might otherwise have played. Not only are the possible choices fed to him within the auspices of the moral luck problem, but the freedom in Kane's system is nothing more than this indeterministic trigger between two determined options – a trigger which is, again, beyond the agent's control.

Kane is not giving us free choice so much as a form of alternate universes scenario, which still cannot give us free choice or moral responsibility. Kane points out that under his thesis the person identifies with the (random) choice he ends up with, but this now means nothing in this debate. Almost everyone in the literature agrees that most criminals identify with the decisions they make. Identification is not the issue: the fairness of blaming people for the cards that were forced on them is. What is at issue is whether the decision they identify with was a free decision, and Kane unfortunately can add nothing here.

$$S_1 \rightarrow O_1 \text{ (no responsibility)}$$
$$S_1 + F_X \rightarrow O_2 \text{ (how now responsible?)}$$

A system is at state S_1: without the intervention of quantum event F_X it would go to outcome O_1 and, as Kane admits, there is no responsibility yet in this system. Due to the intervention of indeterministic factor F_X, however, we get to outcome O_2. So how on earth does this introduce responsibility when it was admitted that the first outcome could not? The character is not even making the choice he truly identified with, because a random event has forced his hand. If anything he is less free – not in the sense of free choice, but purely in the sense of personal control – under the second outcome.

Robert Kane's work is valuable, as least for the author, not only because it is more robust and thoughtful than many other libertarian arguments but also because Kane is driven to positing such constrained free will, as he at least recognises the logical impossibility of the more strenuous could-have-done-otherwise free will suggested by theorists from Kant and John Searle to Roy Baumeister. And due to this recognition Kane has been forced to reflect upon the moral dangers to the belief in standard libertarian free will, and has been willing to draw attention to those downsides, actually distancing himself from such colleagues. Kane's work is theoretically plausible (albeit highly unlikely and untestable) while being practically and morally unhelpful, in contrast with standard libertarian theory, which is simply implausible, while being both morally and intellectually malign. Notwithstanding this greater intellectual rigour, this can only ever be viewed as lesser libertarianism for our purposes, as it doesn't give any of us what we want or need. For hard determinists there is still no formal acknowledgement that all talk of free will appears to be harmful to the less fortunate and will always involve almost deliberately misleading language, while for the free will apologists there is no justification for blame and suffering in Kane's work.

LESSER COMPATIBILISM

Lesser compatibilism can be viewed as a form of compatibilism which avoids the more obvious moral and intellectual errors of a Dennett, a Watson, or a Jonathan Jacobs, but which likewise does so through giving us largely inoffensive conclusions that work for no one. An example is when the compatibilist Susan Wolf tries to tie freedom not to choice but to Reason (spelt with a capital R). The condition of freedom and responsibility, Wolf tells us, is the "ability to act in accordance with, and on the basis of, the True and the Good" (1990, p.71). According to Wolf, you lack true freedom when you veer from the path of Reason. Such arguments have a long pedigree, starting with ancient Greek philosophy, and in Plato's book *Protagoras* there is a discussion of weakness of will (what the Greeks called *akrasia*) as countered by Socrates with his famous dictum that "No one willingly goes to meet evil" (p.95). While the claim that no one does wrong knowingly has always been controversial, the point here is not to defend the Socratic claim but to show that you may be able to use compatibilism to produce an inoffensive, but largely pointless, form of free will. Under a thoroughgoing Socratic view – as reinvented by Wolf – you would effectively get to blame no one: the only ones who are free are those who already know Right from Wrong, and the evidence that they know Right from Wrong is that they are following the path of the True and the Good. Philosophers, under this rather conceited philosophical worldview, could be held responsible, as they alone are guided by Reason and know Right from Wrong, but as they supposedly will never willingly do wrong there is no one around to blame.

Lesser compatibilism doesn't suffer from the typical intellectual failings of mainstream compatibilism, such as the need to argue that "luck averages out in the long run" or that – unknown to biologists – there are actually two forms of human, but lesser compatibilism is not an option for most compatibilists. Compatibilists overwhelmingly feel the need to argue for a system that defends current practice, and if not current practice then at least a theory of desert. Such an overarching goal is indicated by the legal compatibilist Stephen Morse's line that "determinism can neither explain our practices nor ground a theory of desert" (2004, p.431). Lesser compatibilism of the form offered by Wolf thus avoids the standard intellectual and/or moral failings found in the work of Dennett or Watson, but still doesn't get compatibilists to where they want to go, which is a theory of desert and a robust defence of current practice and suffering.

Illusionism

	Can free will and determinism coexist?	Is determinism true (at the human level)?	Do we have free will?
1. Libertarianism	No	No	Yes, but we have no proof
2. Compatibilism	Yes	Yes	~~Yes (but not free choice)~~ Yes, and free choice
3. Illusionism	No	Yes	No, but don't tell anyone

We now turn to an influential third tradition of free will justification, known as free will illusionism. Though compatibilism and libertarianism can be shown to have pedigrees back as far as the ancient Greeks, free will illusionism as a recognised tradition has a relatively recent history. There have been earlier instances of the Christian Church expressing a desire to keep the truth on free will from the public. In addition to Thomas Hobbes's late seventeenth-century assertion that the Church was using the myth of free will to control the masses, the great sixteenth-century Catholic theologian Erasmus wrote that if there should prove to be no free will then only an educated elite should be allowed to possess such dangerous knowledge. While this knowledge "might be treated in discourses among the educated", the lay folk were too "weak", too "ignorant", and too "wicked" to handle such an understanding, said Erasmus (1524/1999, pp.11-12). We need the illusion of free will even if it is only an illusion. Things are pretty shaky as they stand, went Erasmus's argument, so what is the "sense in pouring oil upon the fire?" (p.12). Notwithstanding such instances, open deception on the issue of free will only really entered intellectual thought a decade or so ago in the tradition best represented by the work of the philosopher Saul Smilansky. According to Smilansky, the public are "fragile... plants" who need to be "defended from the chill of the ultimate perspective in the hothouse of illusion" (2002, p.501). Outside of free will theorising this could be seen as drawing upon the well-known philosophical conceit that the lay public cannot be trusted to do what is right, and so their intellectual and moral betters must keep them ignorant of the truth. This view is often traced to the Greek aristocrat Plato, with his argument in *The Republic* that the ideal society would be split into three castes through the inculcation of a powerful foundation myth, or what has become known as the "noble lie". Only those at the very top of society were to be told the true history of their state, and everyone else would have to live in ignorance. Plato's utopia, with its anti-democratic caste system, censorship, and foundation myth, was famously savaged as the prototypical totalitarian state by the philosopher Karl Popper.

Free will illusionism, as in the modern tradition championed by Smilansky, appears to come in two forms: negative and positive. Negative illusionism occurs when theorists stay silent in the face of what can be regarded as public misperception. In contrast, positive illusionism is the deliberate deception of the public, as in Plato's utopia. It is against this intellectual background that Smilansky denies that he has called for positive illusionism – for overt deception – and claims that he has only ever argued for negative illusionism. If the public are naive enough to believe in free will, let us not disabuse them of their mistake when such a mistake helps maintain the existing social order, Smilansky has written. Yet while Smilansky may never have argued for positive illusionism, many others within his tradition have recommended overt censorship over the issue of free will. Calls to suppress the truth on free will seem to occur particularly within the natural and physical sciences, and we will be examining instances in a later chapter when we consider the long-standing involvement of the Western scientific community in the development and maintenance of the free will myth. However, the writing of Smilansky is undeniably the most thoughtful, developed and interesting within the free will illusionist tradition, so we will for the remainder of this section concentrate on Smilansky's work.

Smilansky has himself admitted to concerns about the deception underlying all illusionist defences of free will, but he nonetheless thinks he can find both ethical and democratic grounds for such deception. Free will illusionism standardly assumes the illusion of free will, and building social, economic, and legal systems upon such illusion, is a necessary step, and irrespective of the unfairness and injustice this might create for the victims of such a fraud. Unlike the compatibilism of Dan Dennett and Gary Watson there is no attempt to argue that the problem of moral luck has been solved, and from Smilansky we get instead a justification of the otherwise unanswerable problem of moral luck. For Smilansky – because admitting that free will does not exist would undermine the very possibility of settled existence – we must be willing to pay any price not to let that happen. Even, says Smilansky, at the cost of sanctioning deeply unjust practices. "In practice we commit horrendous injustice on a daily basis, and must do so... This [is the] astounding and grotesque picture of life as a masquerade in which maintaining human dignity depends on... degrading fellow people... What could be more absurd than the moral necessity of the belief in the justness of deeply unjust practices, practices that ought largely to continue and flourish?" (2000, pp. 256, 278-9).

This "astounding and grotesque" picture of the justice of injustice is a moral necessity, stresses Smilansky, where maintaining human dignity depends on "degrading fellow people". In effect Smilansky is offering us what he sees as the only two alternatives.

The first alternative is trying to build a just world and, necessarily, failing. The second alternative is maintaining a deeply unjust – at least at the level of the individual or, rather, certain individuals – and yet, in consequence, politically stable Western world. There is no room for a just world here: under this view the weak and unlucky must of necessity be sacrificed, no matter how disgusting this objectively appears to be. Note, though, that profound injustice *creates* the stability. Thus we are starting to see a glimpse of Smilansky's (deeply Edmund Burkean) moral argument. Nevertheless, the uncomfortable conclusion is that the only "justice" we can have must incorporate deep injustice within it, says Smilansky, and communal justice and fairness require injustice and unfairness directed towards the individual, or at least towards some individuals. This is obviously another example of the utilitarianism we saw in the last chapter, while at the same time Smilansky is offering us a profoundly pessimistic view of mankind. Our cultures have no right to claim a foundation on truth, fairness, and justice, writes Smilansky, and yet we cannot admit this publicly for fear of undermining the free will illusion that keeps society together. Illusionism can offer us only one practical future: injustice towards some individuals and a corresponding need to lie about such injustice – because the alternative, suggests Smilansky, is no more celebrity gossip or reality TV. Stability and economic continuity must be bought at the cost of truth, individual justice and fairness.

We have already considered some of the more obvious problems with utilitarianism and this defence of individual injustice by invoking the greater good and the necessity of sacrificing some for the benefit of others. Problems include not just the fact that almost any atrocity can be so justified but that utilitarianism is not even intellectually coherent as an objective, non-arbitrary, thesis – because advocates are providing their justifications after the fact, rather than in an impartial *a priori* from-behind-the-veil sense.

Smilansky, and other free will utilitarians like Watson and Dennett, have no stake in the game – nothing on the line, we said: they are like the gambler who wants to throw down his chips after the roulette wheel has stopped turning. Smilansky specifically states that his thesis works "for the purpose of establishing a non-arbitrary moral order" (p.285), but again all we are really getting is a form of after-the-fact winners' justice: the justice of those with opportunities over those with no opportunities. Some philosophers, such as Kant and the late Bernard Williams, have not even considered utilitarianism an ethical philosophy at all, but instead a form of anti-ethics, or what is left over when you have given up on morality. In the view of Kant and Williams (and modern Judaeo-Christianity) morality is not a zero-sum game, and one moral wrong and one moral right do not cancel each other out. You are still left, under Smilansky's free will justification, and whatever he may wish to claim to the counter, with one moral *wrong*.

Smilansky has defended illusionism in a number of places, but in his 300-page *Free Will and Illusion* he nowhere mentions that the victims of the illusion may well include more than just offenders. And once (as Smilansky does) you admit that the conceit of free will is being actively used to the detriment of one group there is a real problem with failing to acknowledge that the myth of free will may be being used against a wider pool of the unlucky, for example the "undeserving" poor. He has developed a theory of illusion that by its own admission both recognises and justifies scapegoating, yet without having considered the wider effects of that illusion – the full extent of the scapegoating – which makes Smilansky's programme deeply problematic. We have already seen that the free will myth can be used such that (or at least we can make "room for the thought" that) people with disabilities become responsible for their handicaps, or that the battered housewife is now responsible for her continued toleration of abuse, so where is this being recognised in Smilansky's work? The overarching problem here comes from the fact that utilitarianism is based on supposed calculation (the greatest happiness of the greatest number) but how can Smilansky (or Dennett, or Watson) begin to correctly calculate the balance if one is not adequately summing on both sides of the equation? We shall consider later the wider idea that belief in free will helps to explain vast economic inequalities, and that the more a country clings to belief in free will the greater the inequality one tends to find. In 2000 in the US the net worth of the top 1% of households accounted for more than the net worth of the bottom 95% of households put together. What if the myth of free will helps both create and entrench such massive inequality? It is a short step from blaming offenders for their misfortune to blaming the poor for their misfortune. Smilansky does not consider the danger of wider fallout, or make any attempt to evaluate the full cost of the free will myth. And this, of course, is not to ignore our earlier point against Dennett that scapegoating – or writing some people off – is just as morally odious when it is being done to 1% as when it is being done to 20%. Smilansky has suggested that free will is the only fraud that should be perpetrated on the American public in part because "the threat of political manipulation and the like is less acute here" (p.271). Yet what if the free will myth is already manipulating American political and economic expectations very much in the direction that really benefits, for example, the top 1%? Far from being politically neutral, with "less acute" risk of political manipulation, the free will myth may be one of the most potent and polarising political myths that has ever been used.

Smilansky does seek to deny that his justification for free will illusionism is utilitarianism and the greatest happiness principle, suggesting only that he can give us what is independently "a reasonably just social order" and "a decent socio-political order" (2000, pp. 258, 268). But Smilansky's "reasonably just" is of course identical to Dennett's "fair enough", or what Dennett elsewhere gives as his indifferent "Is is fair? Life isn't fair" guiding maxim. Fairness for the majority can be bought at the cost of unfairness to and discrimination towards the minority, and is anyway to be judged only by the lucky. Dennett was willing, remember, to effectively admit that his definitions of justice and fairness simply discounted questions of injustice and unfairness towards the minority ("dismisses as absurd my claim that it is fair because luck... averaged out in ninety-nine percent of the population"). Smilansky, at least on occasion, refuses to even acknowledge that what is fair for the 99%, or the 80%, may not actually be fair for the 1%, or the 20%. He accepts that it is unfair for the minority, but for him unfairness for the minority does not seem to be real unfairness, which can only be judged at the level of the community. Smilansky's work is thus not simply utilitarianism but is a form of what political philosophers term majoritarianism, also known as the tyranny of the majority, where the majority supposedly get to impose their concepts of fairness and justice on the minority. Dennett and Watson discounted, or plain ignored, the unlucky minority in their estimation of justice: Smilansky, far from ignoring the unlucky minority, almost seems to expect them to express understanding of the injustice they receive, because of the corresponding "justice" that their unjust suffering will allow the community to receive... as if they should recognise that the injustice and unfairness they receive will allow others to live happier and better lives, so they are being selfish when they fail to exult in the injustice directed at them. We mentioned above that Smilansky's work is deeply pessimistic for concepts of human justice and fair play. In many ways it mirrors what we shall see later is the deep pessimism of extreme Calvinism, which will try to get around the free will problem by arguing that human life holds no inherent value separated from God the Creator, and that this fact excuses profound injustice from God (which is directed towards the individual). Smilansky seems to be making a similar argument that all human value arises out of communal living. Hence, if human communal living requires the myth of free will – in his wholly unproven opinion, of course – this then excuses any injustice from the community that is directed towards the individual.

There are other ethical problems with the illusionist position, including an apparent anything goes attitude to defending the myth. Smilansky does not argue that what he is proposing is the truly just, but only the "reasonably just". So how much is too much injustice for Smilansky? If one can ignore almost any injustice in maintenance of the free will myth and its value to the community, why is Smilansky opposed to positive illusionism? Positive illusionism – overtly lying to the public; widespread censorship – is no more obviously unjust than the "deeply unjust practices" that Smilansky is already willing to tolerate. And why just censorship? Why not also violence and extra-judicial killing? It must be extra-judicial for Smilansky, as lawyers and judges – agents of the state and therefore rarely considered by philosophers to be in the top tier of thinkers – must be kept in ignorance of the vital social fraud they are helping to perpetuate. And, if we start down this road, where do we stop? The free will myth "is special" (p.271) for Smilansky – a special case – but Smilansky's argument that this is the only justifiable fraud against the public is not self-evidently true. And if philosophers think that (ethically) they can get away with such free will illusionism despite the underlying injustices, what is to stop (ethically) other groups getting away with their illusions? Why shouldn't other scapegoaters be allowed to get away with their deceptions, and who gets to judge the allowable scapegoating? Why is it necessarily wrong under Smilansky's argument to scapegoat Hispanics or the disabled? If free will illusionism, including "degrading fellow people", is considered morally justified then what exactly isn't permitted in

Smilansky's world – where not only is injustice towards the individual washed away by the wider consideration of the community but the minority are expected to express understanding of the injustice they receive? The illusionist and Harvard psychologist Daniel Wegner says that "sometimes how things seem is more important than what they are" and that it is the illusion of free will that makes us "who we are" (2002, pp. 328, 341), without ever considering the fact that yes, given our widespread enthusiasm for degrading our fellows, this may very well be the problem.

RECAP

We have now covered off the most important and radically alternative traditions of free will justification, and other theories from this point onward are largely variations on a theme. Because, for the defenders of the free will conceit, there are really only three questions to ask oneself.

Libertarianism	Compatibilism	Illusionism
Free choice impossible? NO	Free choice impossible? YES	Free choice impossible? YES
	Down to moral luck? NO	Down to moral luck? YES
		Wider considerations? YES

The first question is about free choice, and whether it really exists. If, like the libertarians, you can convince yourself of the possibility of free choice, there are no further justifications necessary. However, if – like the compatibilists – you can (at least supposedly) acknowledge the lack of free choice, you must then find an acceptable answer to the seeming overarching problem of moral luck. If you can convince yourself that in a world without free choice everything does not just come down to the problem of moral luck – perhaps because skill exists as a spirit-guide elbow somewhere between fortune and misfortune, or because we can split mankind into two forms (where the question of luck becomes irrelevant when considering the not-so-perfect form) – there are no further justifications necessary. But if, like the illusionists, you can acknowledge the lack of free choice and acknowledge the continuing problem of moral luck, you must then decide whether there are other considerations in play that will let you balance off that problem of moral luck.

Illusionism finds this wider consideration in the interests of the majority trumping the interests of the minority, and in the need for social cohesion to outweigh all other moral considerations. Other traditions, the traditions we will now come on to, will find those wider considerations elsewhere. Of course, we have also seen that many writers do not sit comfortably within any single tradition. Libertarians rarely find the need to move, smugly certain that despite the lack of any objective evidence free choice must be possible – although, for the record, Peter van Inwagen has said that if he should suddenly realise that libertarianism was erroneous he would immediately become a compatibilist. In contrast, Dan Dennett and Gary Watson are compatibilists who are sometimes libertarians. Dennett is also a consequentialist who will occasionally argue Saul Smilansky's illusionist position. Even whole traditions can be rather plastic: compatibilism sometimes seems to morph itself into libertarianism, and sometimes into illusionism. But it is time to finish off our investigation by examining the other quasi-traditions of free will justification.

Reactive-attitudinism

For reactive-attitudinists our practices are expressions of our underlying moral attitudes. While in some ways an outgrowth from earlier forms of compatibilism, the late Peter F. Strawson is generally seen as having originated the tradition of reactive-attitudinism in the 1960s. As Strawson put it in *Freedom and Resentment* (1962), our current practices express our natural human reactions, including the "reactive attitudes", and there is no deeper need to justify concepts such as retribution through recourse to ideas like self-origination, could-have-done-otherwise, free choice – or indeed a need to solve the hard problem of moral luck. For Strawson, these natural urges cannot be affected by new insights into determinism and lack of choice, and furthermore should not be affected by such new insights. To attempt to suppress the natural reactions – through (for example) dwelling on the fact that people cannot choose to do otherwise – is to undermine normal human relations. Thus the reactive attitudes of praise and blame are the only justification needed for praise and blame: they are their own justification. Revenge and the infliction of suffering are morally justified by the desire for revenge and the desire to inflict suffering. According to attitudinism, humans have a natural tendency towards revenge and retribution, and we should and will continue to express these sentiments irrespective of whether others had choice over their actions or station in life. While not firmly ruling out the possibility of free choice, irrespective of the truth of free will, Strawson said, we can feel confident that people should and will be prepared to continue to "acquiesce in that infliction of suffering" on offenders (reprinted as 2008, p.34/77).

Strawson's thesis would seem at first glance to bring with it significant ethical and intellectual problems, though it remains deeply influential within philosophical circles. So is attitudinism a stance that can provide an objective and supportable basis for the moral and criminal law, let alone our economic structures? Much has been written in criticism of the reactive-attitudinist thesis, but we can start with Derk Pereboom's (2001) analysis. The first problem, writes Pereboom, is that Strawson appears factually wrong when stating that natural reactive urges cannot be modified by the recognition of determinism. Pereboom cites, for example, even Gary Watson's uncomfortable and ambiguous attitude to the serial killer Robert Harris after Watson was forced to confront Harris's appalling upbringing at the hands of both his parents and the state. Far from being an objective justification of the reactive attitudes in a world without free will, Pereboom shows that attitudinism is actually a mindset founded upon the attempt to cling to blame against the growing realisation that there is no freedom of choice. Attitudinism, says Pereboom, is a defensive rearguard action by apologists for the *status quo* and not an objectively justified ethical platform at all. The immediately obvious objection to the attitudinist position is that it becomes very difficult to square with a morality previously built on belief in free choice. For example, the illusionist Saul Smilansky argues that the reactive attitudes are underlain by a "tacit assumption of libertarian free will" (2000, p.270), while one of the most influential – and thoughtful – of the philosophical attitudinists, UCL's Ted Honderich, admits that we have retributive punishment "based on an assumption of the origination of offences by offenders" (2006). The attitudinist promise that we can and will simply ignore the deeper problem of moral luck and lack of free choice is as practically dubious as it is morally suspicious. The psychologist and illusionist Dan Wegner tells us that uncertainty over the existence of libertarian free will "makes everyone deeply uncomfortable", which is why we need to promote the myth of free choice to the masses in order to ease their consciences (2002, p.336). But Wegner is suggesting that we are in large part uncomfortable with uncertainty over the existence of free will *because* we all know deep down that in the absence of free choice our desire to inflict suffering becomes ethically and intellectually indefensible. Attitudinism seems to be just another thesis built on ingratitude for the great good fortune many of us enjoy through no credit to ourselves, and indifference towards the far greater misfortune others suffer through no choice of their own. There seems to be no concept of fair play within attitudinism: this is philosophy designed for the self-absorbed.

Attitudinism, as with the compatibilism of Dan Dennett and Gary Watson, argues that we need to keep alive the ideals of suffering, desert, and vengeance. But how can it be right that someone with no choice, no option to do otherwise, deserves to suffer? Just arguing that something is a natural reaction (ignoring for the moment wider questions of whether we can modify natural reactions) does not provide it with moral justification – or, in philosophical parlance, "is" does not imply "ought" – as we saw earlier when Bruce Waller recounted the "strike back" response. Christianity has long argued that it would emphatically not be morally or intellectually right to justify suffering in a world without free choice. As the Christian philosopher Alvin Plantinga puts it: "If it isn't possible for me to refrain from doing wrong, then I can't really be responsible for that wrong-doing – not in the relevant sense anyway… The relevant sense involves being properly subject to disapprobation, moral criticism, and even punishment" (2013). Suffering is no longer deserved when choice is stripped away. Attitudinism cannot offer us a coherent theory of desert: desert becomes something partial – something biased – for attitudinists. Under such a biased theory of desert it is apparently right for us to rage against the wrong done to us, or at least the wrongs done to people like us, but not for offenders to act out the rage that comes from the wrongs done to them. The theory of desert has, in the hands of Strawson and as with Gary Watson, been reduced to the plea to be allowed to feel sympathy for those like us and no sympathy for those not like us.

In *Freedom and Resentment* Strawson went on to introduce the idea of different "types" against which to assess the appropriateness of the reactive attitudes. The point here was to describe and justify what philosophers term exempting conditions, which are applied to those who are exempt from calls for vengeance and suffering no matter their behaviour – today the mentally ill, for example. But as Pereboom (2001) has shown (both in relation to attitudinism and more widely) there is no coherent moral nor intellectual rationale to exempt some but not others. Strawson's point in describing types seems to have been to permit fellow-feeling for our former best friend John from the second chapter, but not for the sixteen-year-old hoodlum from Harlem. Strawson noted that the agent who was "peculiarly unfortunate in his formative circumstances" (2008, p.25/66) – arguably, then, the formerly angelic John, who only changed after the dastardly mad professor dripped poison in his morning frappuccino – is set apart and not an appropriate object of the normal reactive attitudes, being one who "tends to promote, at least in the civilized, [sympathetic] objective attitudes" (p.25/66). Yet, as we have seen, all offenders – and the vast majority of non-offenders – have a mad professor somewhere in their past. Pereboom makes the point that it is a feature of our system of morality that when there is no relevant moral difference between two agents you cannot hold one responsible if you are excusing another (2001, p.99). Such "peculiarly unfortunate" circumstances self-evidently apply *across the board* with offenders (and, likewise, the undeserving poor), as otherwise they would not be offenders in the first place.

> "Matters of luck, by their very character, are the opposite of the moral – how can we ultimately hold someone accountable for what is, after all, a matter of luck? How can it be fair that she 'pay' for this?" (Smilansky, 2000, p.45).

Strawson seems to want to not only describe but also excuse and validate the fact that we feel sympathy for our former best friend John but no sympathy for the sixteen-year-old hoodlum from Harlem. Yet, as Pereboom has argued, all such distinctions between the peculiarly unfortunate and the putatively not-so-peculiarly unfortunate are bogus. All such let's-call-this-peculiar versus let's-call-this-not-so-peculiar distinctions are partial and prejudiced. In a universe without free will "luck swallows everything", as Peter Strawson's philosopher son Galen (1998) has recognised. Not luck swallows everything from B_U to BE_U, but excluding parts of E_U. Not luck swallows everything from mental disabilities to our former friend John, but not club feet or the sixteen-year-old hoodlum from Harlem. As with Michael McKenna's essentialism, attitudinism is subtly giving us the excuse for fellow-feeling with the educated drunk middle-class criminal who we can perhaps imagine ourselves as, but not the uneducated working-class criminal we will never try to see ourself as. There is much evidence from social psychology that the more similar we feel to someone the more likely we are to feel compassion and sympathy towards them, with the opposite being the case for those we feel different from. Attitudinism raises the ethical concern that it is far from being a universal objective moral code. Peter Strawson is keen to find a defence of current practices that "we" consider desirable, but exactly who is this "we"? It is certainly not, for example, the we of the more inclusive Christian ethicists. Strawson is assuming population-wide (or at least in-group sect-wide) views of the we, even though the general population has not yet been disabused of belief in free choice, and thus has had no chance to consider the wider ethical questions that Christian theologians have long had to wrestle with. The unwillingness to question the *status quo* is highlighted when Honderich (2007) says that although the free will excuse has served us very well to date in providing a rationale for blame and the infliction of just suffering, if the old "truth" of free choice no longer serves us in this goal then "we need to find another truth".

Simply ignoring the problem of moral luck has consequences for attitudinism. Since the death of Peter Strawson one of the most thoughtful philosophical defenders of the attitudinist mindset has been UCL's Ted Honderich. Honderich celebrates the reassurance provided by the more robust reactive attitudes, including the siren call of retribution, even as he admits that no one can choose to do otherwise. "We want the reassurance of certain moral attitudes", Honderich writes (2006), and the attitudinist position will allow us to persist in the attitudes to others "close to" the attitudes previously tied up with the mystical belief in self-origination. We need to be a little careful here, as in many other parts of his writing Honderich is close to the hard determinist position of Pereboom and Waller. Unlike most of his colleagues he writes clearly on the moral and intellectual failures of both compatibilism and libertarianism. In consequence, Honderich has expressed concern about the appropriateness of justified suffering in a universe without free choice. However, while Honderich has called for new thinking and new attitudes about freedom, he notes (2011) both his own changes of mind here and an unhelpful tendency to still think too much in terms of moral responsibility. Recognising this, it is interesting to consider the further fact that Honderich is well known in philosophical circles as an avowed consequentialist. For a consequentialist the morality of an act lies in its consequences, and not, for example, in its motive. We have already noted that all consequentialism ultimately reduces to the idea that the ends justify the means. There may be an uncomfortably close connection between the standard consequentialist mindset of treating individuals as means not ends (as in "you can't make an omelette without breaking eggs") and the wider reactive-attitudinist indifference to injustice at the level of the individual and often deliberate blindness to the problem of moral luck.

By airbrushing out the problem of moral luck another weakness of mainstream reactive-attitudinism becomes ontological.

Strawson's thesis is all about the justification for resentment when one person is injured by the action of another – people whom he labels "offended parties" (2008, p.21/62). But in a world without origination there is a deep ontological problem with simplistically dividing the world into the offenders and the offended-against. Attitudinism never confronts the problem that if retribution and the need to inflict suffering is to be morally acceptable in a world without free choice then surely it must in all fairness be permitted to the unlucky losers of the deterministic lottery of life. Surely it must also be allowed to those who never chose their station in life, and yet who were the victims of libertarian "moral hardness" and intellectual error, of compatibilist word games if not outright deceit, and of illusionist smoke and mirrors? If violent retribution and delight in the suffering of others is both moral and a reassuring virtue then it's not immediately obvious why P.F. Strawson, Dan Dennett (he of the "Is it fair...? Life isn't fair" bar-room maxims), and Saul Smilansky (to name but three) couldn't be, or couldn't have been, legitimately turned into hamburger by those degraded and unjustly treated under their professional prescriptions. And Smilansky is the first to admit that the treatment of those targeted by the free will myth is both degrading and unjust. When you deny the cathartic experience of that "virtue" to some, and restrict the right to only those like you, you are being discriminatory and partial. No one is denying that it can sometimes be unhealthy, and is often futile, to try to suppress our naturally-felt emotions – even the reactive emotions, like the desire to inflict suffering. When we are slighted we have a natural tendency to strike back, as do rats and monkeys, notwithstanding how unjust that desire to strike back may actually be judged to be. Expressing anger can be psychologically healthy for feelings of individual self-worth (although often anger is not overly healthy), and there will always be venting of such emotions and the desire to vent such emotions. But these considerations can never provide the objective ethical reasons to allow such atavistic emotions to set the agenda for our social, economic, and legal structures. Pereboom also makes the practical point that the profound "moral sadness" one feels when one considers how fortune or misfortune – moral luck – make all the difference to our lives "will be at least as effective in sustaining emotional depth as its more prevalent blame-ascribing counterparts" (2001, p.98).

There is a deeper ontological problem, though, with Strawson's celebration of our natural reactions. Strawson celebrates retribution and the desire to inflict suffering as natural and representative of our true underlying species character. And we have seen Bruce Waller confirming that the strike back response – the need to lash out when hurt, irrespective of wider considerations of fairness or desert – has been observed in our fellow animals, including rats and monkeys. Such a strike back response can also be seen in human infants, who will lash out at their quite blameless mothers when they feel frustrated, angry, or hurt. But there are deep theoretical problems with ever trying to use nature or the natural as a guide for what is moral or right, which is what attitudinism is wholly based upon.

"Meanwhile, Lukaja handed the infant to the alpha male Ntologi, who dragged, tossed, and slapped it against the ground. Ntologi climbed a tree with the infant in his mouth. He waved it in the air, and finally killed it by biting it on the face... Conspicuous competition for meat and meat-sharing was observed as usual. Three adult males and an adult female obtained meat from Ntologi. Two adult females, two juvenile females, a juvenile male, and an infant recovered scraps from the ground or were given scraps. At 13:00, Ntologi was still holding the skin of the carcass" (Hamai *et al.*, 1992, 'New records of within-group infanticide and cannibalism in wild chimpanzees', *Primates*, p.152).

We share 99% of our DNA with the chimpanzees above, when calculated using single nucleotide substitutions. The primatologist Sarah Hrdy was shocked to discover, in groundbreaking work four decades ago, that infanticide was the single greatest source of the up to 83% infant mortality rate within the langur monkey groups she studied at Abu in India (1977, 1977a). Infanticide, Hrdy ultimately realised, was perfectly natural and adaptive behaviour – extremely advantageous for the langur males who succeed at it. Along with more rigorous field study, selfish gene theory – selection at the level of the gene, not at the level of the individual and certainly not at the level of the group – as developed by George Williams in the late 1960s and popularised by Richard Dawkins in the late 1970s, has completely altered our understanding of both nature and natural adaptive behaviour. All the major figures within the development of selfish gene theory, from Williams to John Maynard Smith and Bill Hamilton, as well as popularisers like Richard Dawkins, have come to realise that (to quote Hamilton) "the animal in our nature cannot be regarded as a fit custodian for the values of humanity" (1971, p.219). Or, as Richard Dawkins puts it, "civilized human behavior has about as much connection with natural selection as does the behavior of a circus bear on a unicycle" (Ridley & Dawkins, 1981, p.32). Returning, then, to P.F. Strawson, the natural – one might even say essential – model that mainstream reactive-attitudinism is advancing for mankind doesn't get us far in the morality stakes. Firstly, almost everything that makes us distinctly human seems to be against nature. All the best of our characteristics, with perhaps the singular exception of a mother sacrificing for her child, are seen nowhere in the non-human – the natural – world. Compassion, fair play, justice, charity, kindness: these, as Hamilton and Williams recognised, are not natural world behaviours. They are seemingly the culturally-overlaid rejection of natural world behaviours.

Even the mother sacrificing for her child should give us pause. Equally shocking to Sarah Hrdy as the within-group infanticide were the instances of primate mothers abandoning their butchered infants soon after or even before death. "It is far more likely, however, that desertion reflects a practical evaluation of what *this* infant's chances are weighed against the probability that her next infant will survive" (Hrdy, 1977, p.48). In sharp contrast to langurs, chimps, and bonobos, one of the exemplars of humanity is the way we fight for (and do not desert) our deeply disabled and our dying. Of course there have been (to us, shocking) examples of cultures that despise disability and weakness: from Nazi Germany, where the handicapped were murdered behind closed doors, to the city-states of ancient Greece – including democratic Athens, home to the greatest of the original philosophers – where sick and weak infants were left to die outside the city walls. But we know we are human at least in part because this behaviour is today capable of shocking us. And even in Nazi Germany it was thought best for this to go on behind closed doors, away from publicity, in contrast to the carefree infanticide of the natural world.

Strawson and the attitudinists are choosing with great partiality what they regard as natural and laudable impulses while dismissing out of hand other equally "valid" natural impulses. These impulses are equally valid because – when your yardstick is purely the natural, the essential – you have *no right* to pick and choose between biological impulses. For much of human history – and even today, in many parts outside the West (including India) – extreme violence against women and girls was not only unexceptional but was, where not actively encouraged, then at the very least easily tolerated under religious and social norms. Extreme violence against females by males is also what we get in much of nature, as we shall see later. While some human sexual violence against women is undoubtedly deeply cultural in origin, including the desire to absolutely humiliate an enemy, even here there tends to be a sexual excitement which draws on the same natural urges as acted upon daily by our primate and non-primate cousins. Infanticide was a settled part of ancient Greek and Roman behaviour. Slavery, vicious sexism, and racism are well-established human weaknesses, along with scapegoating, but many of us think we have largely risen above those natural siren calls. And yet Strawson and attitudinism decry what could at least be argued to be the sexual violence and infanticide instincts while worshipping at the altar of the strike back instinct. This is stated in no way to justify sexual violence or infanticide in the human world but is raised purely to make the point that there tends to be no intellectual or moral consistency within attitudinism. Strawson not only displays great partiality in the natural impulses he decides to laud, but he also completely overlooks or even rejects out of hand the anti-natural characteristics that make the human animal unique. Chimpanzees live in "a world without compassion", says the primatologist Frans de Waal (1996, p.83), but this is equally true of squirrels, dolphins, wolves, bonobos, and orang-utans. "There is no charity in nature", writes the geneticist Steve Jones (1999, p.160). It is the things that are not only best about us, but unique to us – our capacity for reason and need for truth, our desire for fair play and justice, our ability to see another's point of view, our toleration, compassion, and charity – that the attitudinist model should be lauding, but these are the characteristics that attitudinism is largely reacting against in its singular homage to partiality ("peculiarly unfortunate"), ignorance and our rat-and-monkey strike back instinct. Human moral progress is at least in part about striving to rise above the animal, but attitudinism appears not to be.

Semi-compatibilism

Semi-compatibilism was developed by John Martin Fischer and Mark Ravizza as a breakaway movement from compatibilism.

Bothered by the obviously-expanding potential problems of trying to argue for the existence of free will (however defined) in a universe deterministic at the human level, and by the accusations of disinformation and word-jugglery, Fischer and Ravizza (e.g. 1998) formulated the argument that while free will (however defined) may or may not be compatible with determinism (or indeterminism for that matter), moral responsibility and blame certainly still were. Semi-compatibilism - at first as advanced by Fischer and Ravizza, but for the last decade largely as advanced by John Fischer alone (as Ravizza was ordained into the Church as Father Ravizza) - holds that moral responsibility and blame do not require self-origination or alternate possibilities. For semi-compatibilism, moral responsibility does not require the possibility to have done otherwise, and requires only control of one's actions - only moderate reason-responsive control - or what Fischer terms guidance control rather than regulative control. Moral responsibility requires that a person is moderately responsive to reason. The agent takes ownership of the mechanism that results in the behaviour by reflecting on the mechanism.

Some compatibilists, including Gary Watson, have doubted that there is any real distinction between compatibilism and semi-compatibilism, but in one important sense semi-compatibilism does seem to be a clear return to the earlier compatibilism of Hume and Locke - as well as to the compatibilism of Harry Frankfurt - where one is either insensible to or indifferent to the problems of winners' justice and moral luck. Semi-compatibilism can thus be contrasted with the compatibilism of theorists like Dennett and Watson, who remain fully aware of the overarching problem of moral luck and thus look to find a solution to the problem, however unsuccessful they may be judged to be. In holding to this stance and in abandoning arguments for free will while retaining concepts of blame and moral responsibility, Fischer and Ravizza of course understood that they were flying in the face of both mainstream Judaeo-Christianity and traditional moral philosophy. Their work was a reaction against both the seemingly unsolvable problem of moral luck and what Fischer terms the standard or common-sense view: "Our commonsense theorizing about our moral and legal responsibility presupposes that sometimes at least we could have done otherwise" (2007, p.72). Fischer and Ravizza's work continues to be influential, largely due to its minimal requirement for only the most basic reason-responsive control. But it suffers from inherent moral problems, which prevent most philosophers feeling comfortable with it, with the greatest concern being precisely that semi-compatibilism openly rejects both the common-sense view and makes no attempt to address the problems of fair play and moral luck. The other traditions we have studied have suggested that answers to the problem of moral luck (and effectively the common-sense view) either lie in the fact that free choice exists – and thus moral luck does not enter into the equation – or that somehow the problem of moral luck can be either solved or at least balanced out and offset. Indeed, by clearly admitting that the deterministic universe we inhabit may well rule out any form of free will, semi-compatibilism was drawing greater attention to the problems of moral luck and the common-sense view. But it was then leaving these thorny issues completely unaddressed. In arguing for the fairness of the reactive attitudes – including contempt and the desire to inflict suffering – in a world without any possibility of self-creation or choice, semi-compatibilism was making no attempt to find the mitigating excuses given by attitudinism and illusionism. The only wider consideration offered by semi-compatibilism is in effect no consideration: semi-compatibilism does not seek to offset the problem of moral luck because semi-compatibilism is wholly indifferent to the problem of moral luck. In a sense what semi-compatibilism is offering us is what the compatibilist George Sher has more recently rejected as the "F" (or "fairness") principle: rejection of what he calls the "bedrock" or "provisional fixed point" moral concept that it is unfair to blame someone for something he could not help (2006, p.60). Unfairness becomes the new fairness for semi-compatibilism, with no wider considerations or extenuating circumstances offered. As with hard compatibilism below, while the honesty of openly admitting to the non-existence of self-creation and free choice is refreshing, the moral paradoxes remain significant.

Fischer has made a distinction between being morally responsible and being blameworthy, but we need not overly dwell on this as most philosophers see little or no important distinction. What is key for us is, anyway, the overarching concern with blameworthiness. Semi-compatibilism appears morally similar to the reactive-attitudinism of Peter Strawson in that it seems to want to justify our tendency to excuse those like us, while condemning out of hand those not like us. This is clearly suggested when Fischer tells us that the pretty, well-scrubbed, and light-skinned female drug smuggler who is just trying to support her family has done wrong "but is not blameworthy" (2007a, p.186). However, this is in contrast to the absolute blame that he suggests attaches to most others including (presumably) the hygiene-deficient and spaced-out male drug runner – who, for cultural reasons, refuses to meet our eye – yet who is also acting to benefit the only supportive family he has ever really known (his gang). Such a distinction is of course wholly arbitrary, exactly as it was with Strawson's "peculiarly unfortunate" formative circumstances, where the world is divided into those we can blame (effectively criminals we don't like and cannot see ourselves in) and those we should not blame (well-scrubbed and articulate criminals we like and can see ourselves – or at least our children – in). Developing this thought, in his 2001 *Living Without Free Will* Derk Pereboom tried to demonstrate that there is no convincing intellectual or ethical rationale for why, in a universe without origination (a universe without free choice) we can blame offenders for their offences when we fail to blame, for example, the insane or the mentally handicapped for the actions they cannot help. Semi-compatibilism argues for the morality of blame in a universe without choice: for the morality of blame in and of itself, with no offsetting considerations. But the corollary to Pereboom's wider point about a lack of justifiable discrimination between the offender and the insane or the mentally handicapped person (or Fischer's pretty and well-scrubbed female drug smuggler) is that when semi-compatibilism refuses flat out to seek to offset or excuse the injustice of blaming someone for something they cannot help, then all less fortunate and at risk groups are potentially put in danger, because there is now no logical place to stop: a purely arbitrary and biased differentiation. P.F. Strawson sought to divide the world into types to try to allow himself (still subjective) protection of certain at risk groups: Fischer has abandoned even this level of protection. In a sense semi-compatibilism is a theory that makes no distinction between the deserving and undeserving poor, however artificial that distinction, because under semi-compatibilism all of the poor are recognised as being undeserving and a drain on the more fortunate. All the poor and less fortunate – except the occasional pretty and well-scrubbed chirpy urchin – are to be blamed for their condition, no matter that their poverty may be down to circumstances completely outside of their control. Misfortune is no longer a mitigating factor, or even a moral consideration, once we have stripped away (and not just excused, as with, for example, illusionism) the principle of not blaming people for something they could not help. Under semi-compatibilism suffering must follow blame. For Fischer and Ravizza life is divided into the lucky winners and the unlucky losers, and the winners not only have no duty to help the losers, they have a right to make the unlucky losers suffer *for being* unlucky losers. Fischer tells us he "is not troubled by" issues of moral luck, winners' justice, and the lack of the ability to have done otherwise. He asks, "Why be disturbed by" such concerns? (2007, pp.69-70).

The problem is that Fischer and Ravizza subscribe to a morality that offers us no objective place to stop, and have therefore given up on any attempt to offer us a non-contingent worldview or impartial moral code. All we have left is subjective prejudice. By arguing for abandonment of the universal fairness principle without attempting to excuse unfairness through wider (or offsetting) moral considerations – such as illusionism's utilitarianism, or attitudinism's natural urges – Fischer and Ravizza have not only abandoned standard morality, they have replaced standard morality with a wholly subjective ethic of praise and blame. Fischer and Ravizza claim the right to blame (or praise) those they wish to blame, such as almost all offenders, but to withhold blame from those they do not wish to blame, such as the insane and the occasional pretty and well-scrubbed offender – yet without any objective right to discriminate between the two groups. To stress again, the argument under semi-compatibilism is not that there is any sort of offsetting rationale for blame and legitimate suffering in the absence of choice. This is not the illusionist argument that wider social concerns offset individual injustice, and this is not the attitudinist argument that our natural attitudes often crowd out what might otherwise be seen as concerns over individual injustice. Illusionism and attitudinism are at least making an attempt to provide a reasoned and – in one very weak sense – a non-contingent, offsetting excuse for blame and the infliction of suffering (notwithstanding the inability to have done otherwise). As Fischer offers no justification for unfairness towards the individual (beyond fairness no longer seemingly being a universal requirement) Fischer's work is fully, and not just partially, open to the charge of being nothing more than winners' justice. It also remains fully open to the associated charge that Fischer and

Ravizza developed their semi-compatibilist thesis after the fact.

There are significant and widely-perceived moral problems to blame and responsibility in the recognised absence of both free choice and alternate possibilities. Hence, while remaining theoretically attractive to many because it looks to set the infliction of suffering bar so low, semi-compatibilism attracts few named supporters and remains a minority tradition within free will theory. It also remains a minority tradition within theology (Father Ravizza notwithstanding) although we may begin to see a parallel between semi-compatibilism, rejection of the universal fairness principle, and what we shall come to investigate as the extreme Calvinist position. Extreme Calvinism will be shown to argue that it is not unfair to blame people (and make them eternally suffer) for something they cannot help, because fairness is a concept that is not relevant. This extreme religious position will utilise a slightly different excuse for unfairness towards individuals. This is not indifference as such, but the argument that fairness is a concept which does not apply to mankind and applies only to God. Extreme Calvinism will justify the "fairness of unfairness" through denigration of human worth in the face of something more exalted, but in some ways the semi-compatibilist fairness of unfairness position seems – at least to the author – to be built upon a parallel denigration of human individual worth.

Hard Compatibilism

We now turn to what we shall call hard compatibilism. Hard compatibilism joins semi-compatibilism in acknowledging, or at least suggesting, that free will cannot exist in a deterministic universe (or indeterministic universe), and hard compatibilism furthermore joins semi-compatibilism in asserting that blame can be attributed in a world without free will. However, where hard compatibilism will separate itself completely from semi-compatibilism, as well as illusionism and attitudinism, is in arguing that while blame can be attributed this can never be a *fair* attribution. This therefore becomes a practical distinction and a utilitarian judgement without further appeals to the justice of that judgement. Unfairness is not the new fairness (the claim of Fischer and Ravizza). Unfairness remains unfairness, but it is all we have – and possibly all we will ever have, at least according to hard compatibilism. Hard compatibilism is another minority tradition, but it needs to be discussed because it will highlight one important new distinction. Hard compatibilism is rare at least in part because it seems to give up on both the idea of moral progress and, probably more crucially, even the possibility of moral progress. Philosophers have an understandable nervousness about being seen to give up on the possibility of moral advancement, and it is difficult to find an academic philosopher willing to sit squarely within this tradition. Probably the closest we come, though, is the influential legal philosopher, UCLA's Peter Arenella. Although otherwise a mainstream compatibilist, in his tellingly-titled paper *Convicting the Morally Blameless*, Arenella writes that "perhaps all this legal rhetoric about 'just deserts' and moral responsibility is just the law's way of legitimating one form of human suffering" (1992, p.1608), and that affixing blame is only there to "soothe our collective social conscience" (p.1533). Hard compatibilism thus combines the first-order indifference to individual injustice of traditions like illusionism, attitudinism, and semi-compatibilism, but without the second-order justifications attempted by those traditions.

The important new distinction referred to above is given voice to by Oxford University's Neil Levy (2011). Levy makes the observation that standard justifications for free will and moral responsibility create what he calls a "double dose" of unfairness and injustice. Firstly there is the poor developmental luck many have to suffer, which is some combination of B_U and/or E_U and/or BE_U, as we investigated at length in the third chapter. Justifications for free will often, although certainly not always, do seem to need to either deny altogether or at least play down such misfortune. Hence, for example, we saw the compatibilist Dan Dennett claiming both that there is no such thing as truly bad luck and that anyway over his long life he had seen just as much misfortune as anyone else. Similarly, the essentialists wish to argue that concepts of misfortune only really apply to one of their two forms of human. In addition, though, we also have illusionism – which can accept the unvarnished truth that some of us do get to live a much more fortunate life than others through no credit to us and no fault of theirs, while simultaneously doing nothing to address such comparative unfairness. To indifference to this *first dose* of developmental unfairness, all of the traditions of free will justification that we have encountered so far add a *second dose* of unfairness. This is the unfairness of claiming that the person was somehow responsible for their first dose of unfairness, or at the very least that blame and suffering are their just deserts. And it is against the background of this double dose of unfairness that we can, and should, contrast the hard compatibilism of Peter Arenella. Certainly Arenella seems relatively indifferent to the first dose of unfairness. (The attribution here of indifference reflects the direction and effect of his professional writing: as with all the thinkers referred to in this book the author makes no comment on their non-academic personality or character, and for all I know each may dedicate all of his or her spare time to *pro bono* work, poor relief and penal reform.) Nevertheless, while academically indifferent to the first dose of unfairness, as a hard compatibilist Arenella refuses to complement that first dose of unfairness with Levy's "double dose" of unfairness by then blaming the less fortunate for their misfortune, or by arguing that suffering is their just desert. This distinction makes the hard compatibilist a very different beast indeed from the semi-compatibilist, reactive-attitudinist, or illusionist.

Having given credit where credit is due – in a non-free will sense, of course – it still remains obvious that hard compatibilism is not, at least for Arenella, a comfortable position to find oneself in. Arenella himself seems to feel the need to back away from the full implications, for example by adding the unconvincing rider that "perhaps" all the legal rhetoric about just deserts is nothing more than an attempt to legitimise human suffering. There is no "perhaps" about it: outside of the (morally highly suspect) rationales of majoritarianism, utilitarianism, and the necessary sacrifice of the unlucky there are no internally consistent rationales for blame. We are indeed always "convicting the morally blameless", as a theorist like Saul Smilansky will admit when pushed into a corner. Similarly, when Arenella notes that determinism would imply that "some moral agents will have a far easier time than others in exercising their moral capacities" (p.1614), this appears to be a slightly half-hearted way of putting over the fact that determinism (or even indeterminism) means that some have no chance at all of not offending. Not a harder time not offending, but no possibility of not offending. Like the qualifier perhaps, "easier time" does not begin to address the full truths of determinism. People no more freely choose to offend than they choose to be poor, or choose to have club feet.

It is perhaps no surprise that Arenella seems to find it uncomfortable fully inhabiting the hard compatibilist space. There are parallels between hard compatibilism and Smilansky's illusionism, as both admit the injustice of blame. Albeit illusionism then seeks excuses for such injustice, which it finds in the greater good, while hard compatibilism does not seek excuses. It is because of such parallels that the hard compatibilist position is even less stable than the illusionist one. Partial truths and single doses of unfairness get you into more hot water in the free will debates than wholesale untruths and double doses of unfairness. We have seen Smilansky wishing to be able to consistently admit to the injustices of the free will myth but being driven to take a step back from this – within illusionism the morally blameless start out as blameless but become blameworthy again once society needs them to be our scapegoats – and the same appears to be true of hard compatibilism. The reason that hard compatibilism is unstable is that blame in the recognised absence of free choice is not only morally problematic but strongly wrong-footing. Hard compatibilism encounters this problem directly, while illusionism encounters it at one remove.

The public is used to thinkers asserting belief in free will and blame together. For all its desire to retain belief in free will, the public can at least understand the argument that in the absence of freedom of choice blame and suffering are unjust. Christianity, for example, has agreed with this latter conclusion for hundreds of years, while nevertheless refusing to examine the evidence against free will. Yet hard compatibilism tries to hold to a destabilising third position – that of blame in the recognised absence of freedom of choice – which illusionism does indirectly and semi-compatibilism does directly, but the latter thereby pays the price in terms of limited philosophical support. In effect, and by having made no attempt to change the sanctions or the language of the process, Arenella, like Smilansky, is not just admitting to convicting the morally blameless but admitting to blaming the morally blameless. "Blaming the blameless" as a tag line for hard compatibilism is fundamentally unsustainable. It smacks of both bad faith and of waving that bad faith in the face of the public. The public has rarely eschewed bad faith but it certainly doesn't want some too-clever-by-half academic like Peter Arenella calling its bad faith to everyone's attention. Dennett asks us all to maintain the moral responsibility system "within limits we take care not to examine too closely" (1984, p.164). Arenella is metaphorically grinning while challenging the public to look more closely: refusing to challenge the system, yet taking away the illusion the system is built upon. While in a sense admirable for refusing to add the second dose of unfairness he is nonetheless still professionally indifferent to the first dose of unfairness. This leaves him in the worst of all possible worlds, as Arenella knows he can expect little gratitude from either free will philosophers or anti-free will philosophers.

Broken Ankles or Stacked Decks?

> "Ultimately, it all comes down to luck: luck – good or bad – in being born the way we are, luck – good or bad – in what then happens to shape us… In the end, luck swallows everything… no punishment or reward is ever ultimately just or fair" (Galen Strawson, 1994, p.16; 1998a, s.6).

We said earlier that for the defenders of the free will conceit, or at least for defenders of the free-will-and-moral-responsibility conceit, there are really only three questions to ask. The first question was about free choice, and whether it actually exists. If, like the libertarians, you can convince yourself of the possibility of free choice, there is no further justification necessary. However, if – like the compatibilists – you can (at least supposedly) acknowledge the lack of free choice, you must then find an acceptable answer to the seeming overarching problem of moral luck and of everything reducing to nothing more than the lottery of biology and environment. If you can convince yourself that in a world without free choice everything does not come down to the lottery of genes and upbringing there is no further justification necessary. However, if – like the illusionists – you can acknowledge the lack of free choice *and* acknowledge the continuing problem of moral luck, you must then decide whether there are other considerations in play that will let you rationalise away that problem of moral luck.

Libertarianism	Compatibilism	Illusionism/ Attitudinism/ Semi-Compatibilism
Free choice impossible? NO	Free choice impossible? YES	Free choice impossible? YES
	Down to moral luck? NO	Down to moral luck? YES
		Wider considerations? YES

Illusionists found this wider consideration in what philosophers term the tyranny of the majority – in the idea that the interests of the majority completely extinguish the interests of the minority – because for illusionists the need for unquestioning social cohesion outweighs all other considerations, moral or otherwise. And we have now completed our review of the "wider considerations" traditions, so we can flesh out the final table. Attitudinism found its wider considerations in our rat-and-monkey strike back instinct, albeit only after rejecting other equally valid instincts and any consideration of the nobler and uniquely human capacities, such as reason and fair play. Semi-compatibilism found its wider considerations in the notion that unfairness is the new fairness, in the belief that there is no requirement for universal fairness, and in the lack of any objective moral code. In a sense semi-compatibilism found its wider consideration in no consideration, refusing flat out to provide an encompassing ethic of fairness or unfairness. In this semi-compatibilism is joined by hard compatibilism: but here the important difference was that the latter refused to acknowledge that unfairness is the new fairness, holding instead to the practical necessity of unfairness without any wider moral justification.

As a general rule, the further to the right you go in the table the less the intellectual error but the greater the moral error. And – whatever their differences – the traditions of attitudinism, semi-compatibilism, and illusionism are cut from the same cloth, which is the belief that the problem of moral luck can't be solved but can be offset, waved away, or in the final instance simply ignored. One point that should not be missed is that for all their intellectual error Dennett and Watson sought to find a solution to the problem of moral luck precisely because they understood how all-consuming the problem is. Watson and Dennett at least acknowledge what is at stake in these debates. However poor or questionable their solutions to the problem of moral luck they recognise that objective morality requires an answer to the problem of moral luck: that it cannot simply be waved away or ignored, as with Frankfurt, Strawson, or Fischer. This said, though, it is the hard compatibilism of Peter Arenella that comes closest to being an intellectually robust tradition of free will and moral responsibility justification. Hard compatibilism does not try to pretend that blame and the infliction of suffering can ever be fair in a universe without free choice. And yet for all its honesty and practical goals hard compatibilism remains intellectually unstable, resorting as it must to waving our hypocrisy in our faces.

Bruce Waller has provided the metaphor that building the world on the free will and moral responsibility conceit is like expecting some people to run a race with broken ankles. This is in many ways an apt metaphor, as upon consideration we realise that races in the modern world are supposed to be largely fair, with competitors deliberately chosen for having similar abilities. We do not race adults against children. We do not even race men against women. And, unlike Sacha Baron Cohen's satire *The Dictator*, we do not give one competitor a gun to shoot anyone who looks like overtaking. We don't force the disabled to complete against the able-bodied in the same race, then give one another knowing grins when the disabled fail to qualify. Instead we form international committees just to establish what forms of disability can compete fairly against other forms of disability. We come up with handicap systems and weight classes to try to level the playing field in sports as diverse as horse racing and boxing. And yet when it comes to free will and moral responsibility attribution the race is anything but fair. But for all that Waller's racing-with-broken-ankles analogy is evocative it fails to tease out the different forms of injustice. Waller's metaphor fails to distinguish a compatibilist from an illusionist from an attitudinist, and they are very different beasts indeed. The – arguably partly reformed – free will illusionist Steven Pinker has approvingly referred (1997) to the free will conceit not as a sporting race but as a "game" – a game, he says, that is akin to a game of cards. So instead of a race with broken ankles let us develop Pinker's allegory here of a card game: specifically an idea that Pinker did not admit to – the idea of a rigged card game.

The libertarian is the player who announces to the world at large that the game cannot possibly be rigged, as you really can have sixty-two cards in a fifty-two-card deck. The mainstream compatibilist doesn't appear to be completely sure how many cards are to be found in a fifty-two-card pack. Is it sixty-two? Fifty-two? Forty-two? He tells us that the game is still fair if up to 20% of players don't get any cards, and that anyway we must be careful "not to examine too closely" the actions of the dealer. The illusionist is the player who quietly acknowledges that the game is rigged, with one player getting cards and another none, but tells us that this is acceptable so long as it is only ever rigged against a minority of players. The reactive-attitudinist argues that whether the game is rigged is irrelevant as we still have a need to deal cards to one player and none to another because we are only truly ourselves when getting self-righteously angry with the no-card player for not winning the hand. The semi-compatibilist refuses to even discuss whether the game is rigged, swipes money from the no-card player, and justifies his actions through there being no overriding principle of fair play. And the hard compatibilist freely admits that the game is rigged and that this is morally unjustifiable, but still shrugs and sweeps up the pot.

The above allegory is certainly more granular then the idea of a race run with broken ankles, and yet we are still missing something important. Both metaphors suggest that those who benefit from the free will myth – and those who suffer under the free will conceit – are part of the *same* race, the *same* game (even if it is an unfair race or a rigged game). Neither metaphor is adequate, though, as to describe us as being in the same game or the same race implies that we all bear some likelihood of cost – just as we all have some likelihood of reward – even if the likelihood is vastly different for different players. But, under the free will conceit, for some there is *nothing but reward* and for others *nothing but cost* (and it was never going to be any way other than this). Philosophers are propagandists for the myth of free will because they get to take the rewards of the myth without paying any of the costs (what is known to economists as "moral hazard"). As Bruce Waller notes, as highly-educated academics philosophers "hold privileged and very comfortable positions in society, and we like to think we justly deserve those special benefits; we've accomplished much, and we are delighted to claim credit for it" (2011, p.307).

> "Waller often resorts to sports examples, provoked perhaps by my example of the marathon with the uneven (but fair) start" (Dan Dennett, 2012).

Philosophers like Dan Dennett try to give the impression, often with crude sporting metaphors, that when it comes to the myth of free will we are all involved in the same race, the same marathon with the uneven "but fair" start – or alternatively "given a head start or held back at the starting line" as Dennett put it (2003, p.274) in his threshold of moral development argument. The truth, though, is that in either a deterministic universe or an indeterministic universe philosophers and most of the rest of us are involved in no race at all. Perhaps the best metaphor, then, is not the runner with broken ankles, nor the reactive-attitudinist getting angry with the no-cards player for not winning the hand. Perhaps in the final instance the best metaphor is the Roman Colosseum. Philosophers are the patricians and the general public the plebeians, with educated and uneducated alike forcing their victims to run the gauntlet in an arena packed with hungry lions while they scream their jaded bloodlust from the seats above, sneering at the spectacle of others dying for their gratification. In Steven Pinker's "game", the free will Games, some sit up high, risking nothing, while guaranteed to win. Others must stand on the sand and risk everything, while guaranteed only to lose.

5

POVERTY IS NOT ACCIDENT BUT DESIGN

> In the Mind there is no absolute, or free, will, but the Mind is determined to will this or that by a cause that is also determined by another, and this again by another, and so to infinity.
> Spinoza, *Ethics* (1677, IIp48 – see Nadler, 2013).

The conceit of free will, however defined and across all its incarnations – libertarian, compatibilist, reactive-attitudinist, illusionist, semi-compatibilist, and hard compatibilist – involves us all in censorship, error, hypocrisy, prejudice, and dissimulation. So what really are the costs of such error and dissimulation, and who pays the greatest cost?

> "*Motive* becomes almost irrelevant; because, in a world without free will, 'luck swallows everything' – Strawson, 1998 – one *effect* of denying the electorate such knowledge is to pretty much ensure that the lucky stay lucky while the unlucky remain unlucky" (Miles, 2013, p.209).

Thomas Halper showed in a 1973 *Polity* essay that attitudes to poverty – including our corresponding compassion towards the poor or lack thereof – have always depended upon our views of personal merit and choice in one's position, but Halper's most worrying conclusion comes when he describes how the main reason for the great longevity and influence of the notorious distinction of the deserving from the undeserving poor "was its profound legitimating power" (1973, p.76). When some are identified as deserving their station through choice rather than luck or accident it becomes not only an excuse not to do anything to help them but, perhaps even more malignantly, it is given as proof that such a society *is* just. The conceit of free choice not only takes away any moral impetus to assist the less fortunate, as their lowly station is no longer seen as misfortune, but the myth then acts to legitimise the whole social order from the very bottom to the very top. The social historian Steve Hindle likewise argues (2004) that the pre-nineteenth-century growth in compassion for at least some of the poor appears to have been matched by the growing reliance on the belief that choice produces the varied stations of poverty. In other words there was now a clear division of the poor into those who are poor through their own choice and continue to deserve no sympathy and the new recognition of those who are poor through no choice of their own so deserve sympathy, with the latter recognition at the same time serving to validate contempt for the former group. And Robert Haggard (2000) actually suggests that the development of the early British welfare state was only possible due to a declining belief in poverty through choice, and the recognition of just how many are at the bottom of the social order because of nothing more than misfortune.

In more recent years the recognition of a substantial deserving poor has declined again, and in June 2009 the Joseph Rowntree Foundation published research showing that up to 83% of Britons think that "virtually everyone" remains in poverty in Britain not as the result of social misfortune or biological handicap but through choice (Bamfield & Horton, 2009, p.23). Because of their belief in the fairness of "deserved inequalities" such respondents were discovered to have become almost completely unconcerned with the idea of promoting greater equality, while at the same time asserting that Britain was a beacon of fairness that offered opportunity for all. According to the JRF report there was a "clear sense" across all the groups surveyed that an individual's situation "is largely of his or her own making". Anyone can make it if they "really try", the great majority of participants asserted (pp.23-24). The 2010 *British Social Attitudes Report* also found that there had been a fall in those supporting any form of wealth redistribution, from 51% in 1994 to 38% in 2010: sympathy was now limited to those who did not choose to live in poverty (NCSR, 2010). Citing this second report, BBC Radio 4's *Analysis* interviewed politicians and commentators to highlight a tendency within the welfare debates to distinguish between those who are poor through bad luck and those who are poor "because of personal choices" (Bowlby, 2010). Free will may just be the primary excuse that many use to legitimise a contempt for the poor which would exist independently of their professed belief in free will, but free will assertion nonetheless provides the ethical fig leaf for such contempt that would be far harder to rationalise (and therefore tolerate) without the myth of free will. The myth of free will doesn't just excuse indifference to poverty. It creates and maintains much of that poverty in the first place.

The influential American Pew Research Center for the People and the Press has concluded that successive Pew Global Attitudes polls "find that at every income level, Americans are far more likely than Europeans to believe that individuals, not society, are responsible for their own failures, economic and otherwise" (Allen & Dimock, 2007). Returning to Haggard's point that the development of the British welfare state required a somewhat declining belief in poverty through choice, then by inference it is at least plausible that the United States lacks a working welfare state in large part because of an even more strongly inculcated belief in the existence of free choice than in Britain. Mink and O'Connor's encyclopedia of the historical, political, and social background to poverty in America tells us that mainstream public discourse since the early nineteenth century has made the distinction between the deserving poor and the undeserving: has raised the issue of worth and merit. Moreover, the book notes that both women and racial minorities have been substantially excluded from the ranks of the deserving poor (2004, p. 226), while the growth in the US of the idea of the undeserving poor coincided with the period of mass immigration of those of non-WASP stock. It is not just adults who are targeted under the free will conceit. The US *Encyclopedia of Children and Childhood in History and Society* includes an entry by social historian Peggy Shifflett asserting that, among other things, the distinction between the deserving poor and the undeserving poor has even been applied to the population of homeless children in the States, estimated to range from five hundred thousand to more than two million (2008). Early twentieth-century runaways – who were viewed, Shifflett tells us, as having chosen to leave their homes – were generally categorised as the undeserving, while she cites studies suggesting that more recent attitudes have not been significantly more tolerant.

In 2009 Jasmine Carey surveyed over 250 undergraduates and found that those who believe in unrestrained free will were significantly more likely to believe in a just world for themselves and others, with just world here defined solely as the tendency "to believe that people deserve the things that happen to them" (2009, p.8). As Carey noted, "the responsibility of free will is necessary for belief in a just world" (p.20). Even those who are trying to defend the free will conceit have provided evidence for the malignity of the myth. The libertarian and social psychologist Roy Baumeister, writing with Andrew Vonasch, unconsciously demonstrated the harmful effects on the poor: "The narrative of the deserving versus undeserving poor is a staunch perennial feature of public debates about welfare, but its only relationship to free will beliefs is that those with higher free will beliefs feel more sympathetic to those who really are trying to lift themselves by their bootstraps" (2013, p.224). If you feel more sympathy towards those trying to lift themselves you are by definition less sympathetic towards those not trying to lift themselves out. Such people are using a *myth*, a *fiction*, to discriminate between the two groups in favour of one and – almost by definition – to the detriment of the other. "People with higher beliefs in free will were more likely to say that 'personal choice' is a cause of poverty [and] people with high belief in free will… actually felt more sympathy towards the person working hard to try to get out of poverty" (p.224). Again, such people are feeling more sympathy towards one group based on an incorrect belief that the other group's members could actually do something about their situation when – in a universe without free choice – they can do literally nothing without assistance. Some have even suggested that blame and a corresponding belief in freedom of choice have, at least in America, been used to move the debate beyond a distinction between the deserving and the undeserving poor and into the territory of whether we ever need feel compassion for the poor. Monica Potts, who writes on poverty and opportunity for *The American Prospect*, writes that the "political and policy discourse about the poor in the United States has centered, to a considerable extent, on whether and how the people who can't make it into the middle class are to blame for their own plight… It's as if the political debate [Michael] Harrington helped ignite has calcified, and we have only two choices: 'You should feel sorry for the poor' or 'You shouldn't'" (2014, pp.103-4).

Free will appears to be the legitimating excuse that is used to ignore the plight of the most unfortunate. Under the free will conceit the world is not now examined to see if it is just, but instead is simply assumed to be just. Henry Ward Beecher, the American nineteenth-century minister, wrote that no man in the United States suffers from poverty "unless it is more than his fault, unless it is his sin", while the early nineteenth-century English politician Edward Bulwer-Lytton wrote that in other countries poverty was seen as a misfortune "but that for Englishmen it was viewed as a crime". Under the mindset epitomised by Beecher and Bulwer-Lytton the existence of poverty is used as proof of a failure of free choice. Referencing the research of Thomas Halper again, some churchgoers have traditionally argued that there are no worthy poor as a just God would not have consigned them to such a horrible fate "if they did not deserve it" (1973, p.75). The poor and unlucky can never win at this game because, thanks to the idea of free will, the existence of poverty becomes the legitimisation of such poverty. As desert morally requires free will, the existence of a segment of society struggling at the bottom is given as proof of free will: they wouldn't be struggling if they did not deserve to be. Such a Kafkaesque inversion of logic brings to mind the contemporary philosophical "proofs" of almost perfect social and economic fairness by the simple expedient of eliminating from the calculus anyone being treated unfairly. And senior figures in the free will debates have often been surprisingly happy to concede that the free will myth blocks both social equality and social justice. Stephen J. Morse is Ferdinand Wakeman Hubbell Professor of Law at the University of Pennsylvania, and has for three decades been the doyen of legal compatibilists; the doyen of those who argue the law must be blind to questions of freedom of choice. Yet, according to Morse, if society were to admit that no one freely chooses their position in life it would necessitate "the wholesale reform of society" (1976, p.1257) and "massive social reforms" (p.1261), "a massive redistribution of wealth" and "social engineering... inconsistent with our system" (1976a, p.1276). Morse tells us that those who wish to query the law's position on free choice are motivated by the desire for "a truly egalitarian democracy" (1976, p.1260), and wish for social reforms "not compatible with a [economically] libertarian and capitalist society" (p.1261). All of which raises the question: under our self-fuelling belief system is poverty less accident than inherent design?

What causes poverty and social and economic misfortune? In every sense it is being dealt a bad hand. Perhaps it is being dealt a bad biological hand but often it is being dealt a bad environmental hand. In a world without free will luck swallows everything, but now we have a system that feeds on itself and legitimises and enhances suffering at the bottom, while privileging those at the top. So what are we to make of platforms that suppress or dissemble over knowledge of what causes poverty and social inequality? Surely, if you refuse to fully recognise what causes poverty – nothing more than a poor biological and, more pertinently, poor environmental hand – you make combating poverty and social exclusion more difficult. We, the fortunate and influential, create the conditions that allow poverty to continue to exist. Then we, the fortunate and influential, create and sustain the public myth that excuses our turning of a blind eye towards that poverty. We continue to run our social systems, including our responses to poverty, from "within limits we take care not to examine too closely", as the philosopher Dan Dennett puts it (1984, p.164). Free will is a belief that hurts the poor and acts to advantage the rich and powerful. It is crass not to recognise the unfair advantage the myth of free will may be giving to some segments of society, very much at the expense of others.

Belief in Free Will Decreases Empathy and Increases Suffering

It was the free will compatibilist Dan Dennett who told us (2012) that his work examines – and, by extension, justifies – all social and economic outcomes: from deprived childhoods to privileged childhoods; from good fortune to bad fortune. It was the free will libertarians Roy Baumeister and Andrew Vonasch (2013) who admitted that people with higher belief in free will saw personal

167

choice as a cause of poverty and felt little sympathy for those seemingly unable to climb out of poverty. Dennett advances the paradigm that we need feel little sympathy for those we naively label the less fortunate because we all get approximately the same breaks in life, and luck averages out in the long run. Gary Watson advances the slightly different social equality argument that "we" all get approximately the same breaks in life because we need not consider that other form of human which just might have received fewer breaks in life.

> "Dennett does not argue that our moral responsibility system is fair; rather, it is *fair enough*... Dennett seems comfortable with 'fair enough', and he can champion such a system and not blink" (Bruce Waller, 2012).

It is the winners, not the losers, who invent the meta-ethical rationales that end up justifying – whatever the original intent – the winners' good fortune and enhanced social position, and not just others' misfortune and social exclusion. It is the winners, not the losers, who see personal choice as a cause of poverty; who argue against luck and for there being two forms of human; who advance arguments that "there is room for the thought" that the lucky can take credit for not having been born with club feet and that the unlucky are to blame for having been born with club feet. It is the winners, not the losers, who can settle for "fair enough" rather than *fair*. The winners here get to write not only the history books but the philosophical and theological primers that define the very terms equality, freedom, opportunity, and fairness; all of which you would have thought runs directly counter to our expressed values. The injunction *Do unto others as you would have them do unto you* has been known as the Golden Rule since the seventeenth century, although the ethic goes back much further than this. Often seen as inseparable from

Christianity, *Do unto others as you would have them do unto you* is a maxim that dates back well over two and a half thousand years. Even Confucianism, frequently regarded as more storytelling and homily than a form of virtue ethics (and sometimes seemingly a system promoting obedience to one's social betters) still grounds such obedience in virtue. Rulers, said Confucius, will be obeyed to the extent they govern with virtue, and central to such virtue was how rulers treat their underlings. When Confucius was asked by Tzu-kung whether there was a single word that could be a guide to conduct throughout life, for rulers and the ruled, Confucius replied "shu" (reciprocity): do not impose on others what you would not desire to have imposed on yourself (c.5th BC/1979, p.135). And *Do unto others* is a maxim central to Judaism, Hinduism, Buddhism, Zoroastrianism and Islam. It is even apparently found within Scientology, and the teachings of L. Ron Hubbard. The idea of *Do unto others* is and always has been central to philosophical concepts of virtue. "Act only according to that maxim whereby you can at the same time will that it should become a universal law without contradiction", the first formulation of Kant's categorical imperative famously states. In other words: don't do unto others except as you would have them do unto you. And while Kant was deeply influenced by Christianity, the same ethic becomes central to secular moral philosophy, such as when in the twentieth century John Rawls (re)introduced into philosophy the concept of *behind-the-veil.*

Under Rawls's analysis a system could be fair if all players were forced to wager from behind the veil of ignorance, not knowing where they would start from. It is a lot easier to argue, as does semi-compatibilism, that there is no duty to be fair to the less fortunate when one is guaranteed of not being among their number. Human nature will push most to urge consideration of the less fortunate if there is a chance they may end up as part of the less fortunate. Hence the purpose of behind-the-veil thinking is to promote real consideration of all positions and points of view, given a lack of knowledge of where one will start. The practical problem, of course, is that we can rarely have such a system, and never in the free will debates. In the free will debates we never start from behind the veil: we always start from different positions of knowledge and power, and therefore many are unlikely to consider fairness from all points of view, specifically when considering fairness from the point of view of the less fortunate. Life's winners, including most senior philosophers, have little incentive to buy into the fairness of behind-the-veil consideration, or even an ethic like *Do unto others*, as they already know they start ahead. They already know whether, to quote Dennett, they were "given a head start or held back at the starting line". They already know that no one can do unto them as they would do unto others.

Within cognitive theory and social psychology there is at present much research into empathy, and our empathic responses to one another. While a very tiny group of humans seem to lack empathic responses entirely – we will later be mentioning research into psychopathy by investigators such as Paul Babiak and Jim Fallon – and a larger group have diminished empathic responses often linked to abusive upbringings, a very common problem found in human groups is where the empathy "gap" is partial and situational. Religions and political ideologies are particularly good at switching off normal empathic responses in specific circumstances (promoting feelings of contempt towards a particular targeted out-group, which drowns out the possibility of empathy). A situational lack of empathy is arguably one of the problems besetting the free will debates and can be seen to exist across a number of the traditions – particularly, perhaps, compatibilism and semi-compatibilism. Hence Gary Watson tells us that the suffering very often endured in childhood by those who go on to lead lives of violence "gives a foothold not only for sympathy, but for the thought that if I had been subjected to such circumstances, I might well have become as vile... This thought induces not only an ontological shudder, but a sense of equality with the other" (2004, p.245). Watson tells us that sympathy, along with outrage, is the appropriate emotional and moral response, and that justice demands that we simultaneously view with sympathy and outrage – "the sympathy toward the boy he was is at odds with outrage toward the man he is... each of these responses is appropriate... Harris both satisfies and violates the criteria of victimhood" (p.244). Yet despite informing us of our binary emotional and moral duty Watson then completely discounts the empathic duty. He tells us that "unless one knew Harris as a child or keeps his earlier self vividly in mind, sympathy can scarcely find a purchase" (p.245). But this does not abrogate the moral duty to feel sympathy, any more than it abrogates the Western law's duty to recognise the offender's status as victim when passing sentence (something it manifestly refuses to do). Watson admits that he has the moral duty to temper outrage with sympathy, but he makes a conscious decision to abandon sympathy (empathy) for pure outrage. Watson is behaving partially, even under his own analysis.

We have seen that essentialists like Gary Watson refuse to treat the offender with the consideration – the ideals of fair play – that they claim for themselves. We have also seen that essentialism is almost certainly not right where it describes the offender as a different form of human. It shouldn't take much to convince us that essentialists, often descended from those settlers that the Harvard historian Bernard Bailyn termed America's barbarous white savages, could once have been induced to commit every atrocity – torture, mutilation, rape, murder – committed by the most shocking serial killer or putative example of that not-so-perfect form of human. It is also not true that it is the offender who "managed to turn himself into a monster" (Dennett), or that the offender "could have acted differently" (Jonathan Jacobs). We need have no particular compassion for the offender to be able to accept that he must still receive the same basic levels of fair play and consideration that we claim for ourselves, and that he has the right not to have people tell untruths about him, just as we demand that people not tell untruths about us. If nothing else, when we refuse him fair treatment – when we refuse to tell the truth about him – it says something deeply worrying and morally unattractive about the rest of us: we, the supposedly perfect form of human. The absence of empathy for others' misfortunes – biological and environmental – is overwhelming within the free will debates. We have already cited the work of the philosopher Richard Double, who has identified what he calls the moral hardness of free will libertarians: their unwavering faith in the righteousness of their worldview no matter the lack of any objective evidence and the pain caused to others. Surely, though, such a judgement of moral hardness – including an absence of empathy or even basic respect for truth, equality of opportunity or fair play – must apply equally to compatibilism, semi-compatibilism, attitudinism, and even free will illusionism? I have already mentioned that I find Dennett's "tough love" excuse for his not-fair-but-fair-enough stance both unconvincing and insincere, with little evidence of even the most basic consideration of others, and an outright refusal to acknowledge his own great good fortune and privileged background or the far greater misfortune of others.

A diminution of empathy and an indifference to cruelty are not the same thing – but they can be linked, perhaps particularly when such diminution of empathy appears ideological in origin. It is important to acknowledge here that even those with a profound biological deficiency in empathy are often still capable of being both kind and highly moral. Cambridge University's Simon Baron-Cohen, one of the world authorities on autism, notes that this is the case for some people with autism and Asperger's, which generally involves diminished empathy. Ritual, rule following, and concepts of fairness are often deeply important in the confusing world that presents itself to those who suffer from these tragic disorders. Returning, though, to our main subject, it has long been recognised within Christian doctrine that the just infliction of suffering becomes very problematic with the absence of freedom of choice. As the great sixteenth-century theologian Erasmus put it, "Why, you ask, is anything attributed to the freedom of the will, then? It is… to prevent calumnies attributing cruelty and injustice to God" (1524, p.93). In other words God could inflict suffering given the existence of free will, but God would appear barbaric (cruel and unjust) if He maintained the torments of Hell in the absence of free will. Just suffering presupposes freedom of choice. Yet the problem remains that Western social and judicial systems often seem to glory in the infliction of degradation, humiliation, and suffering, and in the palpable absence of freedom of choice. Poverty relief is still regularly tied to the denigration and the humiliation of the poor, almost as it was a few hundred years ago, when those receiving poor relief were first badged to mark them off from normal society, and suffering plays a primary role in the Anglo-American penal systems. Yale's Dan Kahan states clearly that the infliction of degradation and suffering on offenders is a major goal of the US penal system, but Kahan is not decrying such a state of affairs: he is a utilitarian who openly celebrates the contempt and violence of the US prison experience. As Kahan writes, "by inflicting countless other indignities – from exposure to the view of others when urinating and defecating to rape at the hand of other inmates – prison unambiguously marks the lowness of those we consign to it" (Kahan, 1998, p.1642). Mark Kappelhoff of the American Civil Liberties Union has referred to the current enthusiasm for shaming punishments as "gratuitous humiliation of the individual" (see Book, 1999, p.655), while the criminologist Dan Markel has noted that public shaming is designed to humiliate and degrade an offender in public (2007).

Due to decades of indifference (and even quiet encouragement by the authorities) rape is now an epidemic within the US prison system. The legal theorist Anders Kaye at the Thomas Jefferson School of Law – and who has himself tied belief in free choice to both anti-egalitarianism and enhanced suffering – quotes David Siegal's *Stanford Law Review* paper on rape in prison and AIDS. "In 1974 it was estimated that of the forty-six million Americans who will be arrested at some time in their lives, ten million will be raped while in prison" (2007, p.416), which would mean that you are many hundreds of times more likely to be raped when incarcerated within the American prison system than you would be outside its walls. Prison rape is such an epidemic that President G.W. Bush was forced to convene a commission to try to stamp it out. According to surveys from both the federally-convened National Prison Rape Elimination Commission and the Bureau of Justice Statistics (BJS, an agency within the Justice Department) a large proportion of the rapes are perpetrated by corrections staff, particularly against women, gay men, juvenile offenders, the mentally ill, the physically small, and those new to life behind bars. In fact some of the most recent BJS reports covering both adults and juveniles (3rd edition NIS, 2nd edition NYSC) conclude that the majority of sexual abuse is committed by corrections staff, and that this is particularly the case within juvenile facilities. Challenging another stereotype, boys are also more likely to be raped by female staff than they are by male staff. All those jokes about dropping the soap in the showers should really become jokes about American taxpayers eager to fund paedophilia and the rape of children. "Americans now recognize sexual abuse as a violent crime with life-changing consequences. Yet the public has been slow to incorporate that perspective into its understanding of sexual violence in correctional environments. Many still consider sexual abuse an expected consequence of incarceration, part of the penalty" (NPREC, 2009, p.25).

The above does not prove that belief in free choice drives these human behaviours of torture, rape, and cruelty but Jasmine Carey has, as noted, provided empirical evidence that belief in free will leads to harsher and more brutal punishment (Carey, 2009). Free will libertarian social psychologists openly admit that reductions in the capacity for free choice, including whether the rule-breaker could have acted differently, "constitute valid reasons for reduced punishment" (Baumeister et al., 2009, p.260). There is an entire philosophical tradition, the reactive-attitudinism of P.F. Strawson, which takes it as read that we need to maintain belief in free choice in order to maintain blame and justifications for suffering. The fear of the reactive-attitudinists that loss of belief in free will means a loss of justified suffering seems supported when Shariff, Baumeister, and Clark claim to have demonstrated that countries with higher beliefs in free will have both higher rates of incarceration and a greater appetite for violent retributive punishment (Shariff et al., in press).

Contemporary Ethics Says That Only Some People Matter

"Consider the biography of any 'self-made' man, and you will find that his success was entirely dependent on background conditions that he did not make and of which he was merely the beneficiary... And yet, living in America, one gets the distinct sense that if certain conservatives were asked why they weren't born with club feet or orphaned before the age of five, they would not hesitate to take credit for these accomplishments." (Harris, 2012, pp.61-2).

Belief in free will means never having to say "Thank you"; means never having to acknowledge your own great good fortune, or the far greater misfortune of others. In a world that reduces to nothing more than biology and environment you can axiomatically have no "self-made" men: all successful men and women are the product of the biological gifts they inherited and the privileged environments they were born into and raised within. Even if you have struggled to make the most of what nature has given you, says the neuroscientist and anti-free will campaigner Sam Harris, you must still admit that your ability and inclination to struggle is part of your inheritance. How much credit does a person deserve for not being lazy? None at all, Harris notes. While it is right to encourage people to not be lazy, and right to discourage laziness, it is morally wrong to blame a person for their laziness when the blind lottery of biology and environment is all that separates the diligent from the indolent. The philosopher Bruce Waller makes similar observations, including how philosophers often overlook this and overwhelmingly fail to point it out. "Typically, we started with advantages – very early childhood education, strong family support – that resulted in more early rewards, and that pattern of reinforcement shaped strong work habits" (2011, p.139). And it is not surprising, says Waller, that those who were nurtured by the moral responsibility system, and who have been very well rewarded by that system, would be outraged by those who wish to look a little more closely at the system and explain that philosophers can actually claim no credit for their strong work ethic.

As the free will illusionist Saul Smilansky has recognised, the hard determinist understanding promotes a sense of equality, a sense of empathy with the less fortunate, and a sense of gratitude for one's privileged position in life: "Realization of the lack of libertarian free will can check harmful forms of feelings of superiority, for this realization presents the anti-luck 'here but for the grace of God' thought overwhelmingly" (1997, p.95). Yet this unwillingness to acknowledge the role that luck plays in life is a siren call to almost all, perhaps for very defensive reasons and no matter the harm it does to the less fortunate. When one fully internalises the understanding that everything in life comes down to biology and environment, and that we can probably expect little help from biology, one faces some disturbing home truths. Abraham Lincoln, that great determinist and critic of the doctrine of free will, once said that Northerners couldn't feel too morally superior to Southern slaveholders because "if we were situated as they are, we should act and feel as they do; and if they were situated as we are, they should act and feel as we do; and we never ought to lose sight of this fact in discussing the subject" (Guelzo 2009, p.39). Similarly, Bruce Waller has noted that given his Southern Baptist upbringing and deep respect for figures of authority he could easily see a younger version of himself as an obedient tormentor in Stanley Milgram's famous psychological experiment, or even as a Nazi prison guard or Abu Ghraib torturer (2011, p.161). Yet such honest self-appraisal is rare among both lay people and philosophers, with the latter (especially) having a tendency to conceit and a feeling that they can do – and always could have done – everything better than everybody else. Philosophers hold privileged and very comfortable positions in society: "we like to think we justly deserve those special benefits; we've accomplished much, and we are delighted to claim credit for it" (Waller 2011, p.307).

In Neil Levy's phrase (2001), advocates of free will and moral responsibility inflict a "double dose of unfairness" on the less fortunate, while simultaneously "double dipping" on reward when we are not only lucky enough to benefit from great good fortune but we seek to claim that such good fortune was somehow always due us. For reasons we have examined we can exempt hard compatibilism from second stage opprobrium, yet the other five free will apologist traditions – libertarianism, compatibilism, illusionism, reactive-attitudinism, and semi-compatibilism – either unconsciously or consciously act to bring about both the first and second doses of unfairness. It is one thing to be indifferent to the problems of the less fortunate, as each of hard compatibilism and the five other traditions mentioned tend to be. But morally it is quite another thing to then seek to blame the problems of the less fortunate on the less fortunate – the second dose of unfairness that Levy refers to. In ethical language it somewhat parallels the distinction between what is called the sin of omission and the sin of commission: the distinction between those whose only sin is failure to stop an act and those whose deeper sin is the commissioning of the act. In another sense it is perhaps the difference between refusing to work in a soup kitchen and standing outside the soup kitchen jeering at and ridiculing the unfortunates who need to use the kitchen to survive.

There is something deeply nasty in that second dose of unfairness, which may at least be avoided in the first dose of unfairness. While belief in free will means never having to acknowledge your own great good fortune or the greater misfortune of others, belief in free will also means ingratitude in a further, even nastier sense, when it encompasses acting to enhance and extend that very misfortune to others. Indeed, Levy may be underselling his case. Both Bruce Waller and the author have shown that the conceit of free will and moral responsibility in a universe without freedom of choice has had a multitude of negative effects, including the lack of genuine opportunity for large segments of society and a meaner support system for the least fortunate. As Bruce Waller argues, it is in large part thanks to the myth of free choice and moral responsibility that most children born into poverty in the United States will die in poverty, with few real opportunities for social or economic advancement. The first dose of unfairness is therefore the unfairness of poor initial developmental luck. The second dose of unfairness is the unfairness of claiming that the person was somehow responsible for their first dose of unfairness, or at the very least that blame and suffering are their just deserts. But a third dose of unfairness is that this same conceit is then invoked so as to widen social inequalities: to deny opportunity to the next generation, to make developmental conditions still worse for the rest in poverty or want, and to actually drive many others into poverty and want. The third dose of unfairness is where the logical outcome is that the net worth of the top 1% of households ends up accounting for more than the net worth of the bottom 95% of households put together. This is not just refusing to work in the soup kitchen; this is not even jeering at those using the soup kitchen; this is deliberately acting to expand the very need for soup kitchens in the first place.

There is something deeply hypocritical about our attitude to misfortune and, in particular, victimhood. Where there is no free will, human behaviour is the product of the interaction of biology and environment. Let us assume, to simplify the lesson, that most antisocial behaviour is the product of poor environment. We shall later be considering rare traits, such as psychopathy, that may have a significant biological component, but even with psychopathy the evidence seems to be that poor upbringing is key to triggering extreme violence and self-destruction. For the moment, though, and for convenience, let us assume a model where antisocial behaviour is the result purely of toxic environment (which will allow us to ignore the extra complication of biology). This assumed, we start to see something very strange when it comes to our understanding of victimhood in a world without free will. As a population we in the West seem to have considerable sympathy for victims, with powerful victims' rights groups, political and tabloid press lobbying, and so on. However, this sympathy seems to disappear the more they become victims. In other words, we have great sympathy for people who are often moderately victimised, but very little sympathy for many (although not all) people who are completely victimised.

In our world without free will, and where antisocial behaviour is hypothesised as largely the product of environment, let us take a character who has been 40% abused, recognising that such percentages are wholly artificial but are being invoked purely to make a point about how we feel empathy with some victims but not others. This is the traditional surviving or escaped victim, whom we tend to feel huge sympathy for. But as 40% of the environment is abusive, this person still lives in a world that is 60% non-abusive. As the psychological profiler Paul Britton told us earlier, this person comes from a pretty bad start – say very poor parents – but still has grandparents to turn to, teachers who help him/her escape, and so on. We consider these people victims when they receive a lesser amount of abuse. (Asserting lesser is meant in no way to downplay their suffering, but is only contrasted to highlight our blindness to even greater suffering.) So what happens when these people, and particularly children, receive far more abuse? We know they receive more abuse because in a world without free will – where behaviour comes down solely (for this hypothesis) to environment – they are the ones who weren't brought back into the fold; weren't lucky enough to get those other options of fine grandparents and excellent teachers. They are, self-evidently, the ones in the 100% abusive environments (bad parents, bad grandparents, bad teachers, useless priests), not the 40% abusive environment (bad parents, good grandparents, good teachers, good priest or social worker). They axiomatically had to be 100% abused because they didn't get any of the ameliorating factors that would have turned their lives around, would have set them on a better path – and we know this because their lives didn't turn around. The others at least benefited from some crucial ameliorating factors and so cannot be said to have been raised in as abusive – as toxic – environments, at least in our hypothetical situation which ignores biology for the moment. Recall the serial killer Robert Harris, who as a child was tortured by his sadistic father, hated by his mother, bullied by merciless classmates, then repeatedly raped from the age of fourteen in an American prison for children. By anyone's reckoning this is as close to a 100% abusive upbringing as you are likely to read about, yet the philosopher Gary Watson feels troubled at his (brief) sense of equality with Harris, his "ontological shudder" and brief feeling that he might have turned out like this had his life been a lot less privileged than it was. Michael McKenna, in contrast, refuses to dwell on the thought that he might have turned out differently, refuses to dwell on the pure luck of biology and upbringing ("the ontological shudder which Watson alludes to has little force"; 2008, p.216). For Harris there were no good grandparents to offset the despicable parents, and although his siblings did feel for their brother they were too terrified of their monster of a father to intervene. For Harris there were nothing but worthless teachers who did not bring the bullying to an end. This was no movie of the week where the priest and the social worker stop the rape and get the warden fired, yet now our sympathy has fallen to zero. We feel sympathy for the 40% abused child, but not the 100% abused child who has already turned, to use Watson's term, "vile". So let us not pretend that we support victims *per se*. We generally only support victims who were lucky enough to be only partly victimised.

It is emphatically not that we recognise they are victims who have been so *extremely and relentlessly* victimised they have been turned into dangerous beings: instead we tend to refuse to accept they are victims in any way, shape, or form. They are instead, according to essentialism, now another form of human. As Gary Watson writes, when mentioning the early life story of Robert Harris, "the sympathy toward the boy he was is at odds with outrage toward the man he is... each of these responses is appropriate... Harris both satisfies and violates the criteria of victimhood", and "an overall view simultaneously demands and precludes regarding him as a victim" (2004, p.244). The morally key words here are "violates" and "precludes". We view victimhood, according to Watson, as digital, not analogue. Violates does not mean that we reduce, water down: that we balance out our sympathy. Precludes means that he has now lost any right to our sympathy or the considerations we still expect, including for people to tell the truth about us. Sympathy, for Watson, is either on or off: digital, not analogue. There is a clear admission from Watson that at some level justice demands that we recognise the victimhood of the offender, because such offenders meet the criteria necessary to be regarded as victims, but at the same time there is the admission that Watson, and most of the public, refuse to view the serious offender as a victim. When offenders (or the poor) are seen as not like us, it doesn't matter how much they have been victimised (beaten, hated, bullied, and raped): we completely and deliberately close our eyes to the fact that they too are victims. Indeed, close our eyes to the fact that it was such victimisation that *wholly* turned them into what we despise – because we shall see later the evidence that even with the most biologically atypical, destructive behaviour almost always requires an environmental trigger. In order to convince ourselves that they are not like us, or that our children could never have been raised to be like that, we tell ourselves stories that are almost certainly completely false. We indulge in the essentialist myths: myths that try to convince us that we never could have been like them, and even that they could never have been like us.

We have already seen Jasmine Carey's study linking belief in unrestrained free will to strong belief in a just world. Just–world beliefs have been extensively studied by psychologists and are sometimes known under the abbreviation BJW – belief in a just world – which means that adherents don't believe the world *should be* just but instead that the world around them – and contrary to much of the available evidence – already *is* just. BJW may seem a very strange mindset to many readers but there are well-known psychological triggers to this quite widespread belief, only some of which revolve around religion and the need to believe in a just

God having designed a just world. But Bruce Waller (2015) goes further when he discusses five of the many academic studies which have demonstrated that the more people subscribe to BJW – the more they believe the world is just – then the more they tend to blame victims. The logic is quite unsurprising, and quite vile. When you believe the world is just because, for example, your religion relentlessly tells you it is so, then you will bend over backwards to try to "prove" the world is just by airbrushing victims out of the picture. Hence people begin to believe that the poor deserve their fate, because God's world wouldn't be just if they didn't deserve to be in such awful poverty – and so, as Carey and Baumeister both found – they must largely have chosen to be poor of their own free will. Non-religious BJW includes what psychologists term biological essentialism, which incorporates the finding that economically and socially successful individuals are often motivated to seek genetic justifications for their elevated social positions in order to avoid feeling sympathy for the less fortunate, and to excuse their society as just and fair. Biological essentialism has been well studied, particularly in America, though also within the Indian caste system, with one finding being that such essentialists were more likely to display prejudice against out-groups and low-status minority groups (research summarised and extended in Kraus & Keltner, 2013). Integrity really does demand that we stop this quite hypocritical talk about victims' rights and recognise that we are interested only in the rights of certain victims: victims who are like us, or those whom we allow ourselves to consider that we might have been like. We touched on an associated hypocrisy earlier when we considered P.F. Strawson's "offended parties" (2008, p.21/62): we argued that in a world without origination and choice there is a deep ontological problem with simplistically and capriciously dividing the world into the offenders and the offended-against. The author also made the further observation that if violent retribution and delight in the suffering of others is both moral and a reassuring virtue it is not immediately obvious why P.F. Strawson, Dan Dennett, and Saul Smilansky couldn't legitimately be turned into hamburger by those degraded and unjustly treated under their professional prescriptions.

A story comes to us through Aristotle that Thales of Miletus, the first recognised philosopher and one of the Seven Sages, got so fed up with his compatriots asking what was the point of brilliance if you don't have two towels to rub together that he decided to shut them up once and for all. Hence he turned to forecasting the long-term weather, bought up all the olive presses he could find, and made a killing on an otherwise-unexpected bumper olive harvest. The point was, according to Aristotle, that Thales was proving that philosophers could be rich, influential, and powerful if they but wanted to be. It is just they can't be bothered, as theirs is a higher and more noble calling. But the sentiment behind this story is complete rubbish. It takes a very different set of skills to be exceptional in business or good on the financial and commodity markets, skills which the vast majority of philosophers do not possess. It takes, for example, interpersonal skills, the ability to sell yourself and a product, the willingness to take risks, a memory for people and minutiae, and (perhaps above all) a certain hunger for economic success. Philosophers become philosophers at least in part because they don't possess these characteristics, but they do possess intellect and an aversion to heavy lifting, and were beneficiaries of stability, relative wealth, and expensive educations. And yet to this day most philosophers would believe Aristotle's story of Thales, and feel that they could be millionaires or top politicians if they but bothered and that – similarly, and again largely incorrectly – their native intellect alone would have saved them from ever having been one of Milgram's unquestioning tormentors, or a Southern slaveholder, or one of Zimbardo's swaggering teenage brutalisers or cowering victims. Philosophers, these keepers of the ethical keys, all too often lack self-awareness while nonetheless possessing a surfeit of conceit – even up to the belief that they were, in Gary Watson's argument, "fated" to succeed in life. They regularly evince little gratitude for their comfortable backgrounds, their involved parents, and their good educations. Philosophers show little willingness to display human fellow-feeling, or "a sense of equality with the other", nor to recognise that others very often are not as blessed as them, nor the vast role that luck, contingency, chance, and privilege play in human life.

6

THE POLITICS – AND ECONOMICS – OF FREE WILL

> You can do what you will, but at any given moment of your life
> you can will only one definite thing and absolutely nothing else
> but this one thing.
> Schopenhauer, *On the Freedom of the Will* (1839, p.21).

Contemporary America, and to a slightly lesser extent Britain, appears to be built upon a belief in free will: built upon a belief in self-reliance in every sense of the term. In the early nineteenth century the English politician Edward Bulwer-Lytton wrote that in other countries poverty was seen as a misfortune but that for Englishmen it was viewed as a crime, while Henry Ward Beecher, the American nineteenth-century minister, echoed this sentiment when he wrote that no man in the United States suffers from poverty unless it is more than his fault: unless it is his sin. The influential nineteenth-century didactic rags to riches novels of Horatio Alger celebrated the free will of the young American male. As Alger put it in *Ragged Dick*, the most famous of his 100 books: "remember that your future position depends mainly upon yourself, and that it will be high or low as you choose to make it". Jodie Allen and Michael Dimock at the Pew Research Center for the People and the Press have reported that successive Pew Global Attitudes polls "find that at every income level, Americans are far more likely than Europeans to believe that individuals, not society,

are responsible for their own failures, economic and otherwise"
(2007). So what exactly is the social and cultural component to
belief in free will?

Free Will and the Politics of the Right

Conservatives, writes the neuroscientist and anti-free will
polemicist Sam Harris, have made a "religious fetish" (2011, p.47)
of self-creation and rugged individualism. Many seem to have
absolutely no awareness of how lucky one must be to succeed at
anything in life, he comments, whereas the disparities in human
luck are both morally relevant and harrowing to contemplate.

> "There is not a person on earth who chose his genome, or the
> country of his birth, or the political and economic conditions
> that prevailed at moments crucial to his progress. And yet,
> living in America, one gets the distinct sense that if certain
> conservatives were asked why they weren't born with club feet
> or orphaned before the age of five, they would not hesitate to
> take credit for these accomplishments" (Harris, 2012, pp.61-2).

It may be true that a belief in self-creation sits deep within certain
traditions of conservatism, and particularly the more economically
libertarian traditions. The arch conservative Charles Murray, with
his stated belief that people may be unequally responsible for what
has happened to them in the past but that all are equally responsible
for what they do next, was a significant influence on Ronald
Reagan. There was a punitive view of the poor from American
conservative figures like Ronald Reagan, and social theorist Robert
Goodin is clear in his belief that the New Right criticism of
welfare provision drew almost exclusively on ethical notions of
moral desert and on personal choice (1988, p.279). Similarly, it is

the American neocon Gertrude Himmelfarb (e.g. 1984) who is most often credited with reintroducing into Western political discourse the earlier division of the deserving poor from the undeserving. "Deserving and undeserving – these terms epitomise the difference between the Victorians and ourselves. The Victorians [weren't afraid to speak] the language of morality" (Himmelfarb, 1995). Margaret Thatcher was a great influence on Himmelfarb, and Baroness Thatcher herself saw morality towards the poor in terms of choice, as was attested to by the veteran BBC political interviewer John Humphrys (2006). When Humphrys interviewed the then Mrs Thatcher early in her career she informed him that freedom of choice, and not love or compassion, was the fundamental message of Christianity. Within Britain numerous commentators on the right have been encouraging the government to take a more moral tone on poverty and unemployment. "The undeserving poor exist," writes Matthew Parris, former Conservative MP and award-winning *The Times* journalist, and we should "trust the unspoken moral instincts of the people, which remain strong and fairly merciless about the undeserving" (2008, p.22). Meanwhile, in a well-covered remark, Herman Cain – one-time front-runner for the Republican presidential nomination in 2012, and the candidate of choice for the hard right Tea Party – said that "if you don't have a job and you're not rich, blame yourself!". Steven Pearlstein of the *Washington Post* suggested that while most Republicans were politic enough to dance around questions of poverty and inequality, Cain was beloved of the hard right because he had no "filter" between brain and mouth, and that this statement was therefore simply the "purest distillation of the attitude of the New Republican Party towards rising poverty and inequality in the United States" (Pearlstein, 2011).

To any assessment of the linkage with political conservatism must be added religious conservatism, some of which is actually paying to promote the free will myth. Many years before Lloyd Blankfein notoriously claimed that he and other Goldman Sachs employees were "doing God's work", the late billionaire financier and conservative John Templeton believed that he was doing God's work on the international money markets. The John Templeton Foundation funds the advancement of the spiritual, including an attempt to forge an "accommodation" between religion, philosophy and science. Views on the Foundation – and in particular its impact on scholarship – are mixed, but some scientists refuse to have anything to do with it, cautious of its motives. As *The Nation* put it in June 2010: "It doesn't help that the foundation is a longstanding donor to conservative think tanks like the Heritage Foundation and the Cato Institute. And while its founder preferred eternal questions to worldly politics, the son who has succeeded him, John Templeton Jr. – Jack – is a conservative Evangelical who spends his personal time and money opposing gay marriage and defending the Iraq War. Since his father's death, concerns have swirled among the foundation's grantees and critics alike that Jack Templeton will steer the foundation even further rightward and, perhaps, even further from respectable science" (Schneider, 2010). In early 2010 the Templeton Foundation gave Florida State University $4.4 million to "investigate" free will, but the Foundation's interest in free will and the effect of the myth on the social order goes back further than this. For instance, the Templeton Foundation had previously funded pro-free will research by implacably libertarian social psychologists, including Roy Baumeister at Florida State – see the funding statements attached to Baumeister et al. (2009) and Stillman et al. (2010) – while the world-renowned physicist Paul Davies, who has called knowledge of the non-existence of free will "one of the world's most dangerous ideas" (2004), was for over a decade on the Foundation's board of trustees. While distribution of Templeton largesse is actually in the hands of the libertarian philosopher Alfred Mele at FSU (and not in the hands of the Foundation) grants have overwhelmingly been directed towards those who either believe in free choice or have argued that it is dangerous to disabuse the public of the idea of free choice. The author is not aware of any grants having been made available to those raising concerns about the damage the myth may be doing to concepts of fair play and social justice. The goal of the Foundation appears to be to advance an accommodation of the conservative-with-a-small-c spiritual and the conservative-with-a-small-and-large-c secular. What is certain is that the goal is not to permit the progressive secular to embarrass or redefine the spiritual.

For one reason above all others it may be true that certain traditions within conservatism are particularly prone to find a need to posit belief in free will. While it is fairly common across all traditions on the right to call for equality of opportunity, this may be especially focused within the economically libertarian right. The right's call for equality of opportunity is regularly contrasted with the left's call for equality of outcome (either wealth and income, or even perhaps just access to healthcare). The focus of the libertarian right, in contrast to (for example) British paternalistic conservatism or Rockefeller Republicanism, is to decry all state intervention, particularly beyond the minimum level required for a putative equality of opportunity. It is of course true that some leftist parties, such as Tony Blair's New Labour, have also championed a quasi-libertarian call for equality of opportunity at the expense of the left's more traditional call for equality of outcome. We should recall, too, the up to 83% of Joseph Rowntree Foundation respondents – across left, right and centre – who actually believe that there is equality of opportunity in Britain today. Nevertheless, the cry that equality of opportunity is all we need probably still finds its most extreme formulation on the libertarian right. There may even be a logical justification for this, if one assumes that the actual intention is to minimise costly social intervention.

(i) Behaviour = B + E

or (ii) Behaviour = b + e + F

If behaviour is as (i), and acknowledged as purely the product of biology and environment, then even the strongest advocate of genetic determinism will automatically tend to permit a greater role for environment than under (ii), where free will is seen to be in play. Even a genetic fundamentalist will tend automatically to ascribe more influence to environment when it is one of only two factors relative to the situation than when it is one of three factors, especially when the third factor can be (and usually has to be) argued to be more determining of behaviour than the first two factors. Where one knows nothing about academic consensus on the relative contributions, a perfunctory examination of the above equations may immediately suggest at least a 50% contribution by E (environment) with another 50% from B (biology) in case (i). In contrast, case (ii) is more likely to suggest that the second factor – now little e to contrast with the supposedly determining factor of F (free will) – merits at most a 33% contribution. Political platforms that are generally associated with minimising state intervention will have an automatic ideological tendency to try to keep e small by championing not just the power and inevitability of biology (b or B) but also belief in free will (F).

The call for equality of opportunity, while on the face of it appearing to be fair and progressive (after all, what could be fairer than a seeming platform of equal opportunity?), may thus be little more than a justification for the *status quo* in a universe without free will. If one already believes that in America "anyone can be president", or buys into the early twentieth-century novelist Thomas Wolfe's famous line that the promise of America gives to every man his chance regardless of his birth, then one will tend to believe that there are not insurmountable inequalities within the existing system, as anyone still has the chance to make it big.

Recall the arch conservative Charles Murray telling us earlier that there is a level playing field in America and that all in America, "black or white, rich or poor" effectively have the same opportunities. "There is in this stance no lack of compassion", he tells us, because "the options are always open. Opportunity is endless" (1984, p.234). The work from which these quotes are taken, *Losing Ground: American Social Policy, 1950-1980*, is credited by the right-wing American Enterprise Institute as being the intellectual foundation for the 1996 PRWORA welfare reform and Work Opportunity Act, a cornerstone of the Republican Party's Contract with America. But for so many in America (or Britain) the truth is that options are not always, *or even ever*, "open". For so many opportunity is not "endless", but completely non-existent. You can make statements such as *Options are always open* and *Opportunity is endless* if and only if you give credence to the myth of the disembodied individual who exists free from the dragging and wholly limiting effects of biology and environment. And because of the actual non-existence of free will, this cry of equality of opportunity becomes an intellectually suspicious banner to rally under in the first place. Suspicious not in the sense that equality of opportunity may not be a very worthy goal as mentioned above. Suspicious in the sense that those who tend to proclaim interest in equality of opportunity (and perhaps in part to decry equality of outcomes) can simultaneously be shown to have little interest in the significant intervention it would take to even begin to bring about such equality of opportunity in a world without free will.

Such equality of opportunity would necessarily require, in a universe without free will, full recognition of the deep importance of environmental intervention, and for two main reasons. The first reason is that once factor F is stripped away it self-evidently turns small e into capital E. While there are a number on the right (and a handful on the left) who have always tried to push B almost to the complete exclusion of E, such a stance has rarely been seen as intellectually persuasive or as anything other than strongly self-interested. The second reason is that when everything comes down to E and B there is the recognition that it is very difficult to do anything about biology directly. Hence, whether one would tend to favour E or B more strongly one is nevertheless largely driven to work through E in order to even attempt to provide a levelling of the playing field and a rudimentary equality of opportunity. The second President Bush may have suffered from both intellectual weaknesses and a train wreck of an addictive personality, but fabulous environmental advantages more than offset any and all of the biological disadvantages that he possessed. In a world without free will equality of opportunity would first require an open acknowledgement that current inequalities are the result of nothing other than unequal biological and environmental inheritances. Equality of opportunity would therefore require large-scale intervention to make up for the different and unequal inheritances. Those with poor biological inheritances would require intervention to get them to a position of equality of opportunity with those who start with better biological inheritances. But those who start with poor environmental inheritances – almost certainly a far more common problem than significant biological handicaps – may require massive intervention to get them to a position of equality of opportunity with those who have better environmental inheritances. Equality of opportunity in a universe without free will would require central and local intervention (and checks and balances) far more profound than the minimal intervention of the Head Start Programs already strongly resisted by the libertarian right. It is not possible to overstate how unjust, regressive, and even ignorant is this belief that for all of us "the options are always open" and that "opportunity is endless", be that when voiced by the American hard right or even by the up to 83% of Britons across left, right and centre canvassed by the JRF in 2010.

Before we examine the corresponding ideological contribution to free will justification from the liberal left it is worth stressing again that belief in free will need not be fundamental to all or even most traditions of conservatism, and certainly not to the more consensus forms of conservatism. No American politician more decisively rejected the conceit of free will than the Republican Abraham Lincoln, and it has been suggested that it was Lincoln's rejection of the myth of free will which partly informed his virtues and his love of freedom: virtues of tolerance, forgiveness, and justice. "Judge not that we be not judged", Lincoln wrote, "with malice toward none; with charity for all" (Guelzo, 1997, pp.78-9). Although fundamentally opposed to the institution of slavery Lincoln accepted that it is a man's upbringing which makes him what he is, even remarking of Southern slave owners that Northerners shouldn't feel too morally superior because "if we were situated as they are, we should act and feel as they do; and if they were situated as we are, they should act and feel as we do" (p.78). Lincoln is thus representative of the more moderate and traditional right-wing attitudes which should be fully capable of accepting that equality of opportunity firstly requires a rejection of the myth of freedom of choice.

Free Will and the Politics of the Liberal Left

While certain traditions within conservatism may have a deep-seated ideological need to champion belief in free will, the left and centre have often behaved just as partially over the issue. Both Gordon Brown and Tony Blair saw the poor in terms of deserving versus undeserving, and commentators have noted that Gordon Brown was significantly influenced by Gertrude Himmelfarb, whose writings he kept to hand and admired greatly (Vallely, 2007; Wilby, 2008). Blair and Brown took the British left with them, with opinion polls suggesting that Labour voters began to make a sharper distinction between the deserving and undeserving poor from the late 1990s. Yet in doing so Blair and Brown were arguably only taking Labour back to its roots, as from the late nineteenth century the working class has had an automatic tendency to make a distinction between those it saw as deserving and those it saw as undeserving.

Will Hutton, the *Observer* opinion writer and key figure (given his early cataloguing of our growing social divide) within the British intellectual left, has encouraged the left to "re-moralise" on the issue of poverty. Hutton, author of a book on the underclass entitled *Them and Us: Changing Britain – Why We Need a Fair Society*, has stated that the left needs to learn to say to some people: "you're in the situation you're in because of personal choices, yes we disapprove and we don't like it" (interviewed in Bowlby, 2010). In *Them and Us* Hutton has written of his desire to drag the left much further into debates about the division of society and about the limiting of opportunity for some, particularly along the lines of desert, or what he likes to call "deservingness" (2010). Choice – this myth of freedom of choice which has always been central to notions of desert and deservingness – is thus the foundation stone of Hutton's recent work. But many parts of the political left have always seen free will as central to their definition of mankind. Existentialism under the leftist Jean-Paul Sartre famously proclaimed that "man is freedom", and that we have the ability to create ourselves from scratch: self-creation; self-origination, in the strongest sense. Left-wing mysticism also seems especially attracted to the conceit of free will, for example the social reformist ideology of Rudolf Steiner (1861-1925), notable for developing something that styles itself as "anthroposophy". Anthroposophy apparently means a creative system which uses natural means to optimise well-being, and Steiner's anthroposophy still finds adherents today. The ethical funder Triodos Bank was reportedly founded as an anthroposophic institution.

We singled out certain of the more market fundamentalist forms of conservatism as particularly attracted to the myth of free will, partly perhaps as an unconscious tool of social control. But elements of the liberal left also seem to be especially vulnerable. Steiner himself was an idealist, in the continental philosophical sense of the word that contrasts with the Anglo-American empiricist tradition. Philosophical idealism, which has a strong tendency to be played out through the political left, may be particularly prone to both flights of metaphysical fancy and grand narratives. Idealism itself harks back to Plato's doctrine of ideas and the concept of ideal forms being seemingly independent of reality. However, there is another intellectual weakness that is found more on the liberal left than the right which may help to explain the attachment of many to the free will myth. This is utilitarianism and its kissing cousin, consequentialism. As we know, utilitarianism is best understood as the greatest happiness principle, while consequentialism says that the value of an action should be judged purely by its consequences: ultimately the argument that the ends justify the means. That the liberal left is far more susceptible to such secular, revolutionary, and holistic mindsets than the right should be a largely uncontroversial assertion. The right has traditionally been deaf to such calls, partly through its own weakness for nationalistic and hidebound religious interpretations. So not only do we have the consequentialist and left-wing philosopher Ted Honderich picking up the free will baton of the late P.F. Strawson, but we also have many avowedly liberal philosophers, including Dennett and Smilansky, advancing basically utilitarian and consequentialist defences of the free will fraud. And the problem with any grand narrative which says that you can't make an omelette without breaking eggs and that sacrifice is necessary (usually the sacrifice of other people, of course) is that it tends to be remarkably good at turning a blind eye to injustice and unfairness at the level of the individual. This does not fully explain why so many intellectuals on the liberal left are first attracted to the free will conceit (we considered one alternative rationale in the last chapter) but it does help to explain why so many are subsequently utterly indifferent to the injustices that permeate the free will fraud and will airbrush out such injustices in their own work.

We have previously noticed that the anti-free will theorist Sam Harris has used dissembling over the free will myth as a stick to beat conservatives (and theists) for their lack of moral and intellectual coherence, yet Harris may be failing to highlight sufficiently that it is often his (and the author's) fellow liberals and atheists who have perhaps behaved worst of all when it comes to dissembling over free will. If for no other reason than the fact that theists and conservatives tend to actually believe in the existence of free choice, while atheists and liberals make up the ranks of the intellectuals who believe not in free choice but in the idea that others – generally perceived as less smart and less ethically reliable than them, of course – need to be made to believe in free will. Yet there is an associated troubling distinction between conservatives and liberals that may not play out in liberals' favour, and that is over the question of partiality and ethical consistency. As we saw above, Herman Cain and the American hard right use the myth of free choice as an excuse to direct antipathy towards both offenders and towards the poor. While in a universe without free will such behaviour is deeply unattractive, it is at least internally consistent. In contrast, liberals appear to display far less internal coherence – and thus, arguably, far less intellectual integrity. As we are nothing more than biology and environment, if you are wont to blame offenders for their offences (which were the result of nothing more than biology and environment), you really are morally driven to blame the poor for their poverty (which was the result of nothing more than biology and environment). To do otherwise is to be arbitrary and partial in your application. Consistency and integrity demand that while free will apologists wish to blame offenders for their offences they must also blame the poor for their poverty. Yet, notwithstanding examples to the contrary that we often have to dig to uncover, liberal philosophers generally want to be seen refusing to blame the poor for their poverty while wishing to continue to blame offenders for their offences. Liberal thinkers, in contrast with conservatives and 83% of the British public, prefer to be partial and biased in their application of blame, notwithstanding that to do so is a purely subjective prejudice. There is, at least in one very limited sense, a sort of savage integrity to the hard right that does not appear to exist on the academic liberal left.

Free Will, Cultural Difference, and the American Dream

The American Dream, a term seemingly first used by the historian James Truslow Adams in 1931 – although the sentiment certainly predates Adams's use – is often seen as underlain by the idea of the self-made man: the man who refuses to acknowledge his debt to anyone beyond himself. The American Dream is the idea that anyone can be president – this national conceit embodied by Thomas Wolfe's line that the promise of America gives to every man his chance, regardless of his birth. But this idea that anyone can be president does not stand up to scrutiny when assessed in the light of the free will debates.

The notion that anyone can be president presupposes the idea of free will – at least when set against the background of contemporary America, with its significant inequalities of opportunity. It is the concept that – whatever limitations have been placed by biology and environment – all Americans could (if they but try hard enough) somehow overcome such limitations: could somehow rise above biological and environmental determinism. The conceit that we can rise above our biology and environment is the very definition of free will, and it is a myth. More than that: it is a myth which inflicts great harm on the unluckiest, because it requires both a blindness to and an indifference to moral luck (because the lucky have a tendency to blame the unlucky for their misfortune and lack of success). The idea that anyone can be president can even be seen as a spiteful and vindictive fraud when one takes away the idea of freedom of choice and places each of us in a chain of causation not of his own choosing and that limits the aspirations of so many unless we actively work to make it otherwise. Now Martin Luther King's view of the American Dream certainly did involve a recognition of the embedded self: of contingency, chance, and the overarching need to provide real opportunity for all if we are to expect most to make anything of their lives. If the American Dream is ever to be a reality, King said in July 1965, Americans must work to make it a reality. God grant that America will be true to her dream, he concluded. The American Dream – when presented by the likes of Herman Cain and Thomas Wolfe – appears to be a social, economic, and political fraud, which acts to hinder opportunity and social mobility. In contrast, the American Dream – when presented by the likes of Martin Luther King – is an impetus to economic advancement and greater social mobility.

"But there is a deep *cultural* connection between strong belief in [free will and] moral responsibility and grossly excessive prison populations, extremes of poverty and wealth, absence of genuine opportunity for large segments of the culture, and inadequate protection of the innocent. The greater the cultural allegiance to [free will and] moral responsibility, the larger and harsher the prisons, the greater the disparity between rich and poor, the weaker the commitment to equal opportunity, and the meaner the support system for the least fortunate" (Bruce Waller, 2015).

To the extent that social historians are correct in the assertion that European welfare states only became possible due to a post-eighteenth-century declining belief in poverty through choice, it does raise the question of whether the United States may lack a working welfare safety net at least in part because of a strongly inculcated belief in the existence of free choice. Certainly there may be a cultural dimension to the strength of belief in free choice (and the need to propagandise that belief to others) with Henrich, Heine, and Norenzayan (2010) summarising the research that Westerners, and in particular Americans, are both more conceited – more self-aggrandising – and more prone to assert what they see as their freedom of choice. This would then raise the question of whether other national characteristics are protected through the myth of free will, in particular differential economic characteristics. According to Citigroup, the top 1% of households accounted for 40% of the financial net worth in 2000 in the US, which was more than the bottom 95% of households put together. On the back of such statistics, Ajay Kapur, chief global equity strategist at Citigroup, wrote a confidential – but now widely-leaked – briefing to the bank's wealthiest investors in October 2005. Sourcing from what it termed the most reliable and credible government and academic sources, the report described the US, UK, and Canada as no longer democracies – from the Greek meaning the rule of the people – but as what it termed plutonomies, from the Greek meaning the law and rule of the wealthy.

The Citigroup research meant the term plutonomy to describe countries with massive income and wealth inequalities. The research contrasted the plutonomies of the US, the UK, and Canada with what it termed the egalitarian bloc of Scandinavia, France, Germany, and other continental European countries (excluding Italy) plus Japan. "The balance of power between right (generally pro-plutonomy) and left (generally pro-equality) is on a knife edge in many countries", Kapur and his team asserted (2005, p.25). What stops the potential social backlash against such open and rising anti-egalitarianism within the plutonomies is that "enough of the electorate believe they have a chance of becoming a Pluto-participant" (p.24). The Citigroup report is of interest both because it mentions the political dimension and because it seems to suggest the necessity to plutonomy of belief in radical self-creation. Kapur and his team noted that the survival of plutonomy effectively required belief in the American Dream as presented by Murray and Dennett: belief in the conceit that we can rise above our embedded selves and our biological and (in particular) environmental limitations. To the extent that this happens to be true, the unravelling of the free will myth may be a significant threat both to plutonomy and to those political persuasions which defend such economic and social inequality. We have already mentioned that Shariff, Baumeister, and Clark claim to have demonstrated that countries with higher beliefs in free will have higher rates of incarceration, stronger appetites for retributive punishment, and lower levels of forgiveness (Shariff et al., in press). Strong belief in free will corresponds to harsher penal attitudes, so is it really any wonder that Kapur's team seemed to identify a strong belief in free will as necessary to maintain plutonomy and harsher attitudes on poverty and inequality?

In his more recent work Bruce Waller (2015) has linked greater belief in free choice and self-creation to greater wealth inequalities, harsher attitudes towards the poor, greater toleration of injustice – including less concern over miscarriages of justice and convicting of the innocent, citing data from the Cardozo Law School-affiliated Innocence Project, Northwestern University's Center on Wrongful Convictions, and even the National Academy of Sciences – and greater indifference to suffering. Waller highlights how bizarre it at first appears that greater indifference to miscarriages of justice is correlated to higher belief in free choice and self-creation. We have already considered the question of empathy, and where we are dealing with indifference to poverty or discrimination free will justifiers often do not seem to share the same social and cultural background as those in poverty or those being discriminated against, so indifference to moral luck is easier to comprehend. But self-creation and moral responsibility theorists tend to be highly legalist (in the sense that this term is used within political theory to mean an excessive veneration of the law) so surely such people could be assumed to be against miscarriages of justice. After all, this is the jailing or killing of those subsequently proved to be innocent. Legalists tend to view themselves as champions of victims – albeit that we have already noted significant hypocrisy in relation to identification of who is a victim – and as very much among life's moral and social innocents. Waller highlights the incongruity that there is no empathy here, either. One reason for this appears to be that legalists tend to be no-smoke-without-fire types and to believe that those charged by the legal system must be guilty of something. In making his assessment of the connection between strong belief in self-creation and moral responsibility and social, economic, and legal exclusion and polarisation, Waller contrasts America and Britain as being at the maximal ends of the belief in self-creation spectrum, with the conservative corporatist countries like Germany and France in the middle and the social democratic corporatist countries like Sweden and Denmark at the minimal end of the belief spectrum. Waller further argues that even within particular countries, the greater the belief in freedom to choose and self-origination the greater the social discontinuity. Thus rugged individualist Texas, writes Waller, "has the highest level of people without access to health care, the most extreme distances between wealth and poverty, some of the worst public schools, and a remarkably meager – even by US neo-liberal standards – system of public assistance. Contrast that with Vermont, where capital punishment was abolished decades ago, and which has excellent public schools, a strong system of health care which is available to almost all its citizens, and a substantial social welfare system" (2015).

It may seem somewhat incongruous to suggest that the United States has bought into the self-origination myth significantly more strongly than any Western European state, given that human self-creation (free will) is supposed to be an idea at the heart of Christianity, and given that Christianity is still a powerful force within many Western European nations. The important difference seems to be that in Western Europe, largely excluding Great Britain, it is far more likely to be lip service which is being paid to the myth of self-creation and free will. Within the European churches which ritualistically invoke faith in God's gift of free will there is nonetheless a strong recognition that poverty, misfortune, and crime are largely social creations outside of any individual's control. And even where misfortune is viewed as strongly biological in origin there is little drive to argue that such susceptibility is chosen or in any way deserved. In addition, and crucially, outside of the churches the political consensus and national institutions tend – at least when ignoring the UK – to act to protect the less fortunate against blame-based regimes built on the notion of self-creation and free choice. Recall that the American Pew Global Attitudes surveys have consistently found that, at every income level, Americans and their institutions are far more likely than Europeans to suggest that individuals and not society are responsible for their economic and other failures (Allen & Dimock, 2007). American institutions – religious, cultural, educational, political – have overwhelmingly been established to deny the reality of the problem of moral luck, whereas European institutions at least partly accept the problem of moral luck, notwithstanding the same holy texts and religious nostrums. Within Western European states the welfare and justice systems often act to protect many against residual calls for social exclusion. This is not always the case, of course. On the issue of prisoner voting rights it is Britain which is standing almost alone in the (typically American) view that it is singularly the offender (and not also the state) which has not just failed but also violated any social contract supposedly built upon principles of opportunity and fair play. We have already seen that Tony Blair and Gordon Brown helped move late twentieth-century Britain towards greater belief in self-creation and heightened contempt for the socially and economically disadvantaged. Nevertheless, even in Britain such national characteristics (vanities?) as a supposedly strong sense of fair play do (at the moment) help to protect the least fortunate against the worse effects of the free will conceit, and they inculcate a healthy scepticism against philosophical calls for censorship and the turning of a blind eye within the free will and moral responsibility debates.

Finally, let us mention that although our analysis has of necessity been restricted to the economically-advanced West – a region which has developed on the back of Judaeo-Christian and humanistic theories of personal freedom, justice, opportunity, and desert – the free will debates are likely to have far wider application. The free will debates are ultimately about luck, conceit, gratitude for one's own good fortune and a recognition of others' greater misfortune, and such understandings will almost certainly have resonance for all arguments around the distribution of resources, fairness, and opportunity. In the economically developing world, where what we so often see is crony capitalism, corruption, scapegoating, rigged social systems, and little more than surface commitment to equality of opportunity – with the violence and frustration that often follows such corruption and inequality – all the issues and problems that are raised by the free will debates in the West must surely apply to at least an equal extent.

Science on Philosophy; or "a Sort of Intellectual Elder Brother"

We have spent much time on the two and a half thousand year philosophical contribution to free will justification (with a few references to the contribution of social psychology over the last decade) but to date we have made little mention of the long involvement of the natural and physical sciences. Originally, of course, there was no distinction between philosophy and what we now call the hard sciences. It was the early Greek philosophers who gave us some of the first physical models of the universe, and Aristotle would have seen himself as much a scientist as a philosopher. Yet once the hard sciences were recognised as separate disciplines it is interesting to note the sometimes deep involvement of scientists within free will propaganda. Although certain of the great scientific minds of the last two hundred years wanted nothing to do with the conceit of free will – and we must mention here Charles Darwin, Darwin's "bulldog" Thomas Huxley, and Albert Einstein – in the early twentieth century it was physicists, and not philosophers, who seemed to be advancing the arguments that the new quantum theory could supply the freedom of choice that religion had always craved. In the 1920s the deeply spiritual British astrophysicist Arthur Eddington wrote that because of both quantum theory and Einstein's theory of relativity science would withdraw its earlier (and classically deterministic) opposition to the concept of free will. Eddington, a great populariser of the new physics, was apparently the inspiration for Alan Turing (the legendary cryptologist and father of computing) to also seek to connect quantum theory with free will. In the 1930s it would most notably be the Nobel Prize-winning physicist Arthur Compton who would argue that quantum fluctuations could ground a two-stage model of free will. And even though many physicists do today appreciate that the randomness of the quantum world can no more give us free choice than determinism can, as recently as 2006 the leading scientific journal *Foundations of Physics* was publishing work by two mathematicians, John Conway and Simon Kochen, which discussed a hypothetical connection between putative human free will and the probabilistic nature of quantum mechanics.

Today it is probably fair to say that the most complex justifications for free will are once again coming from philosophers rather than scientists, but this should not suggest that many influential modern scientists have not jumped on the free will bandwagon with an ideological fervour. The quantum gravity theorist and best-selling science writer Paul Davies – a *Templeton Prize for Progress Toward Research or Discoveries about Spiritual Realities* laureate, and former member of the board of trustees of the Templeton Foundation – has called for the suppression of the growing intellectual recognition that there is no free will. Free will, suggested Davies in a 2004 essay commissioned for the journal *Foreign Policy*, may be "a fiction worth maintaining". Davies has called knowledge of the absence of free will one of the "world's most dangerous ideas", even as he accepts that such knowledge has "more than a grain of truth" to it (2004, pp.36-7). Marvin Minsky is a celebrated cognitive theorist and co-founder of MIT's Computer Science and Artificial Intelligence Laboratory, and in *The Society of Mind* Minsky wrote: "According to the modern scientific view, there is simply no room at all for 'freedom of the human will'... Does this mean that we must embrace the modern scientific view and put aside the ancient myth of voluntary choice? No. We can't do that... Such thoughts must be suppressed" (1986, pp.306-7). Another former MIT figure who was, at least at one stage, influential within the free will illusionist camp is the Canadian cognitive theorist Steven Pinker, now at Harvard. Pinker has admitted that free will is a deception which society must be built upon, although he prefers to call free will "an idealization" rather than pejoratively describing it as a deception (interviewed in Blume, 1998, p.155). The Harvard cognitive theorist Daniel Wegner is another propagandist for the illusion of free will. In his 2002 work *The Illusion of Conscious Will,* Wegner tells us that uncertainty over the existence of free will "makes everyone deeply uncomfortable" (2002, p.336) and that in consequence we should promote the politically expedient illusion of free will to the masses as "sometimes how things seem is more important than what they are" (p.341). As John Horgan, former chief writer at *Scientific American*, puts it: "Science has made it increasingly clear (to me at least) that free will is an illusion. But – even more so than God – it is a glorious, absolutely necessary illusion" (2000, p.161).

Many physicists appear to have continued their 1930s enthusiasm for defending the conceit of free will, including those of the world-class standing of Roger Penrose, Stephen Hawking, and the string theorist Brian Greene. Penrose, writing with the anaesthesiologist Stuart Hameroff (1995), has suggested (in work widely rejected by neuroscientsists and, anyway, logically incoherent) that cellular "microtubules" may be the source of human free will, while Greene has suggested that "it's at least possible" (2004, p.456) that free will might yet find a concrete realisation in physical law. According to Greene multi-universe theory may be the solution to the paradox of free will, but not only is there no evidence for such an assertion, we know from earlier criticism that parallel universes – alternative versions of "you" – offer us absolutely no way out of the free will and moral luck problems. And Stephen Hawking, writing with the physicist Leonard Mlodinow, has suggested that "any complex being has free will – not as a fundamental feature, but as an effective theory, an admission of our inability to do the calculations that would enable us to predict its action" (2010, p.178). While Penrose and Greene are free will libertarians, Hawking is a free will illusionist, and I must stress again that we have no solution to the moral luck problem, and that free will does not exist as either Penrose's "fundamental feature" or as Hawking's "effective theory".

Others who have (mis?)used a scientific platform to defend the false and unjust vanity of free will include biologists of the influence of E.O. Wilson and Richard Dawkins. Dawkins, a close personal friend of the professional free will apologist Dan Dennett, has written that "in practice we can forget about determinism and behave as if we had free will" and has also, and pseudo-scientifically, proposed for the free will debates that "neurones may be amplifiers of fundamentally indeterminate events" (1982, p.11). Meanwhile Wilson has suggested, also incorrectly, that "the paradox of determinism and free will appears not only resolvable in theory, it might even be reduced in status to an empirical problem in physics and biology" (1978, p.77). Another influential biologist making unhelpful statements on free will is the Nobel Prize winner Gerald Edelman, who has written that "a human being has a degree of free will. That freedom is not radical, however, and it is curtailed by a number of internal and external events and constraints" (1994, p.170). Edelman has claimed that the strong psychological determinism proposed by Freud does not hold, that there is even indeterminacy in natural selection, and that indeterminacy is greater in conscious systems. But human beings do not have a "degree" of free will. We are aware of no indeterminacy in natural selection, although this would be irrelevant in any case, and there is no evidence for the assertion that indeterminacy may be greater in conscious systems. Steve Jones, the celebrated evolutionary geneticist once charged with updating (1999) Darwin's *Origin of Species*, has frequently tried to defend the conceit of free will, although in both *The Language of the Genes* and his *In the Blood: God, Genes and Destiny* he gets himself in a terrible muddle over an inability to keep separate the nature/nurture argument and the free will argument.

A few years ago Greg Graffin, a graduate student of the Cornell biologist and anti-free will writer Will Provine, contacted 272 leading biologists and asked for their responses to a number of questions. It was originally called the *Cornell Evolution Project, a Survey of Evolution and Religious Belief* (see www.polypterus.org), and Graffin's list of 272 reads like a *Who's Who* of the great and the good of the last half century of evolutionary biology, from Francis

Crick, James Watson, Ernst Mayr, and George C. Williams to Edelman, Dawkins, and Wilson. Provine tells me that Graffin discovered that while fewer than 5% of these scientists expressed belief in the existence of a god, fully 80% expressed belief in the existence of free will. Due to the way the questions were set this study suggested but did not fully establish that the majority of sampled evolutionists appear to fall within the libertarian camp, rather than the illusionist or compatibilist camps – although in a sense this is beside the point, as for scientists to express any form of support for the myth of free will is both morally and intellectually inappropriate.

> "If the great evolutionists still believe in the myth of free will, why should we trust them on anything?" (a scientist writing to Will Provine, 1 February 2008, and copied to the author, after viewing biologists' responses to the *Cornell Evolution Project*)

Some may suggest that scientists are entitled to their personal beliefs, no matter how bizarre, political, or seemingly illogical, so long as they keep those beliefs private. Others might think that we are better off being aware of the bizarre beliefs scientists subscribe to, but the danger is when they help promote those bizarre, prejudiced, or illogical beliefs to others. Scientists become guilty of bad science when such beliefs harm their scientific objectivity and begin to raise questions, as per the above commentator, over their professional reliability. And it becomes bad science when scientists either express libertarian sympathies and then, like Jones, Greene, Penrose, Wilson, and Dawkins, use their platforms as respected scientists to promote an irrational faith position, or alternatively express illusionist or compatibilist sympathies and then, like Hawking and Pinker, use a quasi-scientific platform to misdirect (unintentionally of course) over the regressive socioeconomics of the free will myth.

The hard sciences do have a somewhat ambivalent relationship with philosophy, often seemingly driven by scientists' views of themselves and others as more or less intellectually trustworthy. On the more supportive side we have the example of Richard Dawkins, who has described the philosopher Dan Dennett as "a sort of intellectual elder brother" on a number of occasions, including when presenting him with the 2007 Richard Dawkins Award (this is not a joke) at the conference of the Atheist Alliance International. On the less supportive side we have rather more scientists who treat philosophy, plus the wider humanities and social sciences, with an animosity bordering on contempt. Stephen Hawking, again writing with Leonard Mlodinow, has declared that philosophy is "dead" and that only scientists can now help us in our quest for knowledge. One of Britain's most respected geneticists, Steve Jones of UCL, has compared the healthy (sexual) intercourse that is science to the self-indulgent masturbation that is philosophy. "For most wearers of white coats, philosophy is to science as pornography is to sex: it is cheaper, easier, and some people seem, bafflingly, to prefer it" (1997, pp.13-14). The theoretical physicist Lawrence Krauss, whose work Richard Dawkins has gushingly compared to *Origin of Species* in its frame-changing importance, doesn't liken philosophy to masturbation but instead likens philosophers to gym teachers – as in the Woody Allen line *Those who can't do, teach; and those who can't teach, teach gym*. Scientists of course "do", without a hint of ignorance or prejudice, according to Krauss. Even non-scientists are starting to get in on the act, with the now ubiquitous Nassim Nicholas Taleb, of post-economic collapse "black swan" fame, seriously suggesting that the social sciences should be shut down and all higher education placed in the hands of apparently more trustworthy hard scientists such as the free will libertarian Richard Dawkins and the free will illusionist Stephen Hawking. At the academic level scientism – once a pejorative term meaning something quite different – is the belief both that the natural sciences are the only valid way to seek knowledge, and that science (and increasingly scientists too when writing *qua* scientists) contains within itself (themselves) a universal competence free from prejudice and self-delusion. One of the first to defend scientism was the chemist Peter Atkins in his 1995 essay *Science as Truth*, but today even some philosophers have defended the glory of scientism, including James Ladyman, Don Ross, and David Spurrett. Scientific method, including experiment, iteration and objective verification, has undoubtedly often operated to keep the natural sciences epistemologically sound (and arguably sounder than certain other academic traditions). However, when students of the methodology of science have raised concerns that scientific method is not the panacea natural scientists frequently suggest it to be they have been met with a deep and abiding hostility. The notorious science wars of the late 1990s represent, among other things, the instance of a continuing view within both the social sciences and the humanities that at least part of modern scientific discourse is driven by social and economic conditions and prejudices, and even myth and superstition. In 1996, in the journal *Social Studies of Science*, Brian Martin argued that a much-lauded 1994 defence of scientific integrity by the scientists Paul Gross and Norman Levitt simply ignored the deeper issues, such as concerns over sources of scientific funding, vested interests, and attitudes to social control and exploitation. Martin, a long-standing investigator of scientific controversies and the suppression of intellectual dissent within the natural sciences, wrote of Gross and Levitt's glorification of natural science as the epitome of rational enquiry, and of their condescending attitude towards the humanities and social sciences (noting that in his experience over twenty-five years quite a number of scientists hold the humanities and social sciences in contempt).

Scientific arrogance and blindness to its own shortcomings does have a long pedigree. In the early seventeenth century Francis Bacon provided an aphorism that has come to be seen by many natural scientists as giving the primacy to scientific method. Bacon, a founding inspiration behind the Royal Society, compared the activities of the bee, the ant, and the spider. Within Bacon's metaphor, the ant is the creature that gathers and consumes, that effectively experiments without understanding. The spider never experiments but simply spins webs out of itself, while the wise bee gathers but then transforms base experiment through effort and discipline. Many natural scientists still see the humanities, and particularly philosophy, as represented by the spider, and the social sciences as largely represented by the ant – whereas the natural scientist is the bee, kept honest and fruitful by the activities and disciplines of science itself. As mentioned, scientific method has helped to keep the sciences comparatively clean when compared with certain other disciplines, but the idea that scientific discourse does not often contain the same ideologies, prejudices, and even ignorance is deeply naive. The free will fiasco has shown that scientists cannot be trusted to tell the truth, at least not when it really matters, either because they are ignorant of the underlying truth or because they are prepared to suppress the truth so as to help maintain the *status quo*. The conclusion seems to be that, as with philosophers, we can trust scientists to tell us the truth *but never when it really matters*. Black holes, electromagnetism, and quantum gravity: yes. Justice, equality and the foundation of ethics: no.

Flattering the Human Animal

John Horgan, former chief writer at *Scientific American*, has written that "free will is something I cherish. I can live with the idea of science killing off God. But free will? That's going too far" (2002, p.3). Which raises the intriguing question of just how far is "too far" when it comes to the truth, and what are the other deep falsehoods that we "cherish" and refuse to see beyond? Sam Harris has suggested that the free will conceit represents a "collective failure of intellectual nerve" (2011, p.46) by scientists and assorted philosophical and religious thinkers but, building on the last section, one question that has always interested the author (1998, 2004, 2005) is whether it is only over free will where we lose our intellectual nerve and flatter ourselves outrageously.

We have discussed the studies of Stanley Milgram and Philip Zimbardo, both of whom produced groundbreaking but controversial work which demonstrated the less-flattering sides to the human character, including aggression and lack of empathy, and it is instructive how critics of Milgram and Zimbardo often invoke free will to try to justify their criticisms. For example, Stephen Reicher of St. Andrews University told the journalist Graeme Green that Zimbardo was wrong to suggest that people lose the ability to judge when in groups. "People can still make choices", Reicher reportedly said (2007, p.19). But the idea of choices as it is being used here – free choice – implies a belief in free will in the libertarian sense: a belief that humans are more than just the product of biology and environment. We have also encountered the Nobel Prize-winning work of Daniel Kahneman, who proved just how irrational we all tend to be. Humans are much less self-aware and reasonable than we like to think of ourselves, and we can easily be fooled and manipulated by both internal and external factors, even by something as seemingly irrelevant as finding a coin in a phone booth. The behavioural economist Dan Ariely (2012) has also made waves summarising research which suggests how naturally dishonest we are – and that, given the opportunity, everyone steals and cheats a little. It is largely being reminded of our honour codes that combats our seeming natural tendency to cheat and steal, and then to self-justify the cheating and the stealing.

So let us now turn our thoughts to the criminally violent. Paul Babiak has shown that psychopaths, that most extreme of psychological formulations, are very common at the top levels of both business and politics. Psychopaths have a natural tendency to be charming, manipulative and intimidating – traits that often stand you in good stead in business and politics. Babiak discovered that there are almost four times as many psychopaths in the highest levels of big business as in the general population. But what makes some psychopaths high functioning rather than violent? Aggressive in business or politics, but not aggressive on the street or in the home? That appears to be largely down to environment. Jim Fallon at UC Irvine is rather unusual among academics who study psychopaths. Fallon is related to the infamous Lizzie Borden, and when checking his extended family history he noted many murderers. When he scanned his own brain and investigated his own genome he found all the markers that have been suggested for extreme aggression, including a total lack of activity over the orbital cortex; a non-functioning limbic system; the MAOA gene; the genetic markers for impulsivity. Yet instead of being a violent criminal, or even a high functioning psychopath within politics, Fallon was a quiet senior academic. Certainly his family had noted his sometimes startling lack of empathy, but Fallon understood that what made all the difference for him was that he had received a loving upbringing. The evidence seems to be that all the unusual brain scans and all the genetic markers offer very little risk unless someone has also come from an abusive background. Yet an area where we seem to be notoriously prone to deceive ourselves – and perhaps to flatter ourselves – is over the relative contribution of biology and environment, in both directions. We predominantly however seem to overplay the role of biology in the variabilities of human life, particularly in moral behaviour. The history of the field of behavioural genetics includes both outright fraud at the highest levels and wild overenthusiasm.

As an example of the latter, only relatively recently has it been noticed that conclusions drawn in behavioural genetics may have significantly underappreciated the role of socioeconomic status in the heritability of IQ (Turkheimer et al., 2003). Traditionally studies have drawn their populations from the affluent classes, where biology may have a high contribution to IQ variability, as all tend to receive a privileged and stable education. Such studies have often ignored the lower socioeconomic classes – arguably far more representative of typical human populations – where biological contribution to IQ variation may actually be relatively minor and environmental contribution rather higher.

Behavioural genetics is undoubtedly a much cleaner field than it was just a couple of decades ago, but even today there is far too little timely verification of the claims made, while oversight of the behavioural genetics industry has sometimes been laughable. In late 2000 the UK's Nuffield Council on Bioethics grandly announced that it had set up a working party to establish the veracity of claims made in behavioural genetics. The Council spent two years investigating the field of behavioural genetics before... asking a behavioural geneticist to write their main conclusion for them. To quote: "A review of research into [the genetic basis of] antisocial behaviour was written by a member of the Working Party Professor Terrie Moffitt [and this paper was] used to inform the Working Party" (2002, p.193). Yet Terrie Moffitt is herself a behavioural geneticist and is married to a behavioural geneticist. This point is raised not as in any way a criticism of Moffitt or her work, but because of the absurdity of spending two years investigating the veracity (or possibly not) of a controversial field, only to ask a leading exponent of the area being investigated to provide the main conclusion. And yet, beyond this, there is also a great deal of ignorance over what genes can and cannot code for among those charged with communicating with the public. Even such august figures as Harvard's Steven

Pinker and the UK's leading science broadcaster Professor Lord Robert Winston have made spectacularly ill-advised claims in the past regarding the findings that can be drawn from twin studies. Steven Pinker, for example, has displayed too little scepticism over the more absurd claims of behavioural geneticists, promoting (1994) the work of one group who went so far as to suggest that there was "evidence" that our genes largely determine both what names we will be given and that we will choose our partners by their names. Posit if you so wish, and as evolutionary psychology does, that genetics makes us look for partners who are tall, or attractive, or rich. But to suggest that genetics makes us look for partners who are called Billy-Bob or Betty is, to be blunt, silly.

One of the more intriguing mysteries of evolutionary biology is whether we are flattering ourselves every time we suggest that morality is an evolved response, that morality exists at the level of our genes, because the problem is that morality exists nowhere in the non-human genetic world. Chimpanzees, to quote the leading primatologist Frans de Waal, live in "a world without compassion" (1996, p.83). What is true of chimps is equally true of squirrels, dolphins, dogs, bonobos, and orang-utans. "There is no charity in nature", writes the evolutionary geneticist Steve Jones (1999, p.160), and for very particular evolutionary reasons. Darwin was aware of the paradox of highly evolved morality, although it was Darwin's great friend T. H. Huxley who was the first to formally recognise the problem. The paradox of an evolved morality is as much of an intellectual headache today as it was in Darwin's time, and has been drawn attention to by the late George C. Williams, father of what he called genic selection theory, or what came to be known a decade later as selfish gene theory (1966, 1988). I must here mention that George C. Williams wrote the Foreword to Miles (2004). This was a kindness and an amazing honour that the author will forever be grateful for, from someone known across all the competing biological camps as one of the nicest and gentlest of senior academics. Others who have highlighted the paradox of an evolved morality include both the other great names within the development of selfish gene-ery, John Maynard Smith and Bill Hamilton, while Richard Dawkins, the most influential propagandist of the work of Williams, Maynard Smith, and Hamilton, has also highlighted the problem. As Hamilton put it: "natural selection... implies concurrently a complete disregard for any values, either of individuals or of groups, which do not serve competitive breeding. This being so, the animal in our nature cannot be regarded as a fit custodian for the values of humanity" (1971, p.219). It seems that everything which is civilized and fundamentally human about us – charity, gratitude, kindness, a sense of fairness and justice – has no correlate outside mankind and should not have come from the natural. Could not have come from the biological.

So the idea (the conceit?) of those like Steven Pinker, Robert Winston and E.O. Wilson that our species evolved to be moral uniquely among the billions of species that have ever existed on this planet – we are *The* Moral Animal, if you recall the title of Robert Wright's 1994 evolutionary psychology work quoted earlier – seems to fly in the face of almost four thousand million years of evolution. The problem is worse than that, though, as it would have required the radical redesign of the mammalian genome, huge leaps (ridiculed by Darwin as saltations) in genetic design space, deleting or inhibiting the behaviours of our ape cousins – including species-wide programming for cannibalism and infanticide – and substituting our new morality-as-a-biological-adaptation coding. But a problem with any attempt to argue that we evolved morality is that what is termed subversion from within would have acted against the trait. As Maynard Smith, the pioneer of what are called evolutionarily stable strategies, or ESSs, first put it in *Nature*: "every time a group possessing the socially desirable characteristic is 'infected' by a gene for anti-social behaviour, that gene is likely to spread through the group" (1964, p.1145). We split from a common ancestor with the chimpanzee six million years ago: a common ancestor that, the evidence strongly suggests, carried the species-wide genetic programming for infanticide and cannibalism.

> "The dominant male, Humphrey, held a struggling infant about 1.5 years old, which I did not recognise. Its nose was bleeding, as though from a blow, and Humphrey, holding the infant's legs, intermittently beat its head against a branch. After 3 minutes, he began to eat flesh from the thighs of the infant, which then stopped struggling and calling. The oldest male, Mike (aged 27-30, formerly the dominant male of the community but now low-ranking), approached and was permitted to tear off one of the infant's feet" (Bygott, 1972, 'Cannibalism among wild chimpanzees', *Nature*, p.410).

We may have out-evolved Maynard Smith's antisocial biological pattern found in every one of our competitor species. This is not strictly impossible, even if it is implausible. The more interesting fact, though, is that this has never been proven (indeed, we do not even have a working model of how it might have happened), and hence many biologists – although not Williams, Maynard Smith, Hamilton, or Dawkins – seem to be simply taking on faith the notion that we must have out-evolved such coding, because the alternative would seem to them to be too awful to consider. So the apparent species flattery proposed by those like Steven Pinker, that morality is a biological adaptation and a uniquely human adaptation, should probably be viewed with a healthy scepticism. Besides, what does morality-as-a-biological-adaptation mean when we have moral philosophers who (at least in the author's opinion) not only don't seem to behave morally, they don't even appear to understand the concept of behaving morally? And what does morality-as-a-biological-adaptation mean when the human animal is quite obviously capable of stunningly awful behaviour on an industrial scale? If morality is a biological adaptation then such a genetic pattern appears to have skipped a few generations in Franco's Spain, with its gang rape to death of teenage girls, its deliberate murder of children in front of their parents, its wholesale slaughter of pregnant women. If morality is a biological adaptation then it seems to be a particularly whimsical adaptation: an adaptation that appears then disappears with monotonous regularity when we have Japanese soldiers raping to death Chinese women and children during the Rape of Nanking, known for amusingly leaving their corpses impaled to the ground with swords, bayonets, golf clubs, and bamboo canes through the genitals (Chang, 1997). The Japanese were so proud of their dehumanisation, bestiality, and extermination that they rather foolishly left behind significant photographic evidence of it to be used at the subsequent war crimes trials: the gang rape to death of pregnant women, and of Buddhist nuns and children younger than ten, the prolonged rape to madness of teenagers, foetuses torn from their mothers' wombs. Hundreds of thousands of civilians raped, mutilated, tortured, and murdered in Nanking within the space of just six weeks by the citizens of what became a few decades later one of the most advanced and peaceable nations on the planet.

So what does morality-as-a-biological-adaptation even mean in the human context? When not just our willingness to do right over what we know to be wrong is open to question, but so is our very awareness of the difference between right and wrong? Two hundred years ago our forefathers appeared not to even understand that it was wrong to treat people of a different skin colour as chattels and beasts of burden, to be mutilated or killed out of hand when they were more trouble than they were worth (literally). Steven morality-as-a-biological-adaptation Pinker himself is descended from ancestors who – at least according to the Pentateuch – raped and butchered children perhaps as young as ten, exterminating entire families and every last infant. Where was morality-as-a-biological-adaptation in those days, then? And even without the roll call from the Pentateuch, is it even plausible that Spanish and Japanese conservatives carry a biological malignity not found in Canadian conservatives? Or not found in American and British liberals, for that matter? When the American essentialist philosopher Gary Watson effectively asks us to leave "room for the thought" that young American soldiers have something biological in them (not cultural, but biological, remember) such that they simply could never have acted as Japanese or Spanish soldiers and paramilitaries emphatically did, how plausible is this really? I ask again, what does morality-as-a-biological-adaptation even mean in the human context, and isn't it perhaps just as plausible that morality is not a biological adaptation, and that we did not out-evolve the bestial indifference (at best) of our chimp cousins? According to Steven Pinker morality is a biological adaptation, but isn't it equally plausible that what is fine in us is simply culture raising us above the animal? When you take away the fiction of free will you are left with just biology and environment. Given the biology carried by our kin the langur and the chimpanzee, and given the behaviour of our ancestors – who if not possessing a malign biology at least did not seem to possess a particularly benign biology – it still seems likely that what saves us from bestiality – and, yes, maybe often what dooms us to bestiality, too – is the cultural.

Adrian Raine is one of the world's top experts on the neuropathology of serial killers. Raine wishes violent crime to be viewed as an illness – a disease – with sufferers to be rehabilitated, where possible, rather than punished. Yet Raine's work is still tainted by his need to see us – or at least most of us – as genetically blessed. Raine (2013) is far too keen to suggest that people like you and me could never have been raised to show the worst behaviours. That "we" are essentially different from "them". While Raine is adamant that the worst forms of behaviour always require an environmental trigger – years of abuse, for example – he starts to get into trouble when he seems to suggest that the worst forms of behaviour always require bad and atypical underlying biology too. Now a distinction must be drawn here between pathological underlying innate biology and pathological subsequently developed biology. Serial killers tend to have very unusual and atypically-developed brains. But the human brain is incredibly plastic and, as Raine notes, years of abuse can easily cause unusual brain development. London black cab drivers have an enlarged hippocampus, which physically grows to a grossly atypical size as they cram into it the knowledge of 25,000 London street names. So significant non-normal brain development does not require a genetic abnormality, just a developmental abnormality. There is evidence that some types of behaviour do have a strong genetic component, but the implications are not quite what Raine and other "neuro-criminologists" appear to believe. Raine and others are wrong where they suggest that we are not all capable of being raised (environmentally "triggered") to display the specific behaviours seen in the worst serial killers: rape, savage butchery, torture, and even the cannibalism of a Jeffrey Dahmer. Neuro-criminologists are also wrong where they sometimes suggest that most criminals have real genetic malignancies: in truth, probably only a fraction do. Raine studies only the worst offenders, so cannot infer from this unique band to the wider prison population (as he has a tendency to do).

However, it is probably safe to say that when the very worst and most shocking behaviours are being displayed by loners (archetypal serial killers), there may often be unusual genetic factors in play somewhere, while when exactly the same shocking behaviours are committed by groups – Japanese, Spanish, maybe even Canadians – there are no unusual genetic factors in play. Although, of course, this raises the intriguing possibility that the genetic difference is little more than a marker for fearless individualism over the conformist herd behaviour most of us display most of the time. Male mallard ducks gang rape to death females of their species. Since the point about natural world rape is to get your genes into surviving offspring, this might suggest that the mallard is a particularly stupid duck. This, however, is just an example of a biological arms race. When other ducks are going in violently, then your seed is going nowhere if you have a tendency to pull back. Hence it is better to go in hard if every other duck is going in hard, and indeed it may pay to go in hardest of all. If the female drowns from all this... well, this was at little cost to the male, and at least other males did not benefit. So when the anti-Communists in Franco's Spain gang raped to death teenage girls, can we say that this was an example of them displaying their "mallard gene"? Should we be worried that conservative teenagers in today's Spain are a hair's breadth from exercising their langur genes, or "going chimpanzee" on socialist youths? If there is indeed a strong genetic component to horrific violence and rape, why are we not taking more of an interest in Spanish conservatives, the wider Japanese population, and Serbian nationalists? And what of Canadian conservatives?

Contrary to the essentialism and contrary to the species flattery of Gary Watson, Steven Pinker, and Adrian Raine, the evidence appears to be that we could all have been raised to display the most appalling behaviours, including torture, rape, mutilation, infanticide, even cannibalism. Whether this has any real link to the fact that we evolved from a common ancestor with the chimp (or the mallard) which also displayed such behaviours is a long way from being resolved, though, as we big-brained humans are so vindictive in our nastiness that we may be taking little direction from the indifferent cruelty of the natural world. So morality may not be a biological adaptation, after all. But there is little appetite to follow such troubling avenues of investigation. Academic science and essentialist philosophy may just be joining theology in the overarching tendency to flatter our species outrageously.

7

THE METAPHYSICS OF FREE WILL

The *causa sui* is the best self-contradiction hitherto imagined, a kind of logical rape and unnaturalness. For the desire for "freedom of the will"... which is unfortunately still dominant in the minds of the half-educated... is nothing less than the desire... to pull oneself into existence out of the swamp of nothingness by one's own hair.
Friedrich Nietzsche, *Beyond Good and Evil* (1886, pp.50-51).

We will never be able to disprove the existence of God, for the simple reason that an (almost) all-powerful creator being cannot be ruled out by either logic or the laws of physics in the same way that free will can be. The author has little wish to be drawn into the tired and seemingly endless arguments between the militant atheists – who display little awareness of the debt of gratitude owed to religion by Western history, intellect, culture, and ethics, and seemingly no willingness to examine the potentially still vital social and moral role religion can play – and their theistic opponents, who show similar intellectual and moral inflexibility. Having said this, it would be insincere and irresponsible for this book not to at least touch upon the metaphysical implications of the free will conceit, because they are going to be significant. For instance, we will never disprove the existence of God, but we can disprove the existence of a God that itself possesses free will. Furthermore, the absence of free will has great implications for the concept of divine reward and punishment, implications which need to be understood both for what they say about us and what they still permit to a hypothetical God. Of course, neither militant atheists nor dyed-in-the-wool theists will be completely happy with the seeming conclusions, but hopefully this suggests that both sides can also take some comfort from the implications. There will be no knockout punches for either side, but the wider free will debates can really only add to both religious and anti-religious understandings.

The author seeks reader indulgence that the metaphysical analysis in this chapter will be overwhelmingly skewed towards Judaeo-Christianity and the Western traditions of irreligion that are largely a reaction against such Judaeo-Christianity. However since it is Judaeo-Christianity, and the atheism that has been a response to it, which has fed and nourished – as well as censored, damaged and confused – the wider free will arguments, such a skewed analysis should in one sense be forgivable. Similarly to the last chapter, where we noted that although our analysis was restricted to the developed West the free will debates would also have great implications outside of the West, we will begin by noting that the lack of free choice is an understanding which must be reconciled in a deeply fundamental way with all metaphysical (and non-metaphysical) systems that try to advance a wider ethical message.

I hope that it is relatively uncontroversial to suggest that you cannot create an ethical system, secular or religious, that is ignorant of – or indifferent to – either fairness or the problem of moral luck. We have already mentioned that the concept of *Do unto others*, often termed the Golden Rule, exists centrally within Judaism, Christianity, Confucianism, Hinduism, Buddhism, Zoroastrianism, Islam, and even Scientology. And the injunction to *Do unto others* speaks to the heart of the problem of moral luck. This problem, and the absence of origination and free choice, creates issues for any ethical – and social, political, economic, or legal – system that incorporates concepts of reward, punishment, justice, fairness, equality, opportunity, providence, the soul, desert, destiny, fate, reincarnation, or karma. There is no encompassing worldview (be it for the individual or the group) that can be left unaffected by the issues of fairness, opportunity, and morality raised by the free will problem: so, while the author can and will make little attempt to specifically address the implications for non-traditional non-Western belief systems, this is not because the implications will not be overarching and profound.

The Doctrine of Free Will is Not Foundational to Judaeo-Christianity

The first point to make is that the definitions of free will and moral responsibility which we have seen advanced by compatibilists and semi-compatibilists often appear to be very different from the definitions of free will and responsibility that the Abrahamic religions have tended to use. Judaeo-Christianity has overwhelmingly defined free will and moral responsibility as the freedom to choose – the ability to have done otherwise – and indeed Dan Dennett tells us explicitly that there is a misplaced reverence for "an absolutist ideal: the concept of total, before-the-eyes-of-God Guilt. The fact that *that* condition is never to be met in this world should not mislead us" into scepticism about the integrity of our institutions of moral responsibility (1984, p.165). Similarly, John Martin Fischer is clear that although we can never be what he calls "ultimately responsible" in the sense suggested within traditional Judaeo-Christianity this should not stop our attempts to ascribe responsibility within the less-than-perfect human world (2006). Notwithstanding the complication that philosophers often wish to define free will very differently from the free choice sense that theologians tend to use, we also have

225

differences of interpretation over when and where religion came to terms with the concept of free choice. There are those who have argued that free will (defined as free choice) was a doctrine which existed within the earliest forms of Christianity. Hannah Arendt, for example, believed that the concept of free will existed right back in the writings of St Paul: but Arendt's argument is not necessarily persuasive, given that the early Church Fathers had to make a conscious effort to find evidence for free will within the teachings handed down by Christ.

It is at least as plausible that free will is not a doctrine which existed within early Christianity. Christianity is an outgrowth of Judaism, and the concept of free will is certainly not foundational to Judaism. While it is true that the idea of free will as free choice is central to modern rabbinical Judaism this is only because contemporary Judaism developed from one of the strands of Judaism that actually incorporated belief in free will. Judaism in the second century BC (the Second Temple period) comprised three sects: the Pharisees, the Sadducees, and the Essenes. Flavius Josephus, the first-century Jewish historian who ultimately Romanised his name after he failed as a Jewish revolutionary, is the main source of available information on these three sects. Josephus recorded that it was over the idea of determinism versus free will, and possibly only over the idea of determinism versus free will, that the three sects were markedly different. The Sadducees thought that all acts of men were free acts, the Pharisees that some acts of men were free acts, and the Essenes that no acts of men were truly free acts (Moore, 1929). A contemporary of Josephus – Philo Judeaus, the Jewish philosopher – also confirms that the Essenes had this attitude to determinism, with Philo writing that the Essenes exempted nothing from the sway of fate. The Essene view of an absence of free will thus appears to have been somewhat different from the understanding of modern philosophers, where the concept of fate has been completely stripped out of the free will and determinism debate. Whatever the impetus behind the Essenes view, though, they did live without belief in free will, and seemingly they did so in a very tolerant and liberal fashion. Josephus, in the final reckoning a Pharisee, spoke of Essene piety: of their diligence and of their fellowship to one another. They were quiet, simple, and kind. "It also deserves our admiration", wrote Josephus, "how much they exceed all other men that addict themselves to virtue, and this in righteousness; and indeed to such a degree, that as it hath never appeared among any other men", he wrote in Book XVIII of his *Antiquities of the Jews*. The Essenes largely disappeared from history at the end of the first century AD and the Pharisee conceit of limited free will is thus today a core tenet of rabbinical Judaism.

Turning from Judaism to Christianity, free will appears to have been first discussed comprehensively by the early Church father and Neoplatonist Origen of Alexandria (185-c.254 AD). Certainly Origen felt the need to make a powerful justification that the concept of free will was inherent within the teachings of Christ, which presupposes the concern that the idea of free will might not have been there in the earliest teachings. In his *On First Principles* Origen provided free will first as a philosophical concept. He then looked to cite biblical texts which he suggested supported the doctrine of free will by inference even if they did not explicitly mention it, before finally seeking to explain away the many passages in the Bible (such as Exodus 4:21 and Romans 8:29) that seemed to deny free will. However, while he defended the idea of freedom of the will, Origen's view of free will was still very different from that of most later Christian scholars. Origen, like Susan Wolf two thousand years later, recognised human freedom in rationality – in Reason with a capital R – thus displaying the influence on him of the Platonic tradition. For Origen, moral ignorance is not to be punished but modified through education.

And although discussed by thinkers including Origen and Jerome, Christian doctrine never truly seemed to incorporate the conceit of free will until the late fourth century when two influential thinkers tried to assimilate it. The first was a British monk, Pelagius (354-c.420 AD), and the second was St Augustine (354-430 AD). Pelagius thought that man was basically good by nature and did not carry original sin from Adam's Fall: he taught that each man was free to choose good over evil. For Pelagius, man – with his unrestrained free choice – could not plead the frailty of the flesh, as his natural will was free to do good without requiring grace or redemption. Augustine, by contrast, thought the choice of good or evil was preordained, and that God's grace was thus an absolute necessity.

Whether the doctrine of free will was inherent in the earliest teachings or tacked on later by the Catholic Church to try to answer such challenges as the Problem of Evil, the idea certainly came to dominate Church thinking after the fourth century. As Erasmus put it: "Why, you ask, is anything attributed to the freedom of the will? It is to prevent calumnies attributing cruelty and injustice to God" (1524, 93). Desiderius Erasmus, the great sixteenth-century humanist and theologian, was clear in his belief that the justness of orthodox Christian practice had been (and had to be) built upon belief in free will. Mainstream religion has almost always had to care about man being free to choose between good and evil because of the difficulty of blame and eternal punishment in the absence of choice.

Extreme Calvinism Offers No Lifeline

So can the determinism of extreme Calvinism offer us any hope of reconciling blame and justified suffering with the modern understanding of no free choice? After all, Luther and Calvin taught that there was no free will, for a somewhat similar reason why the Essenes did: namely, that free will would have provided humans with a space where God was not fully in control. For Luther and Calvin any restriction of God's power was viewed as an intolerable slight on divine authority. So can Lutherism, or at least extreme Calvinism, offer us hope of a reconciliation? Firstly we should say that some theologians recognise that it is not at all certain what Luther and Calvin were arguing for, or that they were indeed advancing the idea that man is never free to choose. The Christian philosopher Alvin Plantinga notes that predestination and determinism are not the same thing: predestination is about salvation and may not necessarily imply what we ordinarily think it might about the ability to choose. "But as Richard Muller, as good a Calvin scholar as one can find, says, 'When Calvin indicates that we are deprived of free choice, he is certainly indicating only that we cannot choose freely between good and evil... He certainly does not mean either that the will... is unfree or coerced in any way; nor does he mean that a person is not free to choose between Merlot and Cabernet Sauvignon'" (2013). However, Plantinga does concede that there are "several" Christian thinkers who have flirted with full determinism at the human level. Hence deeper examination of the extreme Calvinist position is worthwhile, as it may still offer us the potential for expressions of blame and indifference to the problem of moral luck in a world without free choice.

The eighteenth-century Puritan Calvinist preacher Jonathan Edwards is widely regarded as America's most important theologian – Plantinga grandly calls him "perhaps the greatest thinker America has produced" (2013) even as he rejects Edwards's embrace of determinism – and he was an inspiration towards the evangelistic fervour of what has come to be known as the Great Awakening. Edwards himself was writing after the Arminian revolt against the extreme Calvinist stance on predestination. In his 1754 work

Freedom of the Will, supposedly taking his lead from Luther, Edwards defended full theological determinism, arguing that the requirement for Pelagian/Arminian contra-causal self-creating libertarianism would have the effect of limiting God's sovereignty. Edwards did believe that free will existed, but for Edwards such free will was all about character, as our choice will always be what we most desire. Edwards argued we do have choice, but his definition of the term choice was solely that the agent would have chosen to have acted differently if he had possessed a better character. In other words Edwards was giving a standard compatibilist definition of free will without free choice. So could Edwards's justification of free will without free choice ground concepts of blame, (eternal) suffering, and indifference to the problem of moral luck? Yes, it could: but only if we take away individual human worth.

Edwards was not concerned with the problem of moral luck raised by the absence of free choice because – and only because – for Edwards human life held no intrinsic value. For Edwards only God's existence held value, and thus God could do what he liked with his creations. For Edwards it was as pointless to debate the injustice of man's deliberate suffering in the absence of free choice as it was to debate injustice towards any other part of God's Creation. God had already predivided the world into those He would save and those He would damn, and talking about the "injustice" of this or the "problem" of moral luck was pointless, as justice and luck didn't enter into the equation. God, for Edwards, was the only real cause of anything, deterministically arranging all events of every kind throughout the universe. Edwards was arguing against the view that it could ever be unfair to detest, blame, and condemn those who had no opportunity to do otherwise by suggesting that concepts such as unfairness are totally inappropriate when the only judge of fairness – indeed, the only true moral agent and thus the only judge of anything – can be God. Humans were little more than moveable counters – reactive ciphers – in Edwards's Puritan view of God and His Creation.

Of course there was a tradition long before Edwards of seeing humans as little more than God's playthings. According to Isaiah 45:9, we are but the clay which has no right to question the One that fashioned it. Or as Paul put it in Romans 10:20-1, we are potter's clay that could expect little consideration from the potter. The problem though with Edwards's argument, or any potter's clay argument, is that it seemingly has to be built upon the notion that human life holds little or no intrinsic worth separately from God's whimsical plan for it. This view makes it just about impossible to build any form of human morality. It's not certain, for example, that most small children cannot "justly" be horribly mutilated under Edwards's teaching, because if they are not judged to be part of the saved (traditionally, not all or even most of them can be) then nothing that happens to them can necessarily be judged to be unjust. All hopes for universal and objective human codes are immediately lost. Furthermore, even the elect – even the saved – are not valuable in and of themselves, but are just God's favoured toys, to be put back in the box for the next rainy day He feels like playing with them. The problem with the Edwards/extreme Calvinist stance is that it makes Dennett and Watson's disappearance of up to 20% of Western humanity seem positively amiable. Edwards appears to be making 100% of the human population disappear, by turning us from a valued and valuable form of life into nothing more than the bric-a-brac within God's toybox. Edwards achieves moral blameworthiness in the absence of free choice, but at the cost of human worthiness. Edwards's views were deeply controversial even at the time, and he himself admitted that most theologians – those he termed the "modern divines" rather than his ideal of the "reformed divines" – would be both indignant and contemptuous when they saw his defence of free will and just suffering in the absence of choice.

With time, Edwards's views have become harder to justify, not easier, because we largely live in a post-Puritan world where most mainstream religions have embraced the idea of the intrinsic value of individual human life.

Edwards's worldview rests on the need to deny the inherent value of human life largely because of a need to pass that value back to God. God's worth to Edwards was because He is the real and only First Cause, and only He has true free will. So it should perhaps be pointed out that attributing self-origination to God is just as problematic as attributing free will to man. Allocating value based solely on the possession of contra-causal free will does nothing other than push the free will problem back one step, because at the very least Edwards can provide no evidence that God can possess free will, so no evidence that God's existence has value, and thus no argument for why we should be listening to Him in the first place. Edwards's writing combines all the moral and intellectual failings of compatibilism and semi-compatibilism with a seeming betrayal of both God and man. There remains, though, the irony that extreme Calvinism of the sort endorsed by Edwards may in one limited sense be more morally robust than alternative secular theories like compatibilism, attitudinism, or semi-compatibilism. For all its underlying contempt for the value of human life and abased subservience to the ethereal there is one admirable component in Edwards's work which is entirely missing from the work of Dennett, Watson, P.F. Strawson, or Fischer. For all its mankind-abnegating faults, the extreme Calvinism we are considering here is at least objective and non-discriminatory. Edwards suggested that no human had a right to expect justice or fairness, and that all human life held no intrinsic worth. In direct contrast to this Dennett, Strawson, and Fischer, as well as essentialists like Watson, like to suggest that only some of us have the right to expect considerations of justice, opportunity and fairness.

"Attributing Cruelty and Injustice to God"

> "Why, you ask, is anything attributed to the freedom of the will, then? It is… to prevent calumnies attributing cruelty and injustice to God" (Erasmus, 1524, p.93).

Religious doctrine, and certainly Christian doctrine, would appear to have a serious problem with the possibility of Hell in the absence of free choice. Augustine knew this and was therefore driven to assert some form of free will, given that Christianity seemed to impose certain moral duties upon man. As Augustine understood it, God's eternal punishments would be unfair if man is not at liberty to follow freely but is in fact constrained. Of course, even given belief in free will, Hell has often been recognised as a troubling concept for Christianity. The Church father Origen was one of the first to hold to the conviction that notwithstanding freedom to choose a moral Christianity would be incompatible with the idea of eternal suffering. According to Origen, God's love was so strong that it would bring all souls, even the Devil, to ultimate salvation – and that all would eventually see the light, even if this takes many aeons. Knowledge of God will eventually broach even the hardest heart. Yet while the existence of Hell can be a problem for a loving Christianity even in a universe that hypothetically permits free choice, the idea of Hell becomes far more difficult to reconcile with the non-existence of free choice.

Philosophical justification for the existence of free will tries to hold on to the everyday concepts of blame and moral responsibility, yet there has been almost no attempt by contemporary philosophers to argue that we possess what has been called "Guilt-in-the-eyes-of-God". Dan Dennett, for example, argues (1984; 2014) that we have just enough free will to excuse human ideals of punishment and a low-level infliction of suffering, but he states clearly that we could never have the level of responsibility sufficient to excuse the eternal punishments of Hell. Yet Dennett justifies low-level suffering because he thinks that he has a solution to the otherwise troubling problem of moral luck. When we realise that Dennett and Watson fail to offer us any solution to the problem of moral luck even low-level suffering becomes unjustified, let alone the Christian notion of eternal suffering. There are people who believe, the eminent Oxford and Harvard philosopher Derek Parfit writes, that although our wrong acts are merely events in time (and are causally inevitable) we could deserve to be sent by God to suffer in Hell. But, suggests Parfit, this can only be justified by minimising, indeed ignoring, the cost of human suffering. Parfit continues:

"Of those who believe that we can deserve to suffer, some would give this counter-argument:

(W) God makes some people suffer in Hell.
(X) God is just.
Therefore
(R) we can deserve to suffer.
But we don't, I believe, know that (W) is true.
If we believe in a just God, we must accept either
(Y) God acts justly in making wrongdoers suffer in Hell, though it is unintelligible how such acts can be just,
or
(Z) God does not make anyone suffer in Hell.

Of these two claims, we would have more reason, I believe, to accept (Z). If God does not make anyone suffer in Hell, it may be surprising that so many people believe that God does act in this way. But we can understand how these people might have come to have this false belief, and we cannot understand how a just God could make anyone suffer in Hell. We can deserve many things... but no one could ever deserve to suffer" (2011, pp.271-2).

(Y) is a reformulation of the (for instance, Jonathan Edwards's) idea that human life holds no intrinsic value and thus it is meaningless to talk about problems like moral luck or unjust suffering. But most modern monotheistic religion has come to completely reject the idea that a just God would treat human life as valueless and meaningless in and of itself. If there is no free will and yet Hell still exists, then (following Erasmus) God would be shown to be both cruel and unjust because He would be treating humans with scant regard to the cost of human suffering or the value of human life. As Parfit points out, if we have to choose between claims (Y) and (Z) we would have far more reason to accept (Z), because – as we do lack contra-causal free will, and as we are in no way responsible for our own character – we cannot understand how a just God could make anyone suffer in Hell (assuming only human life to be valuable). In a universe without free will we can deserve many things, argues Parfit, including praise and the kind of blame that is merely moral dispraise, but no one could ever deserve to suffer.

Yet while it is impossible to reconcile the existence of the cruelties of Hell (or at least a populated Hell) with the divine valuing of human life in a universe without free will, Heaven becomes a headache too. While the possibility of eternal reward is not incompatible with a just and fair God in the way that the possibility of suffering is, the problem now becomes one of understanding who would get to go to Heaven. Parfit suggests that we can deserve gratitude and praise – though not blame or suffering – in a world without free will, in the sense that we can admire, applaud, be grateful for, and even reward the bravery we witness in someone without needing to believe that such bravery was self-created or did not rely on a fortuitously-created personality. And Heaven could theoretically exist whether or not we more deeply "deserve" praise and reward, in the same way that a theme park like Alton Towers could exist whether or not we "deserve" roller coasters in the deeper sense. However, the issue we will always have is over the justice of permitting entry to Heaven to some and not others in a world without free will. Dennett told us that there is a misplaced reverence for "an absolutist ideal: the concept of total, before-the-eyes-of-God Guilt" (1984, p.165). God, or at least a moral God, cannot blame and justify suffering. But just as He cannot blame and make suffer in this world without free choice, He cannot praise (or at least He cannot praise some and not others) because of exactly the same argument. There is no before-the-eyes-of-God *guilt*, but equally there can be no before-the-eyes-of-God *reward*. Either we all get rewarded, or none of us do. Hitler goes to Heaven or nobody does. Surely we have to conclude that Heaven, to the extent it even exists, is either going to be very full – Alton-Towers-on-a-summer-bank-holiday full – or completely empty? Just suffering is ruled out, but so is the partiality of eternal reward.

The story of Ebenezer Scrooge is supposed to be a largely Christian allegory of damnation and redemption, and a wonderful and moving tale it is indeed, even when performed by the Muppets. Yet this great story of Christian redemption is a classic example of the problem of moral luck, and the injustice of Hell or a Heaven with a dress code. As we know, Scrooge is the very worst of men, a selfish miser with a heart of stone: indifferent to the injustice of poverty, suffering, and the lack of hope and opportunity all around him in Victorian London. But the damned shade of Jacob Marley visits one evening, and Scrooge eventually comes to see his life in terms of the effect of his actions and inactions, and in terms of how he will suffer if he does not change. Having seen the error of his ways, and the pleasure of human interaction and kindness, Scrooge becomes the best of men. As Dickens wrote in *A Christmas Carol*: "He became as good a friend, as good a master, and as good a man, as the good old city knew, or any other good old city, town, or borough, in the good old world. Some people laughed to see the alteration in him, but he let them laugh, and little heeded them... His own heart laughed: and that was quite enough for him". But the problem with the tale as a morality play is one of moral luck. Scrooge was the worst of men who became the best of men, and thus he escaped Hell, because he received sufficient external intervention. He was frightened, coaxed, and cajoled into changing his ways. Marley continued to forge his chains in Hell because he was unlucky enough never to have received such lessons. Neither deserved the attention or inattention of the Christmas shades – the ghosts of Christmas Past, Present and Future – but one got them and was saved, while the other did not get them and was damned. There is absolutely no fairness in this, and pure moral luck. Even for the essentialists – who will completely miss the point of Dickens's story when they nevertheless try to claim, *Ah, yes, but there was something essential in good old (bad old) Ebenezer such that he was always going to benefit from the visitation, whereas Marley would never have changed his ways* – the point still becomes: how fair is this? After the last chapter we know that almost certainly with enough visitations, or early enough visitations, Marley could have changed – because we know that all essentialists themselves appear to be descended from slavers, rapists, reavers and butchers if you go back far enough – so where does it become fair that three visitations in your fifties is the right maximum level in a universe without free choice? That Scrooge was lucky enough to get the three at fifty he needed in order to change, while Marley was unlucky not to get the six at forty that would have changed him? Even if, and contrary to what we appeared to see in the last chapter, there was something essential in Marley such that he would never have changed even if the spirits visited him nightly from the age of ten, how is this anything other than unfairness that Marley has to suffer because he was unlucky enough to be born with this essential badness? What is supposed to be a wonderful allegory of the power of

Christian redemption becomes a morality play broken on the problems of moral luck, justified suffering, and the partiality of salvation and reward.

So the problem is this: who would deserve entry to Heaven in a universe without free will? If we start by saying that it is self-evident that really bad people could never deserve to go to eternal reward, the first question then becomes this: where do we even draw a line? Heaven is supposed to be a reward for virtue; but who is truly virtuous, at least in the Judaeo-Christian tradition? For seventeen hundred years Christian theologians have made God appear cruel and unjust through the heterodox doctrine of free will. Surely no traditionalist since the third century merits entry to Heaven, as otherwise God would be rewarding failure, ignorance and betrayal? St Augustine and Thomas Aquinas never merited entry to Heaven. And yet why not? Augustine and Aquinas cannot be blamed for their betrayal of God. They never wanted to betray God: they were just unlucky enough to be raised in periods where it was difficult to make sense of the facts. Yet if Augustine and Aquinas get to go to Heaven despite their betrayal of God – their betrayal of Christianity – where will the line be drawn? Why not Judas Iscariot, another great betrayer of God? Well, Judas knowingly betrayed God, while Augustine unknowingly betrayed God. Really? That the notion of free will is a potential intellectual and moral fraud had been known to mankind, or at least to its scholarly centres, for centuries before Augustine was around, so you could argue this was close to wilful blindness, and therefore wilful betrayal. Yet even if we do allow there to be a distinction between knowing and unknowing betrayal of God, Judas deserves no greater blame than Augustine because his knowing betrayal was no more free than Augustine's unknowing betrayal. If you are going to reward one with Heaven, why not the other, because it will be unjust to make any real distinction between the two? And if Judas goes to Heaven, why not Cassius and Brutus, Dante's two other great sinners in the innermost circle of Hell? And if Cassius and Brutus, why not also Osama bin Laden and Adolf Hitler?

And if we all get to go to Heaven, is this only after we admit our mistakes? The moral necessity, in a universe without free choice, of Hitler or bin Laden going to Heaven if others do is one thing. The idea of Hitler striding through the pearly gates in his trademark jackboots and leather coat, or bin Laden refusing to first hand over his Semtex and AK47, is quite another. The jackboots would surely have to be removed, literally and figuratively. But if we have to admit our moral and intellectual mistakes first this will require a complete character transplant, and not just for Hitler and bin Laden but perhaps also for many contemporary philosophers. So who, in a deeper sense, is being admitted? Is Hitler without the jackboots still Hitler, or bin Laden without the Semtex still bin Laden (as this appears to be a complete personality wipe)? And yet who deserves to have their personality, however vile a personality, wiped in a universe without free choice? The personality is the individual in the most fundamental way. If the personality doesn't get admittance then the individual doesn't really get admittance, either. How fair is that? Our personalities change and mature over a lifetime, but this is very different from saying that a personality needs first to be rewritten. And yet of course Hitler cannot be admitted with the jackboots, or bin Laden with the Semtex, because that would be deeply offensive in so many ways (and rewarding immorality). The idea of Heaven itself thus appears to be a paradox. Yet if we start at the other end when considering who gets to enter Heaven, thinking not about the very evil but about the very good, we face similar problems. We might feel on safer ground suggesting that the deeply angelic deserve entry, but what have such people actually done to deserve eternal reward? Generally they were lucky to be smart and educated in the first place, came from nurturing families, and were lucky to be lucky (to have been exposed to the teachers and ideas that allowed them to champion human progress, or challenge received wisdom). The non-existence of free choice does not rule out the possibility of reward in Heaven in the same way that it does rule out the possibility of suffering in Hell, but it still calls for some radical rethinking of the concept of the partiality of eternal reward.

Will Provine of Cornell University, one of America's longest-standing academic critics of the conceit of freedom of the will, calls the Christian belief in free will the "fangs" of an otherwise beautiful and morally positive religious system (pers. comm., 1 Feb 2008). While it is difficult not to agree with his point, monotheistic – and monist – religion unfortunately seems to contain within itself the seeds of its own moral and intellectual corruption. Monism, unless taught very carefully and thoughtfully, tends to be pregnant with the assumption of free will, notwithstanding what we may have said earlier about the doctrine of free will not being foundational to Judaism or Christianity. Monism is the idea that everything, including evil, comes from a single God, in contrast to dualism, where good tends to come from God and evil from some sort of malign anti-God figure. Christianity and Judaism are thus both monist and monotheistic religions, yet the problem with attributing the existence of evil to God rather than some form of anti-God is that the faithful may always try to find a way to relieve the monist God of responsibility for that evil. So, the argument goes, God gave man free will to decide between good and evil: evil is no longer God's problem but man's problem. Monism tends to lean towards internally corrupting into a way to blame mankind – or parts of mankind – simply to avoid blaming an omnipotent God. Recalling the words of Erasmus, cruelty and injustice have now been attributed back from God to man, in order to get a supposedly omnipotent God off the hook for the Problem of Evil. It is particularly depressing that the conceit of free will seems almost pregnant within monist religion as it is only by abandoning belief in free will that we can get all that is supposed to be best in Judaeo-Christianity. In *The Spontaneous Self: Viable Alternatives to Free Will*, Paul Breer noted that:

> "Much of the behaviour that Western religion defines as virtuous and exhorts us to emulate will arise spontaneously when we give up our belief in agency. I refer to humility, patience, forgiveness (acceptance), turning the other cheek (non-defensiveness), not craving or clinging to objects or people, not seeking our own glory, and not protesting adversity. If 'virtues' of this kind seem out of reach to most of us, it is primarily because we insist on seeing ourselves as the causes of our own behaviour" (1989, p.143).

Shariff, Baumeister, and Clark claim to have empirically demonstrated Breer's point that countries with higher belief in free will have lower levels of forgiveness, that most Christian of virtues (Shariff et al., in press). Breer's claim – that Christian virtues often seem out of reach to us primarily because we see ourselves as a First Cause (and thus rarely acknowledge our debt to others and to what has gone before) – still needs to be validated, but it is difficult not to at least see the argument. Breer goes on to claim that the concept of free will (with its conceit of self-made First Causes) naturally breeds egocentricity, and advises that the myth of free will inculcates defensiveness, pride, and disdain for others (plus the ready excuse to give up on others and minimise any sense of obligation to our fellows – sentiments supposedly opposed by the mainstream Christian virtues). Breer's claim that rejection of free will inculcates the Judaeo-Christian virtues was also noted by Einstein, both before the Spinoza Society in 1932 and when corresponding with a colleague in 1948. Einstein had found recognition of the absence of choice a continual consolation in the face of life's hardships and an unfailing wellspring of tolerance and love of one's neighbour. "I cannot hate him, because he *must* do what he does," as Einstein put it (Jammer 1999, p.87). The Stoics recognised over two thousand years ago that one of the benefits of an acceptance of determinism at the human level was a calmness of the soul and equanimity in the face of life's trials, while it is the free will illusionist Saul Smilansky who has written that acceptance of the hard determinist picture "presents the anti-luck 'here but for the grace of God' thought overwhelmingly" (1997, p.95). And even if Breer is largely wrong about the spontaneous emergence he describes, we will nevertheless still be forced by our rehabilitated institutions to behave morally and fairly once we abandon our attachment to the myth of free will. Liberal religion may have far less to fear from the death of the free will conceit than it may imagine, and much to celebrate.

Irreligion and Religion As Equally Morally Flawed

"Everything happens through immutable laws... There are persons who, frightened by this truth, admit half of it, as debtors who offer half to their creditors, and ask respite for the rest. 'There are,' they say, 'some events which are necessary, and others which are not'" (Voltaire, *Philosophical Dictionary*, 1764, pp.100-101).

On 10 April 2008, at its annual Voltaire Lecture, the British Humanist Association – Vice President one Richard Dawkins – allowed its invited speaker Raymond Tallis to explicitly link humanism with belief in free will. Tallis, a physician and philosopher, stated that: "The notion that we humans are in an important sense free – and in this regard different from any other living creature – is central to humanism" (2008). Tallis's lecture was a bizarre anti-materialist and anti-scientific polemic against "what we feared: that our brain is calling the shots", and Tallis rounded off with his contention that "intentionality is entirely mysterious and not, at any rate, to be explained in terms of the processes and laws that operate in the material world". Oh, really? The lecture was the most extraordinary confusion of fatalism and determinism, of conflation of libertarianism and compatibilism, and of a failure to accept the scientific consensus or recognise the difference between the free will problem and the entirely separate nature/nurture debate. Quite what Voltaire, ardent materialist and tireless critic of the free will conceit, would have made of his name being co-opted into a BHA tirade seeking to separate mankind from the rest of the natural world is anyone's guess, but institutional humanism has a long track record of being on the wrong side in the free will debates. Corliss Lamont was a Marxist philosopher who became president emeritus of the American Humanist Association, and in 1977 was named Humanist of the Year. In *The Philosophy of Humanism* Lamont counselled all fellow humanists to reject the idea of a deterministic cause-effect sequence within the human brain. Humans, he wrote, were genuine First Causes of events. As with Tallis, Lamont had a tendency to confuse determinism and fatalism and, like most libertarians, gave the subjective sensation of free choice as his objective proof of free choice. While few secularists are as extreme in their anti-materialism as Lamont and Tallis, we have already seen that a number of the most influential intellectual atheists are simultaneously ardent propagandists for the irrational myths of free will, including both Dan Dennett and Steve Jones.

Jim Al-Khalili, physicist, broadcaster and atheist, has written that, while believing in God is fine by him, "we still have a long way to go if we are to rid the world of the bigoted attitudes held and injustices carried out in the name of religion" (2013). While one can surely agree with Al-Khalili on this, it is not enough to just slightly distance oneself from what he calls the zealotry of sections of the militant group known as the New Atheists, including leading lights Dennett and Richard Dawkins. It is not enough for Al-Khalili, now President of the BHA, to suggest that the New Atheists have "laid the foundations" upon which the "New, New Atheists", as he calls them – those who have gone beyond the one-sided zealotry of Dawkins and Dennett – can now build. Because if we, the non-zealots, have a moral and intellectual duty to face up to the bigoted attitudes held and injustices carried out in the name of religion, surely we also have a moral and intellectual duty to face down the bigoted attitudes held by and injustices carried out in the name of both humanism and militant atheism? It is atheists like Dan Dennett, and not theists, who have openly written off the least fortunate 20% in America when defining concepts of equality, opportunity, and fair play. It is humanists like Gary Watson, and not the religious, who have split mankind into two forms, and written that "there is room for the thought" that we (the physically blessed) can take credit for our great good fortune, with the distasteful corollary that those who are born physically and mentally different may somehow be to blame for their handicaps and misfortunes.

It is humanists and intellectual atheists who have behaved at least as badly as – if not worse than – theists, when it comes to the free will conceit. Theists tend to be libertarians, actually believing – quite erroneously, of course – that free choice may be possible. Humanists and atheists, in contrast, tend to overwhelmingly make up the ranks of the compatibilists, attitudinists, and illusionists. It is humanists and atheists who tend to be not ignorant of the problem of moral luck, but indifferent to the problem of moral luck. It tends to be humanists and atheists who do not care that some of us are born vastly more lucky than others, and who do not care that some are born and raised in great misfortune, with absolutely zero opportunity. "In fact, I will argue, it is seldom that we even *seem* to care whether or not a person could have done otherwise" (Dennett 1984, p.133). Theists at least have the excuse that they have tended to be wrong because they didn't know any better: they started from the misunderstanding that free choice was possible. Many of the most profoundly intellectual humanists and atheists have been wrong despite knowing better: have deliberately looked the other way and taken "care not to examine too closely" (p.164). This is a very significant moral difference. Furthermore, where theists have been misguided in positing freedom of choice, the motivation has at least appeared to be the pursuit of external justice, however misplaced that pursuit might have been. When Erasmus noted that the conceit of free will protected God from criticism, it was in order to try to make sense of a confusing (and confused) God-centred worldview. When Jonathan Edwards used the free will conceit to turn humans into worthless ciphers, it was in order to try to make sense of a confusing (and confused) God-centred view of the world. Such religious justification of the free will conceit, objective and justice-seeking even if profoundly misguided, often seems to be the opposite of the prejudiced and subjective "Is it fair?... Life isn't fair" indifference to injustice displayed by many of the militant atheists. So it is not enough for Jim Al-Khalili to reaffirm the call to arms against "the bigoted attitudes held and injustices carried out in the name of religion" while refusing to confront the bigoted attitudes held and injustices carried out in the name of humanism and militant atheism.

We saw in a previous section that monism may have an inbuilt tendency towards moral corruption, yet we have now seen that humanism and atheism may be just as unsafe a pair of moral hands. The truth of course is that often there are the same intellectual and moral weaknesses, just as there are similar intellectual and moral strengths – as is perhaps only to be expected, given that they share such common roots. The leftist philosopher Jürgen Habermas upset many of his atheistic colleagues when he supported, in 1999, Nietzsche's insight that the values of modern secular humanism are the direct intellectual legacy of Judaeo-Christianity. "Universalistic egalitarianism, from which sprang the ideals of freedom and a collective life in solidarity, the autonomous conduct of life and emancipation, the individual morality of conscience, human rights and democracy, is the direct legacy of the Judaic ethic of justice and the Christian ethic of love... To this day, there is no alternative to it. And in light of the current challenges of a postnational constellation, we continue to draw on the substance of this heritage. Everything else is just idle postmodern talk" (2006, pp.150-151). Religion has been, and continues to be, capable of great wickedness and a lack of compassion just as it has been (and continues to be) capable of great goodness and overwhelming compassion. Such ambivalence is true, too, of humanism, which has driven forward vast intellectual and ethical inquiry even as it often remains blind to its own irrationality, prejudice, indifference, and consequentialism. We may have little option but to conclude that both moral and intellectual probity require a dynamic and creative tension that will involve theist as much as atheist, philosopher as much as scientist, and conservative as much as liberal.

8

WE ARE NOT ALL EQUAL
BEFORE THE LAW

Whenever people are punished, the scope of injustice is overwhelming.

Saul Smilansky, *Free Will and Illusion* (2000, p.256).

To what extent is it true to say that the Western law is built upon the presupposition of free choice? H.L.A. Hart, Professor of Jurisprudence at Oxford, was one of the most influential legal philosophers of the modern age, in particular as regards the relationship between law and morality. "Nonetheless," wrote Hart, "most lawyers, laymen and moralists... would conclude that what the law has done here is to reflect, albeit imperfectly, a fundamental principle of morality that a person is not to be blamed for what he has done if he could not help doing it". Choice to do or avoid the act in question, Hart continued, is "the only thing that renders human actions praiseworthy or culpable" (1968, p.174). But in saying this Hart was also contradicting himself, as he simultaneously suggested that he could reconcile freedom and determinism, though some legal scholars – for example, Alan Norrie, in a 1983 paper in the journal *Legal Studies* – have pointed out that Hart's understanding of the idea of choice did not truly reflect an understanding of the constraints posed by determinism.

Yet Hart's seeming confusion helps to underscore the profound difficulty for the law of a world without free choice. As Saul

Smilansky has written, Hart appears clear that whether or not he thought he could reconcile the present Anglo-American criminal law with determinism he seemed pessimistic that he could ever reconcile Anglo-American criminal justice with determinism. "What I have written concerns only *legal* responsibility and the rationale of excuses in the legal system in which there are organized, coercive sanctions", wrote Hart. "I do not think the same arguments can be used to defend *moral* responsibility from the determinist" (1968, p.53). Hart seemed to understand that the law may not be threatened by determinism and the lack of free choice but that the possibility of justice or fairness within that system of law is. Smilansky points out that this distinction would make it "very problematic" for the legal system (2000, p.86), partly because we have a tendency to flatter ourselves, and we don't like understandings that challenge our belief in our own probity and moral and judicial integrity. Today, the underlying assumption of free choice still exists unchallenged in many corners of the criminal law. English law seems to presume the existence of *liberum arbitrium*, of freedom of the will – of the idea that people can have chosen to have done otherwise. Quoting the QC Helena Kennedy, one of the most influential legal scholars working in the public eye in Britain today, and speaking on Radio 4 to UCL's Steve Jones: "I think that we'd still hold on to the idea that in each and every one of us, for the most part, we're able to exercise free will" (2011). In his history of the legal trial, barrister Sadakat Kadri notes that while there would always be debate over exactly what free will meant, "Europe's theologians and lawyers always agreed that innocence and guilt depended on the rational exercise of free will" (2005, p.159). Richard Oerton, a lawyer who has worked at the Law Commission, the law reform body established by Parliament, writes that the idea of free will as free choice, "is central to the" English and Welsh criminal law, and that judges "quite clearly" believe that the offender could have done otherwise (2012, p.69). Oerton notes that section 142 of the Criminal Justice Act

2003, in declaring for the first time by statute the aims of sentencing, makes it clear that retributory punishment based on the assumption of freedom of choice is the primary goal of the criminal justice system. Or as Eric Metcalfe, barrister and director of human rights policy at the all-party British law reform organisation JUSTICE, put it: "A world in which human beings lacked free will would require a radically different conception of criminal responsibility" (pers. comm., 16 July 2004).

In contrast with the UK it is often said that the US criminal law is officially compatibilist, and thus indifferent to questions of freedom of choice (the ability to have done otherwise). Yet even with the American law there is evidence that the current system, federal and state, presupposes freedom of choice and despite what may otherwise be claimed. The late Chief Judge David Bazelon, one of the leading modern American legal causal theorists and a pioneer in the field of mental health law, argued that "it has been asserted repeatedly [by the law] that only a free choice to do wrong will be punished" (1976, p.389). Attorney Robert Gulack writes that when the District of Columbia established a definition of criminal responsibility over fifty years ago that did not assume the reality of free will, the courts threw out that definition later on and went back to a definition relying on the assumption of free will (2004). Gulack further notes that in New Jersey today it is against the law to doubt the existence of free will in the courtroom: you can't even bring it up, he suggests. And according to the online version of the Dean's Law Dictionary, the former dean of Harvard Law School Roscoe Pound asserted that "historically, our substantive criminal law is based upon a theory of punishing the vicious will. It postulates a free agent confronted with a choice between doing right and doing wrong and choosing freely to do wrong". Turning to the US Supreme Court we find that in the 1952 case of Morissette v. United States it was stated that "it is as universal and persistent in mature systems of law as belief in freedom of the human will and a consequent ability and duty of the normal individual to choose between good and evil". Similarly the 1978 Supreme Court case of United States v. Grayson stated that "a deterministic view of human conduct [] is inconsistent with the underlying precepts of our criminal justice system".

And yet challenges to the stated presumption of legal compatibilism have not been without their own problems. Bazelon, and modern causal theorists like Anders Kaye at the Thomas Jefferson School of Law, have tended to misunderstand determinism. In particular, they have sought to keep alive the idea of "partial determinism". Law professor Michael S. Moore has termed (partial) causal theory "degree determinism" and has said that "to speak of being partly determined or partly free makes as much sense as to speak of being partly pregnant" (1985, p.1116). The partly pregnant joke only half works here, though, because Moore is wrong to suggest that human actions could not contain both a deterministic element and an indeterministic element, at least in theory and aside from considerations of decoherence. Degree, or partial, determinism as a legal theory is completely unhelpful: not because human thought processes cannot contain an indeterministic component, but because we can never be free. And yet resistance to the deterministic understanding by even the self-styled causal theorists appears just as deeply held as it is by Moore himself. For example, Anders Kaye seems positively unnerved by the thought of complete determinism, such as when he writes that absolute determinism is a "dangerous" and "devastating" belief, and that this concern should drive us towards partial, or degree, determinism. "The result is a prudent partial determinism," Kaye says, arguing that his and Bazelon's work makes no claims "as to whether other or all acts are determined acts" (2005, pp.1119-23). The resistance to accepting the impossibility of free choice seems as great within the causal theorists as we shall find it to be with supposed legal compatibilists like Michael S. Moore.

An Examination of the Legal Compatibilist Position

"Once, it was common for criminal theorists to say that the criminal law takes the originationist approach to responsibility. Today, however, it is more common to say we have a compatibilist criminal law" (Anders Kaye, 2007, p.367).

Stephen J. Morse is Ferdinand Wakeman Hubbell Professor of Law at the University of Pennsylvania, and he has for more than three decades been the doyen of legal compatibilists: the doyen of those who appear to argue that justice can be blind to questions of freedom of choice; indifferent to questions of true desert. And yet when you actually analyse his work he regularly claims the opposite. Morse freely acknowledges that "hard determinism can neither explain our practices nor ground a theory of desert" (2004, p.431), while he tells us approvingly that "most theorists believe that a moral decision for conviction requires... an actor who 'could have done other'" (1976, p.1257). "All of us choose our behavior" (p.1251), Morse tells us, "behavior *is* a matter of choice" (p.1252). We are all capable, he says, "of that most human capacity, the power to choose" (p.1268). It is choice, Morse tells us, and choice alone, which means that "convicted criminals deserve the punishment society allots to their offenses" (p.1266). Morse, the senior figure within the stable of the legal compatibilists, apparently believes in both the possibility of free choice and that free choice is absolutely necessary to ground a theory of desert and justify retributive practices.

On closer analysis Morse is more confused and confusing about the free will question than he initially appears, even suggesting that real freedom of choice is compatible with complete determinism. How can Morse possibly accept that the universe is deterministic at the human level but still believe in freedom of choice? "Determinism does not entail a finding of compulsion or absence of choice", Morse writes (1984, p.1488). Free choice simply must exist, Morse tells us, as the "vast majority" born into poverty do not break the law (1976, p.1254). Morse appears to believe that human life is made up of three factors – biology, environment, and free will – because, for Morse, two of those three factors have no possible nuances. Hence without free will all exposed to poverty, Morse seems to argue, would commit crime – or all exposed to poverty would not commit crime, as biology and environment are supposedly identical for all. Ignoring basic points about differential biology here, behavioural geneticists stopped arguing three decades ago that any two humans can ever have shared the same environment, recognising the importance of what is called non-shared environment. Two brothers will share certain experiences – same parent, same school – yet have just as many unique experiences: relationship with parents, their sibling, teachers, and friends. No two humans, not even the most closely-raised identical twins, have ever shared the same upbringing, as to do so they would have had to have looked out from the same pair of eyes. Many raised in poverty do not commit crime not because they differentially exercise that third factor, their free will, but because all humans have unique experiences of just two complex and interacting factors: the genetic and environmental worlds. Morse appears to be woefully blind to the wonderful contingency of human life and, like many who defend free choice, Morse gives surprisingly little value to human individuality. "Determinism", says Morse, "does not entail a finding of compulsion or absence of choice". Unfortunately for Morse an absence of choice is exactly what determinism implies. So quite patently it does matter to the law whether free choice exists – at least according to Morse, the senior theorist within the compatibilist tradition. You can only coherently say free choice is irrelevant to the law – the legal compatibilist position – if the existing theory of desert is applicable to both the situation where free choice exists and to the situation where free choice does not exist. If you admit that if free choice does not exist the existing theory of desert does not work then the legal compatibilist framework was nonsense to begin with.

Another legal compatibilist who tries to argue the law does not require freedom of choice (but whose own work seems to require freedom of choice) is Michael S. Moore. Moore is author of *Placing Blame: A Theory of the Criminal Law*, which is apparently one of the leading modern statements of the retributivist theory of punishment. But, despite claiming to be a compatibilist, Moore clearly calls for a libertarian requirement to justify the current legal position. It is because individuals could have done otherwise, says Moore, and it is because individuals have a degree of freedom of choice that current practices, including retributivism, are just. Moore is patently giving us a libertarian interpretation of the law here, based on a belief in could-have-done-otherwise – based on a belief in an element of free choice – but Moore's argument for could-have-done-otherwise is no more valid than any other libertarian argument that has been proposed. Moore argues that an individual could have done otherwise "*if* he had chosen (or willed) to do otherwise" (1985, p.1142). This is an argument which philosophers have previously debated but is one that they have largely given up on, because to say an individual could have done otherwise *if* he had willed to have done otherwise is logically like saying a dog would have a curly tail *if* it was a pig. As we saw in an earlier chapter (when we looked at this argument in slightly more detail) conditionality is not applicable here, as no individual ever could have willed to have done otherwise in either a deterministic universe or an indeterministic universe. At any particular moment an individual could only have willed to have done otherwise if his biology or experiences to that date had been different. Hence an individual could only have done otherwise if, in effect, he had happened to have been a different person. There is no ability to have done otherwise for the individual offered here and hence any claims that an individual could have done otherwise are axiomatically false. And yet Moore, nominally a compatibilist, claims that could-have-done-otherwise *at the individual level*, and not at the *alternative person* level, is necessary for the law's infliction of deep suffering because "what could be more unfair than punishing someone for something he could not help?" (1985, p.1112). Moore goes on to emphasise not only the injustice of retribution in the absence of the ability to have done otherwise, but his belief that the law is indeed originationist (the claim of those, like Bazelon, that he has always vehemently denied): "The law demands more than that we *pretend* people are free and thus hold them responsible *as if* they were" (p.1122). This tendency (for those who are nominally compatibilists to turn out to have serious problems with justifying a robust platform of legal compatibilism) appears widespread. To quote another highly influential legal compatibilist R. Jay Wallace, it is the "default position" of society that "it would not be justifiable to hold people morally responsible for what they do if determinism were true" (1994, p.222).

An intelligible legal compatibilism would thus seem to require theorists to stand up and say what Dennett says, which is that he does not (and the law should not) "care whether or not a person could have done otherwise" (1984, p.133). This would at least be an internally coherent legal compatibilist position, but what we get from Morse and Moore is emphatically not the compatibilist argument that the law does not care whether or not a person could have done otherwise. For Morse could-have-done-otherwise is the only explanation that can "ground a theory of desert". For Moore could-have-done-otherwise is a prerequisite because there is nothing more unfair than "punishing someone for something he could not help". And for Wallace could-have-done-otherwise is key, as everyone seems to understand deep down that "it would not be justifiable to hold people morally responsible" in the absence of the ability to have done otherwise. Dennett, and not Morse or Moore, is the one giving us the coherent argument of legal compatibilism. Why is Dennett able to make the coherent legal compatibilist argument when Morse and Moore cannot? The difference between Dennett and Morse and Moore is apparently that Morse and Moore know they need to give a theory of justice that at least appears to apply to 100% of the population. In contrast, Dennett's (or Watson's) theory of "justice" begins by simply writing off the least fortunate 1 to 20% of the population. Hence, could-have-done-otherwise becomes largely irrelevant – as you are then left only with the 80 to 99% who never needed to have done otherwise to have successful lives.

> "Dennett does not argue that our moral responsibility system is fair; rather, it is *fair enough*... Dennett seems comfortable with 'fair enough', and he can champion such a system and not blink" (Bruce Waller, 2012).

As H.L.A. Hart recognised, there is a vast difference between defending a system of law and defending a system of justice. Morse and Moore need to be seen to at least try to defend a system of justice. Dennett, the great utilitarian and proponent of "Is it fair? Life isn't fair" aphorisms (and the sacrifice of others) needs only defend a system of law.

Let us turn now from Stephen J. Morse and the arch retributivist Michael S. Moore as putative champions of a system of justice, and examine instead some of the more uncomfortable statements that come along with legal compatibilists' desire to nevertheless defend current practice in a deterministic universe. Firstly, there is a serious question mark over intellectual coherence. So, for example, Morse has written that legal compatibilism has no moral case to answer "even if determinism is true – and we shall never know" (2004, p.348). Yet we do already know that at the human level determinism is true, even were we to assume indeterminism at the subatomic level. Human actions are not the result of indeterminism due to decoherence, but putting this to one side a human action which was the result of an indeterministic event would still therefore have a causal trigger (see Chapter Three), be no less determined than if it were the result of biology and environment, and be no less prone to the core could-have-done-otherwise problem that Morse admitted to above. Morse also writes that "I claim that the explanation of human action is still mysterious, despite the herculean efforts of the metaphysicians" (1994, p.1588), but human action is not at all mysterious in that it comes down to the complex interaction of two factors: biology and environment. There is no mystery at all here. There is complexity, certainly, but no mystery. Remember that legal compatibilism is supposed to be able to acknowledge the truths of determinism, of the lottery of biology and environment – so the question remains why Morse is so adamantly opposed to accepting the truths that scientific compatibilism and philosophical compatibilism would admit to. Such seemingly wilful blindness to modern intellectual life by senior theorists does the US law no favours.

Equally unappealing is where legal compatibilism downplays the widely-accepted logical implications of determinism. Morse has written that even if one accepts determinism is true "how hard is it not to offend the law? The criminal law sets very low standards; it asks very little of us... it is simply not that hard to obey" (1984, pp.1498-9), and "we are all capable of obeying the law" (p.1504). But this is the entire point under discussion, and the lack of free choice would make it physically impossible in this or any other universe for a particular individual to have acted otherwise without the aid of external intervention or a different upbringing. Morse may believe in libertarian free will, but he is head of a school that professes to be vindicated even if free choice does not exist. Hence, just asking *How hard is it not to offend the law?* is, in the opinion of the author, deeply questionable and prejudicial when the law itself is supposed – under the wider understanding of legal compatibilism – to already be able to accept the meta-ethical limitations of determinism (including that an actor could not have chosen not to offend) and yet still be able to accommodate such determinism within a compatibilist theory of desert. In his classic 1968 *Punishment and Responsibility: Essays in the Philosophy of Law*, seen as a cornerstone of penal philosophy and criminal law theory, H.L.A. Hart stated that what is called the choice theory of punishment was appealing for many reasons, one of which was that it gives citizens the reassuring impression that they can avoid punishment by making prudent choices. Yet logic tells us that such prudent choices are simply not possible for a substantial section of the population, so in this sense choice theory is recognisably partial, self-serving, and perhaps even duplicitous.

We must also ask to what extent it is at all meaningful to assert that the law is compatibilist (and therefore indifferent to the question of free choice) when both juries and voters overwhelmingly and mistakenly believe in the existence of choice. The Harvard and Princeton psychologists Joshua Greene and Jonathan Cohen have written: "We argue that current legal doctrine, although officially compatibilist, is ultimately grounded in [moral] intuitions that are incompatibilist and, more specifically, libertarian... At present, the gap between what the law officially cares about and what people really care about is only revealed occasionally" (2004, pp.1775-6). Greene and Cohen point out that Morse himself admits that the public's moral intuitions may actually be libertarian, and that once the public realises that there is no libertarian free will it may demand significant change. The experimental compatibilist Eddy Nahmias has admitted that even his own studies appear to show that between two thirds and three quarters of the most highly-educated subjects (college students) think that at any given moment people can choose to do otherwise. In one scenario 67% thought that we are always free to choose and in another 76% thought so (Nahmias et al., 2005). Some legal compatibilists have already accepted that even partial recognition of a lack of free choice may force us to promote a less brutal judicial system, with Morse for example admitting (1994) that worries over free choice already show the need for limited reform of the current system. Moreover, the legal compatibilist tradition does not appear to be economically and socially neutral. Anders Kaye points out that the legal compatibilist approach is more conducive to the use of state violence against the disadvantaged than an approach which recognises the absence of choice. In his paper *The Secret Politics of the Compatibilist Criminal Law* Kaye notes that the disadvantaged tend to be "disproportionately – though not exclusively – people of color... This is also the group with the most reason to criticize and challenge the social order... It follows that the compatibilist criminal law will more frequently punish the disadvantaged" (2007, pp.418-9), and that compatibilist criminal rhetoric is not politically neutral and that it acts "to disempower those at the bottom of the social order" (p. 368).

What Would Be a Morally Robust Legal System?

"What could be more unfair than punishing someone for something he could not help?" (Michael S. Moore, 1985, p.1112).

One of those who does hold to the line that the current US penal practices can be compatible with a lack of free choice is the hard compatibilist Peter Arenella. As we have seen already, Arenella is a legal theorist who accepts that determinism would mean that "some moral agents will have a far easier time than others in exercising their moral capacities" (1992, p.1614). Arenella's argument, which somewhat echoes the earlier concerns of H.L.A. Hart, is that while it is possible to reconcile present legal and penal practices with the lack of choice in a brutal pragmatic sense, you cannot invoke a moral case for doing so. Affixing blame has no deep moral legitimacy, according to Arenella, and is simply there for the utilitarian need to "soothe our collective social conscience" (p.1533). Derk Pereboom reminds us that no less a character than John Stuart Mill similarly remarked that (given the problem of moral luck and the realisation that none of us make our character) "as a refuge from this view, 'men imagined what they called the freedom of the will – fancying that they could not justify punishing a man whose will is in a thoroughly hateful state unless it be supposed to have come into that state through no influence of anterior circumstances'". The point being, says Pereboom, that legal systems search for "beliefs that justify the violence they carry out" (2001, p.210). And the more violent the system, the more firmly theorists can thus be expected to cling to quasi-mystical justifications for such violence. Or, as Arenella prefers to put it, "perhaps all this legal rhetoric about 'just deserts' and moral responsibility is just the law's way of legitimating one form of human suffering" (1992, p.1608).

A lack of free choice can neither explain our practices nor ground a theory of desert, says Stephen J. Morse (2004). So one of the ethical effects of recognition of a lack of free choice must surely be radical revision of the current penal system and its sanctions, and in particular the indifference to cruelty and suffering seemingly engendered by belief in free choice and recognised in the work of, among others, Carey and Baumeister. After all, as the philosopher Ted Honderich notes, "retributive desires are attached to the idea that the person in question... could have done other than the thing he did" (2002, p.473). The lawyer Richard Oerton quoted earlier goes on to argue that retributivism is "inseparable" from belief in free choice, that the term retributive justice is "a contradiction in terms" in a universe without free choice, and that basing the English and Welsh criminal law on the incorrect belief that we act under freedom of choice is "… well, let's call a spade a spade; it's savagery, cruelty" (2012, pp.130-6). And the evidence does appear to show a deep connection between belief in could-have-done-otherwise and the idea of justified suffering. Rape in the US prison system, and quasi-official toleration and even celebration of such rape, has become such an embarrassment that there is now a federally-convened National Prison Rape Elimination Commission. US prison rape is no longer viewed as an unfortunate and unintended by-product of close incarceration, because for many Americans it appears to have become an accepted and endorsed part of the retributivist prison experience. "Americans now recognize sexual abuse as a violent crime with life-changing consequences. Yet the public has been slow to incorporate that perspective into its understanding of sexual violence in correctional environments. Many still consider sexual abuse an expected consequence of incarceration, part of the penalty" (NPREC, 2009, p.25). Or as a *Washington Post* editorial put it after the NPREC report was released, "A culture that jokes about prison rape perpetuates the expectation that rape is a legitimate part of the prison sentence. It is not" (Washington Post, 2009). Toleration of prison rape appears to be part of a wider American satisfaction with the brutalisation and humiliation of offenders. Yale Law Professor Dan Kahan is a leading exponent of the shaming and degradation of prisoners, and he has written that "by inflicting countless other indignities – from exposure to the view of others when urinating and defecating to rape at the hands of other inmates – prison unambiguously marks the lowness of those we consign to it" (Kahan, 1998, p.1642). Kahan here cites without demur another legal theorist's description of criminals as "scum" and the "filth" of humanity, and writes of the importance of cruelty within the penal process, identifying himself with Jeremy Bentham, the late eighteenth-century philosopher who likened criminals to excrement. The free will debates exemplify the unwillingness to feel gratitude for one's own great good fortune in life or acknowledge others' far greater misfortune, and it is difficult not to conclude that were the deep problem of moral luck to be widely appreciated it would have a profound effect on the language that society would feel comfortable to tolerate.

Legal scholars like Michael S. Moore, and philosophers like Dennett, P.F. Strawson, and Smilansky, like to suggest both that the law cannot be changed and that it would actually be unjust to build a legal system upon the recognition that there is no freedom of choice. Moore in particular is noted for his arguments that suffering and retributivism are not only just but that we honour criminals when we make them suffer grievously. So presumably the more we make them suffer, the more we are honouring them. In fact Bruce Waller has pointed out that the notorious Christian apologist C. S. Lewis made exactly this argument that "however severely" we punish criminals we are honouring them as persons "made in God's image". And, in response to the philosopher Angela Smith's argument that not punishing criminals would be a "patronizing and disrespectful stance", the normally placid Waller is driven to deep scorn: "Locking [Robert] Harris in a cage until we drag him out and strap him down in an execution chamber: this shows respect for him as a human being. But recognizing that Harris is, like all of us, shaped by forces that were ultimately beyond his control: that is a patronizing and disrespectful stance" (2015). Recall that Waller shows that it is countries with the strongest beliefs in freedom of choice and self-creation which not only demonstrate the least respect for those at the bottom of society but which have overwhelmingly fewer protections for the innocent or controls against miscarriages of justice. Belief in free will makes a society more, not less, indifferent to all injustice and miscarriages of justice. Both Angela Smith and Daniel Dennett express horror at the excesses of the American penal system – horror at the deliberate cruelty, the executions, the indifference to mass rape, the life sentences for minor offences, the vindictive incarceration of non-violent offenders alongside violent offenders simply to destroy their and their families' lives, as well as the widespread conviction of innocents – but Smith and Dennett profess that the excesses are nothing to do with them and their justifications of free will and moral responsibility in the absence of free choice. But how true is it that the excesses are nothing to do with philosophers? The author would argue that if it can be shown that there is a strong link between belief in free choice and cultural vindictiveness or the celebration of suffering, and if it can be shown that philosophers are either turning a blind eye to the evidence against free choice or asserting manifest untruths – such as the "absurd" (Waller) argument that "luck averages out" in human life – then, yes: at that point the excesses of the system are very much something to do with philosophers. When you throw a hand grenade into a crowded room and then lock the freaking door you don't get to claim that the resulting carnage was nothing to do with you. Beyond penal injustice, given that it has been suggested that internal (including essentialist) self-causation arguments are increasingly used to try to justify social inequalities, "to constrain upward mobility in society" (Kraus & Keltner, 2013, p.258), and to reject restorative social policies, it can also be asked to what extent the philosophical justifiers of internal self-causation arguments are a contributory factor towards destitution and rising economic inequality. Bruce Waller (1990, 2011) has drawn a clear distinction between being responsible and taking responsibility. In a universe without free choice philosophers will never be responsible for their words or their actions, which were the inevitable result of their biology and upbringing. However, the world might be a less cruel and unjust place if philosophers started to take responsibility for their words and their actions.

"A world without punishment is not a world any of us would want to live in", Dennett writes (2008, p.258). But Dennett is helping to legitimise the excesses of the current system when he refuses flat out to acknowledge that you can have incarceration without needing to assert free will or blame. Ironically, it is actually his fellow utilitarians who have suggested for hundreds of years now that you can have incarceration once you have given up on blame. In a world without free choice many offenders still remain very dangerous people, whom society has a right to be defended from. Similarly, the insane and people with contagious diseases may not be to blame, but we nevertheless feel we have the right to segregate them for the protection of the wider society. Derk Pereboom and Bruce Waller have gone to great lengths to make the case that moral codes still exist in a world without the recognition of free will, distinguishing for example between character fault (that someone has a dangerous character) and blame fault (that someone can be blamed for having a dangerous character).

> "When the assumption that wrongdoers are blameworthy is withdrawn for hard incompatibilist reasons, the conviction that they have in fact done wrong could legitimately survive."
> (Pereboom, 2001, p.212).

Smilansky suggests that ending the free will myth is "presented to us as an 'all-or-nothing' choice" (2000, p.225), whereby without the myth (according to Smilansky) we lose the right to imprison. But, again, this is nonsense. In a world without free choice morality still allows us prisons – even life imprisonment for the most damaged individuals who will remain forever dangerous. It just does not allow us torture and execution, or to turn a blind eye to and even raise a cheer for prison rape. It does not allow us to describe criminals, or the "undeserving" poor, as scum, filth and excrement, or to take pleasure in cruelty and suffering, or to write off the interests of the unluckiest 20% of the population. Both Pereboom (2001) and Waller (2015) argue that treatment strategies for offenders tend to be far more effective than moral responsibility advocates like Dennett and Smilansky wish to admit, and more effective than traditional strategies. Robert Martinson's 1974 review *What Works?* was arguably the most influential article contributing towards a scepticism of rehabilitation and a backlash against penal reform in the US criminal justice system in the 1970s and 1980s. Pereboom notes that not only has Martinson's review been widely criticized as deeply flawed but that Martinson himself has now retracted all his original claims, having become convinced that "such startling results are found again and again... for treatment programs" (2001, p.181).

Dennett, seemingly pathologically blind to the right to still incarcerate in a world without free will (Clark, 2012; Dennett, 2012; 2012a; 2014), has challenged Bruce Waller to come up with a better legal system than the current American ones, federal and state. But a point that free will justifiers like Dennett continually miss is that under Dennett's personal code of ethics the public has the absolute moral right to be protected from those who would do it harm only when it starts to deal fairly with the unlucky. Hence, this makes the current system in need of change even under Dennett's own working assumptions. So, and for the sake of argument, let us allow Dennett's contention that with the recognition of no free choice we will have difficulty morally legitimising a penal system that simultaneously keeps the public safe through incarceration. Under this new hypothesis incarceration may be necessary for public safety, but may always have to be judged to be at least partially an unjust act against the offender who could not have done otherwise. Incarceration, in other words, is judged to be practically necessary but nevertheless morally unjust. We thus have irreconcilable ideals: the requirement for public safety cannot be reconciled with perfect justice, at least under this working assumption. The point is that even if this is the case, the current system is the worst of all possible worlds.

Under the present system (let us call it the Dennett-Moore system) we have two injustices and one practical good. We have the first injustice (we are allowing it to be called injustice to test the Dennett-Moore hypothesis) of incarceration in a world without free choice, and the second injustice of, like Dennett and Moore, being blind to the problem of moral luck. Both are set against the practical good of public safety. But the Dennett-Moore system still carries with it this second injustice of practical blindness to the problem of moral luck and injustice of blame in a world without opportunity and free choice. Dennett seems to want to suggest the second injustice goes away if we don't talk about it – just disappears when "we take care not to examine too closely", but this is utter nonsense. The second injustice does not disappear when Dennett turns his blind eye. Under the Dennett-Moore system we have two injustices and one practical good. But where we change our attitudes and begin to admit the problem of moral luck and that free choice does not exist, while nevertheless recognising that public safety cannot be achieved at the same time as perfect justice, we have taken away one of the two injustices. We still have the first injustice (hypothetical, remember, as we are granting the Dennett-Moore argument in order to test it) of incarceration in a world without free choice, but we have stopped the second injustice of dissembling over free will, of needing to pretend that anyone could ever have done otherwise. We retain the practical good, but lose one of the two injustices. Under the Dennett-Moore system we had two injustices and one practical good, but by throwing away the Dennett-Moore system we reduce the equation to only one injustice and still one practical good. But we can go further. Even though we (hypothetically) retain one injustice, we have at least ameliorated that single remaining injustice by reducing the human suffering attached to it. After all, Baumeister and Carey have both found a link between belief in free will, could-have-done-otherwise, and greater indifference to cruelty and suffering. We will have reduced the harm (the quantum of unfairness) of the remaining injustice by taking away much of the cruelty and enhanced suffering that is embedded within the free will and could-have-done-otherwise myths.

A final point. Let's say that we ultimately agree that we can't come up with a better system than the one Dennett supports, which is that of no true consideration being given to the problem of moral luck. Let's suggest that we are forced to agree that from a practical perspective the current system is so superior that this must be allowed (under some practical utilitarian calculus) to offset all its ethical failings. But this would still in no way morally justify the current system that Dennett champions. Most philosophers today promote a system that has no ethical justification outside of majoritarianism, consequentialism, and indifference to individual injustice. Hence, even if we decide together that we can't formulate a practically better system this would still leave us with the overarching moral and intellectual duty to stop professing – and to stop our philosophers and theologians professing – that the current system was in any way a moral or just one. We may agree that the current system has the greatest utility but it will never be an ethical system. We would still be morally required to put an end to the current turning of a blind eye, and we would still be required to put an end to the palpable untruths (such as that in human life "luck averages out in the long run", that "everyone comes out more or less in the same league", or that it is the person who "managed to turn himself into a monster"). The one thing that moral and intellectual integrity will never allow is the continuation of silence over the current system, and of pretending that injustice at the individual level adds up to justice at the social level.

The legal philosopher Peter Arenella has told us that a lack of free will would mean that "some moral agents will have a far easier time than others in exercising their moral capacities" (1992, p.1614). This is a vast, and strictly incorrect, understatement. In a world without free will some of us find it not harder but literally impossible – at least without external intervention – to meet the obligations placed on us by the law. There's the rub. The law places obligations which it knows in advance that only some can meet and yet stoops to the injustice of pretending that all could meet such obligations, such as when it asserts that "the criminal law sets very low standards; it asks very little of us... it is simply not that hard to obey" (Morse, 1984, pp.1498-9). The criminal law may ask very little of Morse, but of others it asks what is well beyond their physical and psychological capacities. We are not all equal before the law, and the law asks far more of some than it does of others. We have designed a system that some have no option but to fail, only for us to take cruel pleasure and vindictive excitement in arguing, wholly falsely, that this is not the case.

> "I agree with [Miles's] analysis that a world in which human beings lacked free will would require a radically different conception of criminal responsibility" (Eric Metcalfe, Director of Human Rights Policy, JUSTICE, pers. comm., 16 July 2004).

The upshot, as H.L.A. Hart recognised, is that in this quasiclassical deterministic universe that humans inhabit we have a system of law but we do not have a system of justice. "St. Peter", writes Stephen J. Morse, "may wish to do greater 'fine tuning', but the law should not" (1984, p.1499). In other words (according to Morse) God and St Peter may care about fairness and justice, but you and I and the law should not.

SUMMARY - BELIEF IN FREE WILL MEANS NEVER HAVING TO SAY "THANK YOU"

For the defenders of the free will conceit there are only three questions to ask oneself. The first question is about free choice, and whether it actually exists. If, like the libertarians, you can convince yourself of the possibility of free choice, no further justifications are necessary. But if, like the compatibilists, you can acknowledge the impossibility of free choice, you must then decide how seriously you take the problem of moral luck – the pure lottery of biology and upbringing. If you can convince yourself that in a universe without free choice everything does not just come down to moral luck, no further justifications become necessary.

Libertarianism	Compatibilism	Illusionism/ Attitudinism/ Semi-Compatibilism
Free choice impossible? NO	Free choice impossible? YES	Free choice impossible? YES
	Down to moral luck? NO	Down to moral luck? YES
		Wider considerations? YES

However, if (like the illusionists) you can acknowledge the impossibility of free choice and acknowledge the continuing problem of moral luck, you must then decide whether there are other, wider, considerations in play that will let you wave away the unfairness of moral luck.

> "Is [the system] fair enough not to be worth worrying about? Of course. After all, luck averages out in the long run" (Dan Dennett, 1984, p.95).

Illusionism found those wider considerations in majoritarianism and the belief that the interests of the majority completely extinguish the interests of the minority, because for illusionism the need for social cohesion untroubled by questions of conscience trumps any other imperative (moral or otherwise). Reactive-attitudinism found those wider considerations in the supposed truth of our rat-and-monkey strike back instinct, albeit only after rejecting any evaluation of the nobler, and uniquely human, capacities of impartial justice or a sense of fair play. Semi-compatibilism found its wider considerations in the idea that unfairness is the new fairness: in the belief that there is no requirement for universal fairness.

At its most fundamental, free will justification is the inability to admit that others have been, or will be, less lucky in life than you. Belief in free will – be that belief in free will as free choice, or belief in a free will that eschews free choice – means never having to say "thank you": it means never having to acknowledge your own great good fortune, or recognise the far greater misfortune of others. Free will justification is also, though, an inability to recognise or speak the truth. When John Searle, Roger Penrose, Roy Baumeister, and Kathleen Vohs tell us that people can, or at least may be able to, stand outside their biology and upbringing and freely choose to do otherwise in the deep libertarian sense this is not (and could never be) true. When Stephen J. Morse and Michael S. Moore tell us that determinism does not entail an absence of choice, and that could-have-done-otherwise conditionality is applicable at the level of the individual, this is not true. When Dan Dennett tells us that luck averages out in human life and that in America all – rich or poor, black or white – get approximately the same breaks, this is not true. When Dennett and Saul Smilansky tell us that morality allows us to wholly discount the rights of the minority, this is not true. When Gary Watson says that there is room for the thought that you and I can take credit for our wonderful health and fine characters – with the deeply distasteful corollary that it is to others' discredit when they are born diseased or into a toxic environment – this is not true. When Watson and Michael McKenna tell us that there are two biologically distinct forms of human, and that we owe no sense of fellow-feeling to the less-than-perfect form, this is not true. When Dennett writes that it is the person who has "managed to turn himself into a monster", or when Watson writes that "the thought is not 'It had to be!'", or when Jonathan Jacobs writes that it is "not exclusively a matter of bad constitutive luck" and that the individual "could have acted differently", these statements are not true. And when Dan Dennett, Harry Frankfurt, Peter Strawson, Saul Smilansky, John Fischer, and Stephen Hawking tell us that the absence of free choice does not raise, or at least can find an ethically acceptable answer to, the deep problem of moral luck, this is not true.

We can get drawn into endless arguments about the "correct" meaning of origination, of coercion and control, of freedom of choice, and of could-have-done-otherwise. But nothing in the free will and moral responsibility literature can answer to the fairness of blame and suffering when some of us – through no credit of our own – are born and raised lucky, and some of us – through no fault of their own – are simply born and raised unlucky. And nothing can justify what Oxford's Neil Levy has called the "double dose" of unfairness that free will justification brings with it. The first dose of unfairness is the poor developmental luck some have to suffer through no choice of their own. But the second dose of unfairness is when we add the further injustice of claiming that the person was somehow responsible for their first dose of unfairness, or at the very least that blame and suffering are their just deserts. It should surely be sad enough that some have to endure the slings and arrows of outrageous fortune, while many of us – generally the wealthier, the better-educated, the more attractive, the lighter-skinned – coast though life with barely a hiccup. But to then feel the pressing need to tell untruths about those who suffer misfortune: what does this say about us? To bear false witness about those who didn't get the breaks we did, to make up stories about how they freely chose their own misfortune? When free will philosophers like Smilansky and Dennett tell us that justice for the 99%, or the 80%, wholly extinguishes injustice for the 1%, or the 20%, using arguments "we take care not to examine too closely", what does this say about us? When free will theorists like Gary Watson state that we don't need to extend consideration to those not like us, and we stay silent, what does this say about us? And when philosophers like Fischer and Ravizza tell us that there is no requirement for universal fairness, and we don't call them on this, what does this say about us?

Bruce Waller has observed that "there is a deep *cultural* connection" between strong belief in self-creation and free choice and extremes of poverty and wealth, and an absence of genuine opportunity for large segments of the culture. The greater the commitment to these conceits, the more the "absence of genuine opportunity… the greater the disparity between rich and poor, the weaker the commitment to equal opportunity, and the meaner the support system for the least fortunate". What is surprising is not that Waller can claim this. It is that so few are willing to admit the profound logical connection he recognises. When the influential conservative social commentator Charles Murray tells us that there is indeed a level playing field in America, and that rich and poor, black and white, get just as many chances in life, his evidence and his argument is equality of opportunity. "The options are always open. Opportunity is endless," writes Murray. Yet what *The Bell Curve*'s author is claiming is no different from what compatibilists like Dan Dennett, Gary Watson, Jonathan Jacobs, and George Sher are writing. "Everyone comes out more or less in the same league", say the philosophers. "Many of the differences that survive are, in any event, of negligible importance" and "count for nothing", they suggest. "The thought is not 'It had to be!'", they assert. The differences between people "are rarely so pronounced as to have" the effect of making any course impossible, they profess. Genes and culture are not limiting because the person can rise above his biology and upbringing: he has "created and unleashed" himself, they intone. The options are always open, and opportunity is endless, says the author of *The Bell Curve*. The options are always open, and opportunity is endless, say the philosophers. But in a universe without free will – however you define that term – the uncomfortable truth is that for many there was no level playing field, no equality of opportunity. For some the options were *never open*; the opportunity was *non-existent*.

Everyone does not come out "more or less in the same league". The differences that survive are not "negligible". They do not "count for nothing". It is the differences that survive which absolutely and in every way determine our economic successes and our economic failures, our social successes and our social failures, and our moral successes and our moral failures. The thought is entirely "It had to be!" None of us is a disembodied self who gets to rise above the dragging and wholly limiting effects of biology and environment. Yet the myth – the scapegoating prejudice – of the self-made man joins arch conservative social commentator to liberal philosopher in privileging the lucky and taking away the opportunities, the equality, the dignity, the freedom – even the lives – of the unlucky.

> "Is it fair, he keeps asking, to hold both of them responsible? Life isn't fair" (Dennett, 2012).

Life is not fair. And if we leave it up to the priests, the rabbis, and the philosophers, it never will be.

BIBLIOGRAPHY

Al-Khalili, J. [2013]: 'Believing in a God is fine by me', *New Statesman*, (27 March). Available at http://www.newstatesman.com/lifestyle/religion/2013/03/god-dead-long-live-our-souls

Allen, J.T. and Dimock, M. [2007]: 'A nation of "haves" and "have-nots"? Far more Americans now see their country as sharply divided along economic lines', *Pew Research Centre for the People & the Press*. Available at http://pewresearch.org/pubs/593/haves-have-nots

Arenella, P. [1992]: 'Convicting the morally blameless: reassessing the relationship between legal and moral accountability', *UCLA Law Review*, 39, pp. 1511-1622.

Ariely, D. [2012]: *The (Honest) Truth About Dishonesty: How We Lie to Everyone – Especially Ourselves*, London, HarperCollins.

Aristotle [c.4th B.C.]: *Ethics*, trans. J.A.K. Thompson, (1976) London, Penguin.

Bailyn, B. [2012]: *The Barbarous Years: The Peopling of British North America: The Conflict of Civilizations, 1600-1675*, (2013) New York, Vintage Books.

Balaguer, M. [1999]: 'Libertarianism as a scientifically reputable view', *Philosophical Studies*, 93, pp. 189-211.

Bamfield, L. and Horton, T. [2009]: *Understanding Attitudes to Tackling Economic Inequality*, York, the Joseph Rowntree Foundation. Available online at www.jrf.org.uk

Barrett, P.H., Gautrey, P., Herbert, S., Kohn D. and Smith, S. (*eds.*) [1987]: *Charles Darwin's Notebooks, 1836-1844: Geology, Transmutation of Species, Metaphysical Enquiries*, transcribed and edited by Paul H. Barrett and others, Cambridge, Cambridge University Press.

Baumeister, R.F., Masicampo, E.J., and DeWall, C.N. [2009]: 'Prosocial benefits of feeling free: Disbelief in free will increases aggression and reduces helpfulness', *Personality and Social Psychology Bulletin*, 35, pp. 260-268.

Bazelon, D.L. [1976]: 'The morality of the criminal law', *Southern California Law Review*, 49, pp. 385-405.

Berlin, I. [1971/2013]: 'Isaiah Berlin on Machiavelli', *New York Review of Books*. (Reprint of November 1971 article to mark 50th anniversary of NYRB.) Available at http://www.nybooks.com/articles/archives/2013/mar/07/isaiah-berlin-machiavelli/

Blume, H. [1998]: 'Reverse-engineering the psyche: Evolutionary psychologist Steven Pinker on how the mind really works', *Wired*, 6.03, March, pp. 154-155.

Bókkon, I., Vas J. P., Császár, N., and Lukács, T. [2014]: 'Challenges to free will: transgenerational epigenetic information, unconscious processes and vanishing twin syndrome', *Reviews in the Neurosciences*, 25, pp. 163-175.

Book, A.S. [1999]: 'Shame on you: An analysis of modern shame punishment as an alternative to incarceration', *William and Mary Law Review*, 40, pp. 653-686.

Bowlby, C. [2010]: 'The deserving or undeserving poor?' *British Broadcasting Corporation*. (B.B.C. Magazine review of Bowlby's Radio 4 Analysis episode Who Deserves Welfare? broadcast 18 November.) Available at http://www.bbc.co.uk/news/magazine-11778284

Breer, P. [1989]: *The Spontaneous Self: Viable Alternatives to Free Will*, Cambridge, Massachusetts, Institute of Naturalistic Philosophy.

Bygott, J.D. [1972]: 'Cannibalism among wild chimpanzees', *Nature*, 238, pp. 410-411.

Carey, J. M. [2009]: 'Development and validation of a measure of free will belief and its alternatives,' postgraduate thesis at the *University of British Columbia*. Available at U.B.C. website http://circle.ubc.ca/handle/2429/12588

Chang, I. [1997]: *The Rape of Nanking: The Forgotten Holocaust of World War II*, (1998) London, Penguin.

Clark T.W. [1999]: 'Free will and naturalism: A reply to Corliss Lamont', *The Humanist*, 50, pp. 18-24. Available at www.naturalism.org/freewill1.htm

Clark T.W. [2012]: 'Exchange on Bruce Waller's *Against Moral Responsibility*'. Available at
http://www.naturalism.org/Wallerexchange.htm

Confucius [c.5th B.C.]: *The Analects*, trans. D. C. Lau, (1979) London, Penguin.

Davies, P. [2004]: 'Undermining free will', *Foreign Policy*, 144, September / October, pp. 36-37 (published as one of *Foreign Policy*'s World's Most Dangerous Ideas essays). Also published as: 'In defence of the ghost in the machine', *Australian Financial Review*, 3 September 2004.

Dawkins, R. [1982]: *The Extended Phenotype: The Gene as the Unit of Selection*, (1983) Oxford, Oxford University Press.

Dennett, D.C. [1978]: *Brainstorms: Philosophical Essays on Mind and Psychology*, (1981) Cambridge, Massachusetts, The MIT Press.

Dennett, D.C. [1984]: *Elbow Room: The Varieties of Free Will Worth Wanting*, (1996) Cambridge, Massachusetts, The MIT Press.

Dennett, D.C. [1995]: *Darwin's Dangerous Idea: Evolution and the Meanings of Life*, (1996) London, Penguin.

Dennett, D.C. [2003]: *Freedom Evolves*, London, Allen Lane.

Dennett, D.C. [2008]: 'Some observations on the psychology of thinking about free will'. In J. Baer, J.C. Kaufman, and R.F. Baumeister (*eds.*) *Are We Free? Psychology and Free Will*, New York, Oxford University Press, pp. 248-259.

Dennett, D.C [2012]: 'Daniel Dennett reviews *Against Moral Responsibility* by Bruce Waller'. Available at
http://www.naturalism.org/DCDWallerreview.htm

Dennett, D.C. [2012a]: 'Exchange on Bruce Waller's *Against Moral Responsibility*'. Available at
http://www.naturalism.org/Wallerexchange.htm

Dennett, D.C. [2014]: 'Reflections on *Free Will*', 24 January. Available at
http://www.naturalism.org/Dennett_reflections_on_Harris's_Free_Will.pdf

de Waal, F.B.M. [1996]: *Good Natured: The Origins of Right and Wrong in Humans and Other Animals*, Cambridge, Massachusetts, Harvard University Press.

Double, R. [1991]: *The Non-reality of Free Will*, New York, Oxford University Press.

Double, R. [2002]: 'The moral hardness of libertarianism', *Philo*, 5, pp. 226-234.

Edelman, G. [1994]: *Bright Air, Brilliant Fire*, New York, Basic Books.

Einstein, A. [1954]: *Ideas and Opinions*, (1982) New York, Three Rivers Press.

Erasmus, D. [1524]: *Discourse on Free Will*, trans. E.F. Winter, (1999) New York, Continuum.

Fischer, J.M. [2006]: 'The cards that are dealt you', *Journal of Ethics*, 10, pp. 107-129.

Fischer, J.M. [2007]: 'Compatibilism'. In J.M. Fischer, R. Kane, D. Pereboom and M. Vargas (*eds.*) *Four Views on Free Will*, Malden, Massachusetts, Blackwell, pp. 44-84.

Fischer, J.M. [2007a]: 'Response to Kane, Pereboom, and Vargas'. In J.M. Fischer, R. Kane, D. Pereboom and M. Vargas (*eds.*) *Four Views on Free Will*, Malden, Massachusetts, Blackwell, pp. 184-190.

Fischer, J.M. and Ravizza, M. [1998]: *Responsibility and Control: A Theory of Moral Responsibility*, Cambridge, Cambridge University Press.

Frankfurt, H. [1971]: 'Freedom of the will and the concept of a person'. In Gary Watson (*ed.*) *Free Will*, (2003) Oxford, Oxford University Press, pp. 81-95.

French, P.A. [2001]: *The Virtues of Vengeance*, Lawrence, KA, University of Kansas Press.

Goodin, R.E. [1988]: *Reasons for Welfare: The Political Theory of the Welfare State*, Princeton, Princeton University Press.

Green, G. [2007]: 'Is there a devil inside?', *Metro*, 3 May, p. 19.

Greene, B. [2004]: *The Fabric of the Cosmos: Space, Time, and the Texture of Reality*, (2005) London, Penguin Books.

Greene, J. and Cohen, J. [2004]: 'For the law, neuroscience changes nothing and everything', *Philosophical Transactions of the Royal Society of London B*, 359, pp. 1775-1785.

Gross, P.R. and Levitt, N. [1994]: *Higher Superstition: The Academic Left and its Quarrels with Science*, Baltimore, Johns Hopkins University Press.

Guelzo, A.C. [1997]: 'Abraham Lincoln and the doctrine of necessity', *Journal of the Abraham Lincoln Association*, 18, pp. 57-81.

Guelzo, A.C. [2009]: *Abraham Lincoln As a Man of Ideas*, Carbondale, Illinois, Southern Illinois University Press.

Gulack, R. [2004]: 'Free will: The last great lie'. Available online at the Ethical Culture Society of Bergen County website at www.ethicalfocus.org/index.php?mpage=34/Free_Will.htm

Habermas, J. [2006]: *Time of Transitions*, Cambridge, Polity Press.

Haggard, R.F. [2000]: *The Persistence of Victorian Liberalism: The Politics of Social Reform in Britain, 1870-1900*, London, Greenwood Press.

Halper, T. [1973]: 'The poor as pawns: the new "deserving poor" & the old', *Polity*, 6, pp. 71-86.

Hamai, M., Nishida, T., Takasaki, H. and Turner, L.A. [1992]: 'New records of within-group infanticide and cannibalism in wild chimpanzees', *Primates*, 33, pp. 151-162.

Hameroff, S. and Penrose, R. [1995]: 'Orchestrated reduction of quantum coherence in brain microtubules: A model for consciousness', *Neural Network World*, 5, pp. 793-804.

Hamilton, W.D. [1971]: 'Selection of selfish and altruistic behaviour in some extreme models'. In W.D. Hamilton (*ed.*) *Narrow Roads of Gene Land: Volume I,* (1996) Oxford: W.H Freeman, pp. 198-227.

Harris, S. [2011]: 'The free will delusion', *New Statesman* (19 December), pp. 46-47.

Harris, S. [2012]: *Free Will*, New York, Simon & Schuster.

Hart, H.L.A. [1968]: *Punishment and Responsibility: Essays in the Philosophy of Law*, New York, Oxford University Press.

Hawking, S.W. and Mlodinow, L. [2010]: *The Grand Design: New Answers to the Ultimate Questions of Life*, London, Bantam Press.

Henrich, J., Heine, S.J. and Norenzayan, A. [2010]: 'The weirdest people in the world?', *Behavioral and Brain Sciences*, 33, pp. 61-83.

Himmelfarb, G. [1984]: 'The idea of poverty', *History Today*, 34, pp. 23-30.

Himmelfarb, G. [1995]: 'From Victorian virtues to modern values', *American Enterprise Institute Bradley Lecture Series*, Washington, AEI Publications.

Hindle, S. [2004]: 'Dependency, shame and belonging: badging the deserving poor, c.1550-1750', *Cultural and Social History*, 1, pp. 6-35.

Hobbes, T. [1682]: *Behemoth; or, the Long Parliament*, (1969) Chicago, University of Chicago Press.

Honderich, T. [2002]: 'Determinism as true, compatibilism and incompatibilism as both false, and the real problem'. In Robert Kane (*ed.*) *The Oxford Handbook of Free Will*, Oxford, Oxford University Press, pp. 461-476.

Honderich, T. [2006]: 'After compatibilism and incompatibilism'. Article prepared after the 2006 INPC conference on 'Action, Ethics and Responsibility', and available online at Ted Honderich's Determinism and Freedom Philosophy Website at www.ucl.ac.uk/~uctytho/

Honderich, T. [2007]: 'Determinism's consequences: the mistakes of compatibilism and incompatibilism, and what is to be done now'. Notes for a lecture delivered at the Max Planck Institutes, and available online at Ted Honderich's Determinism and Freedom Philosophy Website at www.ucl.ac.uk/~uctytho/

Honderich, T. [2011]: 'Effects, determinism, neither compatibilism nor incompatibilism, consciousness'. In Robert Kane (*ed.*) *The Oxford Handbook of Free Will* (Second Edition), Oxford, Oxford University Press, pp. 442-456.

Horgan, J. [2000]: 'Free will'. In John Brockman (*ed.*) *The Greatest Inventions of the Past 2000* Years, London, Phoenix, p. 161.

Horgan, J. [2002]: 'More than good intentions: Holding fast to faith in free will', *The New York Times*, Science section, 31 December, p. 3.

Hrdy, S.B. [1977]: 'Infanticide as a primate reproductive strategy', *American Scientist*, 65, pp. 40-49.

Hrdy, S.B. [1977a]: *The Langurs of Abu: Female and Male Strategies of Reproduction*, (1980) Cambridge, Massachusetts, Harvard University Press.

Humphrys, J. [2006]: 'What I found out about God'. Available at http://www.telegraph.co.uk/news/uknews/1537677/What-I-found-out-about-God.html

Hutton, W. [2010]: *Them and Us: Changing Britain – Why We Need a Fair Society*, London, Little, Brown Book Group.

Jacobs, J.A. [2001]: *Choosing Character: Responsibility for Virtue & Vice*, Ithaca, NY, Cornell University Press.

James, W. [1884]: 'The dilemma of determinism'. In William James (*ed.*) *The Will to Believe and Other Essays in Popular Philosophy*, (1956) New York, Dover Publications, pp. 145-183.

Jammer, M. [1999]: *Einstein and Religion: Physics and Theology*, Princeton, Princeton University Press.

Jones, J.S. [1994]: *The Language of the Genes*, London, Flamingo.

Jones, J.S. [1996]: *In the Blood: God, Genes and Destiny*, (1997) London, Flamingo.

Jones, J.S. [1997]: 'The set within the skull', *New York Review of Books*, 54, (6 November), pp. 13-16.

Jones, J.S. [1999]: *Almost Like a Whale:* The Origin of Species *Updated*, London, Doubleday.

Josephus [c.1st A.D.]: *Antiquities of the Jews*, trans. W. Whiston. Available online at www.ccel.org/j/josephus/works/

Kadri, S. [2005]: *The Trial: A History from Socrates to O.J. Simpson*, London, HarperCollins.

Kahan D.M. [1998]: '*The Anatomy of Disgust* in criminal law', *Michigan Law Review*, 96, pp.1621-1657.

Kahneman, D. [2011]: *Thinking, Fast and Slow*, London, Allen Lane.

Kane, R. [2002]: 'Free will: New directions for an ancient problem'. In R. Kane (*ed.*) *Free Will*, Malden, Massachusetts, Blackwell, pp. 222-248.

Kane, R. [2007]: 'Libertarianism'. In J.M. Fischer, R. Kane, D. Pereboom, and M. Vargas, *Four Views on Free Will*, Oxford, Blackwell Publishing, pp. 5-43.

Kant, I. [1788]: *Critique of Practical Reason*, trans. L.W. Beck, (1956) Indianapolis, Bobbs-Merrill.

Kapur, A., Macleod, N. and Singh, N. [2005]: 'Equity strategy – plutonomy: Buying luxury, explaining global imbalances' (16 October) Citigroup Global Markets.

Kaye, A. [2005]: 'Resurrecting the causal theory of the excuses', *Nebraska Law Review*, 83, pp. 1116-1177.

Kaye, A. [2007]: 'The secret politics of the compatibilist criminal law', *Kansas Law Review*, 55, pp. 365-427.

Kennedy, H. [2011]: Interviewed by Steve Jones for 'The Jukes: Bad Blood or Bad Science?', (23 May) BBC Radio 4.

Kraus, M.W. and Keltner, D. [2013]: 'Social class rank, essentialism, and punitive judgment', *Journal of Personality and Social Psychology*, 105, pp. 247-261. Available online at: http://www.krauslab.com/SES.essentialism.JPSP.pdf

Kymlicka, W. [1990]: *Contemporary Political Philosophy: An Introduction*, Oxford, Clarendon Press.

Lamont, C. [1949]: *The Philosophy of Humanism*, (1997) Washington DC, Humanist Press.

Levy, N. [2011]: *Hard Luck: How Luck Undermines Free Will and Moral Responsibility*, Oxford, Oxford University Press.

Lloyd, S. [2012]: 'A Turing Test for free will', *Transactions of the Royal Society A*, 370, pp. 3597-3610. Available at doi: 10.1098/rsta.2011.0331

Markel, D. [2007]: 'Wrong turns on the road to alternative sanctions: Reflections on the future of shaming punishments and restorative justice', *Texas Law Review*, 85, pp. 1385-1412.

Martin, B. [1996]: 'Social construction of an "Attack on Science"', *Social Studies of Science*, 26, pp. 161-173.

Maynard Smith, J. [1964]: 'Group selection and kin selection', *Nature*, 201, pp. 1145-1147.

McKenna, M.S. [2008]: 'The limits of evil and the role of moral address: a defense of Strawsonian compatibilism'. In M.S. McKenna and P. Russell (*eds.*) *Free Will and Reactive Attitudes: Perspectives on P. F. Strawson's 'Freedom and Resentment'*, Farnham, Ashgate Publishing, pp. 201-218.

Miles, J.B. [1998]: 'Unnatural selection', *Philosophy*, 73, pp. 593-608.

Miles, J.B. [2004]: *Born Cannibal: Evolution and the Paradox of Man*, London, IconoKlastic Books. Foreword by George C. Williams.

Miles, J.B. [2005]: 'The accidental creationists: Why evolutionary psychology is bad for the teaching of evolution', *Reports of the National Center for Science Education*, 25 (May-August), pp. 23-32.

Miles J.B. [2013]: 'Irresponsible and a disservice': The integrity of social psychology turns on the free will dilemma', *British Journal of Social Psychology*, 52, pp. 205–218.

Miles J.B. [2013a]: 'The integrity of social psychology turns on the free will dilemma: Reply to Baumeister, Vonasch, and Bargh', *British Journal of Social Psychology*, 52, pp. 231–237.

Mink, G. and O'Connor, A. [2004]: *Poverty in the United States: An Encyclopedia of History, Politics, and Policy*, ABC-CLIO.

Minsky, M. [1986]: *The Society of Mind*, New York, Simon and Schuster.

Mlodinow, L. [2012]: *Subliminal: How Your Unconscious Mind Rules Your Behavior*, (2013) New York, Vintage Books.

Moore, G.F. [1929]: 'Fate and free will in the Jewish philosophies according to Josephus', *Harvard Theological Review*, 22, pp. 371-389.

Moore, M.S. [1985]: 'Causation and the excuses', *California Law Review*, 73, pp. 1091-1149.

Morissette v United States [1952]: MORISSETTE v. UNITED STATES, 342 U.S. 246. Available online at http://supreme.justia.com/cases/federal/us/342/246/case.html

Morse, S.J. [1976]: 'The twilight of welfare criminology: a reply to Judge Bazelon', *Southern California Law Review*, 49, pp. 1247-1268.

Morse, S.J. [1976a]: 'The twilight of welfare criminology: a final word', *Southern California Law Review*, 49, pp. 1275-1276.

Morse, S.J. [1984]: 'Justice, mercy, and craziness', *Stanford Law Review*, 36, pp. 1485-1515.

Morse, S.J. [1994]: Symposium paper: 'Culpability and control', *University of Pennsylvania Law Review*, 142, pp. 1587-1660.

Morse, S.J. [2004]: 'Reason, results, and criminal responsibility', *University of Illinois Law Review*, 2, pp. 363-444.

Murray, C. [1984]: *Losing Ground, American Social Policy, 1950-1980*, (1994) New York, Basic Books.

Nadler, S. [2013]: 'Baruch Spinoza'. In E. N. Zalta (*ed.*) *The Stanford Encyclopedia of Philosophy* (Fall 2013 Edition). Available online at http://plato.stanford.edu/entries/spinoza/

Nagel, T. [1979]: *Mortal Questions*, Cambridge, Cambridge University Press.

Nahmias, E., Morris, S., Nadelhoffer, T. and Turner, J. [2005]: 'Surveying freedom: Folk intuitions about free will and moral responsibility', *Philosophical Psychology*, 18, pp. 561-584.

N.C.S.R. [2010]: '26th British social attitudes report,' *National Centre for Social Research*. Available at http://www.natcen.ac.uk/study/british-social-attitudes-26th-report

Nietzsche, F. [1878]: *Human, All Too Human*, trans. M. Faber & S. Lehmann, (1994) London, Penguin.

Nietzsche, F. [1886]: *Beyond Good and Evil*, trans. R.J. Hollingdale, (1990) London, Penguin.

Norrie, A. [1983]: 'Free will, determinism and criminal justice', *Legal Studies*, 3, pp. 60-73.

Nozick, R. [1981]: *Philosophical Explanations*, Cambridge, Massachusetts, Harvard University Press.

N.P.R.E.C. [2009]: *National Prison Rape Elimination Commission Report*, (June). Available at the DoJ's National Criminal Justice Reference Service website, *www.ncjrs.gov/pdffiles1/226680.pdf*

Nuffield Council on Bioethics [2002]: *Genetics and Human Behaviour: the Ethical Context*, London, Nuffield Council on Bioethics.

Oerton, R. [2012]: *The Nonsense of Free Will: Facing Up to a False Belief*, Kibworth Beauchamp, Matador.

Papineau, D. [2008]: 'Power and consciousness on the Clapham omnibus', *The Times Literary Supplement*, January 16.

Parfit, D. [2011]: *On What Matters, Volume 1*, Oxford, Oxford University Press.

Parris, M. [2008]: 'The undeserving poor exist – just don't say so', *The Times*, July 12, p. 22.

Pearlstein, S. [2011]: 'Hermanomics: Let them eat pizza', *The Washington Post* (October 15). Available at
http://www.washingtonpost.com/business/economy/hermanomics-let-them-eat-pizza/2011/10/11/gIQAgTOmmL_story.html

Pereboom, D. [2001]: *Living Without Free Will*, Cambridge, Cambridge University Press.

Pereboom, D. [2007]: 'Hard incompatibilism'. In J.M. Fischer, R. Kane, D. Pereboom and M. Vargas (*eds.*) *Four Views on Free Will*, Malden, Massachusetts, Blackwell, pp. 85-125.

Pinker, S. [1994]: *The Language Instinct: The New Science of Language and the Mind*, (1995) London, Penguin.

Pinker, S. [1997]: *How the Mind Works*, (1998) London, Penguin.

Plantinga, A. [2013]: 'Bait and switch: Sam Harris on free will', *Books &*

Culture: A Christian Review. Available at http://www.booksandculture.com/articles/2013/janfeb/bait-and-switch.html

Plato [c.4th B.C.]: *The Republic*, trans. D. Lee, (1974), London, Penguin.

Plato [c.4th B.C.]: *Protagoras and Meno*, trans. W.K.C. Guthrie, (1956), London, Penguin.

Potts, M. [2014]: 'The other Americans', *Democracy*, 32, Spring, pp. 100-106. Available at http://www.democracyjournal.org/pdf/32/the_other_americans.pdf

Preston, P. [2012]: *The Spanish Holocaust: Inquisition and Extermination in Twentieth-Century Spain*, London, HarperPress.

Raine, A. [2013]: *The Anatomy of Violence: The Biological Roots of Crime*, London, Allen Lane.

Ridley, M. and Dawkins, R. [1981]: 'The natural selection of altruism'. In J.P. Rushton and R.M. Sorrentino (*eds.*) *Altruism and Helping Behavior: Social, Personality and Developmental Perspectives*, Hillsdale, NJ, Lawrence Erlbaum, pp. 19-39.

Sartre, J-P. [1943]: *Being and Nothingness*, trans. H.E. Barnes, (1958) London, Methuen.

Schneider, N. [2010]: 'God, science and philanthropy', *The Nation*, (June 21). Available at http://www.thenation.com/article/god-science-and-philanthropy

Schopenhauer, A. [1839]: *Prize Essay On the Freedom of the Will (Royal Norwegian Society of Sciences Winner)*, trans. E.F.J. Payne, (1999) Cambridge, Cambridge Texts in the History of Philosophy.

Searle, J.R. [2000]: 'Consciousness, free action and the brain', *Journal of Consciousness Studies*, 7, pp. 3-22.

Searle, J.R. [2001]: 'Free will as a problem in neurobiology', *Philosophy*, 76, pp. 491-514.

Searle, J.R. [2007]: 'Neuroscience, intentionality and free will: reply to Habermas', *Philosophical Explorations*, 10, pp. 69-76.

Shariff, A.F., Schooler, J., and Vohs, K.D. [2008]: 'The hazards of claiming to have solved the hard problem of free will'. In J. Baer, J.C. Kaufman, and R.F. Baumeister (*eds.*) *Are We Free? Psychology and Free Will*, New York, Oxford University Press, pp. 181-204.

Shariff, A.F., Karremans, J.C., Clark, C.J., Luguri, J.B., Baumeister R.F., Ditto, P.H., Schooler, W.S., Greene, J.D. and Vohs, K.D. [in press, under revision at *Psychological Science*]: 'Diminished belief in free will increases forgiveness and reduces retributive punishment'.

Sher, G. [2006]: *In Praise of Blame*, New York, Oxford University Press.

Shifflett, P.A. [2008]: 'Homeless children and runaways in the United States'. In E. Craig (*ed.*), *Encyclopedia of Children and Childhood in History and Society*, The Gale Group, Inc. Available online at www.faqs.org/childhood/Gr-Im/Homeless-Children-and -Runaways-in-the-United-States.htm

Skinner, E.A. [1995]: *Perceived Control, Motivation, & Coping: Individual Differences and Development Series Volume 8*, Thousand Oaks, California, Sage Publications.

Smilansky, S. [1997]: 'Can a determinist respect herself?' In C.H. Manekin and M.M. Kellner (*eds.*) *Freedom and Moral Responsibility: General and Jewish Perspectives*, College Park, University Press of Maryland, pp. 85-98.

Smilansky, S. [2000]: *Free Will and Illusion*, Oxford, Oxford University Press.

Smilansky, S. [2002]: 'Free will, fundamental dualism, and the centrality of illusion'. In Robert Kane (*ed.*) *The Oxford Handbook of Free Will*, Oxford, Oxford University Press, pp. 489-505.

Stillman, T.F., Baumeister, R.F., Vohs, K.D., Lambert, N. M., Fincham, F.D., and Brewer, L.E. [2010]: 'Personal philosophy and personnel achievement: Belief in free will predicts better job performance', *Social Psychological and Personality Science*, 1, pp. 43-50.

Stillman, T.F. and Baumeister, R.F. [2010]: 'Guilty, free, and wise: Determinism and psychopathy diminish learning from negative emotions', *Journal of Experimental Social Psychology*, 46, pp. 951-960.

Strawson, G. [1994]: 'The impossibility of moral responsibility', *Philosophical Studies*, 75, pp. 5-24.

Strawson, G. [1998]: 'Luck swallows everything: Can our sense of free will be true?', *Times Literary Supplement*, 26 June, pp. 8-10.

Strawson, G. [1998a]: 'Free will'. In E. Craig (*ed.*), *Routledge Encyclopedia of Philosophy*, London, Routledge. Available online at www.rep.routledge.com/article/V014

Strawson, P.F. [1962/2008]: 'Freedom and resentment'. In M.S. McKenna and P. Russell (*eds.*) *Free Will and Reactive Attitudes: Perspectives on P. F. Strawson's 'Freedom and Resentment'*, Farnham, Ashgate Publishing, pp. 19-36.

Tallis, R. [2008]: 'Is human freedom possible?', *British Humanist Association Voltaire Lecture 2008*, 10 April. Available online at the British Humanist Association website www.humanism.org.uk

Turkheimer, E., Haley, A., Waldron, M., D'Onofrio, B. and Gottesman, I.I. [2003]: 'Socioeconomic status modifies heritability of IQ in young children', *Psychological Science*, 14, pp. 623-628.

United States v Grayson [1978]: UNITED STATES v. GRAYSON, 438 U.S. 41. Available online at http://supreme.justia.com/cases/federal/us/438/41/case.html

van Inwagen, P. [1983]: *An Essay on Free Will*, Oxford, Oxford University Press.

Vallely, P. [2007]: 'Gertrude Himmelfarb: Brown's guru', *The Independent*, 3 November. Available online at www.independent.co.uk/news/people/gertrude-himmelfarb-browns-guru-398800.html

Vohs, K.D. and Schooler, J.W. [2008]: 'The value of believing in free will: Encouraging a belief in determinism increases cheating', *Psychological Science*, 19, January, pp. 49-54.

Voltaire [1764]: *Philosophical Dictionary*, (2008) Charleston, BiblioBazaar.

Vonasch, A. and Baumeister, R.F. [2013]: 'Implications of free will beliefs for basic theory and societal benefit: Critique and implications for social psychology', *British Journal of Social Psychology*, 52, 219–227.

Wallace, R.J. [1994]: *Responsibility and the Moral Sentiments*, Cambridge, Massachusetts, Harvard University Press.

Waller, B.N. [1990]: *Freedom Without Responsibility*, Philadelphia, Templeton University Press.

Waller, B.N. [1999]: 'Deep thinkers, cognitive misers, and moral responsibility', *Analysis*, 59, pp. 44-47.

Waller, B.N. [2006]: 'Denying responsibility without making excuses', *American Philosophical Quarterly*, 43, pp. 81-89.

Waller, B.N. [2011]: *Against Moral Responsibility*, Cambridge, Massachusetts, The MIT Press.

Waller, B.N. [2012]: 'Exchange on Bruce Waller's *Against Moral Responsibility*'. Available at
http://www.naturalism.org/Wallerexchange.htm

Waller, B.N. [2015]: *The Stubborn System of Moral Responsibility*, Cambridge, Massachusetts, The MIT Press.

Washington Post [2009]: 'A prison nightmare. A federal commission offers useful standards for preventing sexual abuse behind bars', *Washington Post* (23 June). Available at
http://www.washingtonpost.com/wp-dyn/content/article/2009/06/22/AR2009062202550.html

Watson, G. [2004]: 'Responsibility and the limits of evil: Variations on a Strawsonian theme'. In G. Watson (*ed.*) *Agency and Answerability: Selected Essays*, New York, Oxford University Press, pp. 219-259.

Wegner, D.M. [2002]: *The Illusion of Conscious Will*, Cambridge, Massachusetts, The MIT Press.

Wiener, N. [1948]: *Cybernetics*, New York, John Wiley.

Wilberforce, S. [1860]: '*On the Origin of Species*, by Charles Darwin', *Quarterly Review* (reviewed anonymously), 108, pp. 225-264.

Wilby, P. [2008]: 'Gordon and Gertrude: Brown should resist his penchant for US gurus', New Statesman. Available at
http://www.newstatesman.com/society/2008/03/british-brown-himmelfarb

Williams, B. [1972]: *Morality: An Introduction to Ethics*, Cambridge, Cambridge University Press.

Williams, G.C. [1966]: *Adaptation and Natural Selection: A Critique of Some Current Evolutionary Thought*, Princeton, Princeton University Press.

Williams, G.C. [1988]: 'Huxley's *Evolution and Ethics* in sociobiological perspective', *Zygon*, 23, pp. 383-407.

Wilson, E.O. [1978]: *On Human Nature*, Cambridge, Massachusetts, Harvard University Press.

Wilson, E.O. [1998]: *Consilience: The Unity of Knowledge*, New York, Knopf.

Wolf, S.R. [1989]: 'Sanity and the metaphysics of responsibility'. In J. Christman (*ed.*) *The Inner Citadel: Essays on Autonomy*, Oxford, Oxford University Press, pp. 137-151.

Wolf, S.R. [1990]: *Freedom Within Reason*, Oxford, Oxford University Press.

Wright, R. [1994]: *The Moral Animal: Evolutionary Psychology and Everyday Life*, (1996) London, Abacus.

Zimbardo, P.G. [2007]: *The Lucifer Effect: How Good People Turn Evil*, (2008) Rider & Co, London.

INDEX